A Failure to Thrive

My Personal Account of the Canadian Blood Disaster

Leslie Sharp

authorHOUSE®

AuthorHouse™
1663 Liberty Drive
Bloomington, IN 47403
www.authorhouse.com
Phone: 1 (800) 839-8640

© 2019 Leslie Sharp. All rights reserved.

No part of this book may be reproduced, stored in a retrieval system, or transmitted by any means without the written permission of the author.

Published by AuthorHouse 01/22/2019

ISBN: 978-1-5462-7461-2 (sc)
ISBN: 978-1-5462-7462-9 (e)

Library of Congress Control Number: 2019900136

Print information available on the last page.

Any people depicted in stock imagery provided by Getty Images are models, and such images are being used for illustrative purposes only.
Certain stock imagery © Getty Images.

This book is printed on acid-free paper.

Because of the dynamic nature of the Internet, any web addresses or links contained in this book may have changed since publication and may no longer be valid. The views expressed in this work are solely those of the author and do not necessarily reflect the views of the publisher, and the publisher hereby disclaims any responsibility for them.

Contents

Dedication vii
Acknowledgement ix

A Fresh Start 1
A Failure to Thrive? 9
The I.C.U. 21
Is It Just Me? 34
Crisis 47
It's Complicated 67
Seeking Truth 85
Priorities 96
Stepping It Up 115
Escape and Corruption 127
Our Peruvian Lifesaver 143
A New Beginning 158
The Silver Lining 167

Epilogue 181
About the Author 195

Dedication

This book is dedicated to all families living with chronic disease and to the loved ones they have lost.

Acknowledgement

A Failure to Thrive is dedicated to my three children – Tyler for your constant love and encouragement, Ashley for your love, support and great suggestions, and Jarad for your love and for taking me on this crazy journey with you since the day you were born.

Thank you to my Lord and Savior without You in my life, I could not have relived this experience. You are faithful even when I did not know you were there.

Thank you to Dr. Jose Cabanilla's for saving Jarad's life.

Thank you to Brad Clarke for funding the research, and giving us A4+.

Thank you to Dr. Michelle Brill Edwards. I am so grateful to have had you as a mentor as I learned the truth.

Thank you to John Nelson. You pushed and prodded me along my path so that today I can say "I did it!"

And lastly, thank you to all of my family and friends. You have been most patient.

CHAPTER ONE

A Fresh Start

The sun was hot as I backed our navy blue Buick Regal out of my parents' North Delta driveway. Tears trickled down my cheeks, as I waved goodbye to our three children—11-year-old Tyler, 8-year-old Ashley, and 6-year-old Jarad. They were so excited about spending their spring break with Mom and Dad, but I knew that I was going to miss them so much. I told myself that it would just be easier this way—we would be able to get a lot of work done and besides Peter and I needed this alone time. Even if we fell exhausted in to bed each night, at least we will be alone and together.

My husband, Peter, had gone on to Penticton ahead of the family. He had been there for more than a week now. He was eager to begin renovating our newly purchased home. Peter was really looking forward to his new posting and was anticipating finally achieving his dream of becoming a traffic accident analyst. He had big plans for his career in the Royal Canadian Mounted Police (RCMP), in this "big" city.

This move reminded me of my family's first transfer. I am the youngest daughter of an RCMP officer family. My Mom, a nurse, had gone on ahead of us, as she had committed to work at the hospital. My sister and I watched our belongings being loaded into the moving van; we ran wild, briefly, in our empty house, and then Dad, my sister and I climbed into the car and headed north.

Growing up I loved all the feelings that surrounded a move and fresh start in a new city, a new home and a new school. With the RCMP life, we moved frequently, and I enjoyed the many fresh starts in new towns and cities. Although I believe all this moving around helped form my shy and reserved personality, I wouldn't have traded the experience thus gained. As a child I was always serious, and that hasn't really changed much.

Funny, I thought, Jarad is now the same age as I was when our family made that first move from Langley to Williams Lake. However, that's where our similarity ended. I had been healthy my entire childhood, which unfortunately I cannot say about Jarad and his myriad of health issues.

As I was totally alone on this drive, I could listen to my favorite music, stop when I wanted to look at the spectacular scenery and think about my future. Sure I knew where I was headed physically—Penticton was 248 miles northeast from my parents' home—but emotionally, I was not sure where I was at with my husband.

I became temporarily lost in thoughts of our first encounter—a blind date set up by my cousin, Joan and her husband Gerry. Both worked at the Richmond RCMP detachment and knew both Peter and me. Then I smiled as I remembered our dating days, how carefree we were then! I thought about Pete's desire for a dozen children. He talked of his dreams, his goals, and I saw his ambition. At the time I was not sure I wanted any children; I had a great career and so did he. But it did not matter then . . . we had our lives stretched before us.

As I drove through Hope, I took one last spin past our old home. Empty now, only the memories were left. It was with mixed feelings that I drove back onto the freeway and headed northeast. I briefly reviewed what I liked about Hope—a small town where you got to know all of your neighbors, the proximity to my parents (only a 1 ½ hour drive), great friends, good school, inexpensive to live and relatively close to the children's hospital versus what I did not like: namely the limited services.

Although hopeful of the positive changes ahead of us in Penticton, the past was very much staring me in the face. Jarad had been diagnosed at five weeks of age as a failure to thrive, and at seven years old that label remained. Over the past seven years, Jarad had had open heart surgery, closed heart surgery, unexplained rashes, and respiratory infections, as well as complications and severe allergic reactions. Tyler had Type 1 diabetes since he was seven years old and required daily finger pokes and insulin shots.

The trauma from our children's medical conditions was mounting, and Pete faced unfulfilled promises at work that built stress and then a financial crisis that caused a definite shift in our relationship. I believe he was frustrated and I was not sympathetic to his needs. This put our already strained relationship on thin ice. There were many problems we faced and most, I believed, centered on our lack of communication, which we've been working on.

I thought back to our first hurdle shortly after Tyler was born when Peter became withdrawn. Weeks later, Peter finally admitted that he felt helpless to protect his new son, and his thoughts were paralyzing him. It was clear Peter wanted to be a hands-on daddy but something was keeping him from it. There were emotional barriers preventing him from getting close, when it was clearly evident that protection was what Pete wanted most. What he was experiencing was beyond new-parent anxiety, far deeper and more traumatic. Poor guy, I thought, whatever this demon from his past, it had now stepped in as a barrier in our relationship, too.

While living in White Rock, Peter had voiced concerns that he felt left out since our new son had come home from the hospital, especially while I focused on breastfeeding and being a first time Mom to our new baby. I was exhausted, from all the sleepless nights. Peter was back working 12 hour shifts and our intimate life suffered, which in turn I did nothing for meeting his needs. I had little time for Peter, our first baby consuming my attention. A vicious cycle, I am sure, but think all new families experience it. It appeared that my strong husband was more fragile than I had ever imagined.

A few years later, somehow I got the thought in my head that if we had another baby, things would improve, and in no time I was pregnant again. I relished all of the attention bestowed on me—complete strangers smiled and asked so many questions as I answered, "I am due at the end of September; no, we do not want to know the sex of the baby as long as it is healthy, that's all that matters." But again I think Peter was feeling even more left out and ignored, by me, after Ashley's birth.

Sadly Peter continued to withdraw and while he was at work or away on assignments, all the family responsibilities rested solely on my shoulders. We talked less and I became more engaged with being a full-time stay-at-home mother to our two children. I doted on our children, making a detrimental mistake that would take a lot of work to recover from.

The more I saw our train swiftly careening off the tracks; the more I focused on mothering, the further engrossed Peter became with his work and taking police courses, and the more he appeared to withdraw from his family. And then at work he suffered major disappointments. Neither of us was happy at this time in our lives.

So when Tyler was three and Ashley one, we went to a Marriage Encounter weekend to try to restore our battered relationship. The time alone that weekend, combined with the great communication we shared, gave us both renewed hope for our future together. When the weekend was over, we drove away from the facility, Rosemary Heights, with both of us happy and hopeful we now had the tools that would enable our marriage to survive.

But six weeks later we learned that I was pregnant once again. More pressure at a time when everything was still rocky. How could we have been so foolish? The unplanned pregnancy led to a birth that changed our lives forever.

Immediately after his birth, Jarad was whisked away to an incubator with its heightened oxygen flow. He remained there for almost forty-eight hours because his blood-gas numbers indicated a problem. Meanwhile my maternal instincts continued to warn me that something was seriously wrong with Jarad, especially when they told me we had to leave the hospital two days later. I did not want to leave, but I failed to adequately explain what was fueling my fears. The staff assured me that medically everything was okay with him, but I wanted to remain in the safety of the hospital. This was such a different reaction to my first two deliveries, where I begged to go home just hours after giving birth.

Concentrate on driving, I told myself. Pay attention to the road. I needed a break, I decided, and pulled off into the Lodge at Manning Park. I got out of the car and walked around, clearing my head by enjoying the beauty, the crisp air, and all of the activity in the park. There was a family of four, probably fellow travelers, who were eating breakfast at one of the picnic tables. After visiting the restroom and getting a bottle of juice, I decided to take a short walk. My head was clouded with so many memories; I really needed the fresh air and wilderness to clear my head.

Returning to the car, I put on a sweater; it was ten degrees cooler in the park. The chill in the air woke me up, and I was ready to get on with my journey. Catching a glimpse of the family as I drove out of the parking lot, I thought back over the past few years as Peter began to distance himself from the children and I. He would get wrapped up in Highway patrol job, his accident-training course, and his hockey. Eventually these activities filled his days and nights.

When discussing children in the early days of our marriage, we agreed that if and when they arrived that I would stay home and raise them; neither of us could envision our children in daycare. With Peters shift work—two twelve-hour days, two twelve-hour night shifts—this would be possible, if my Mom was available a day or possibly two each week. We made it work with me taking occasional day off until a month before Ashley was due to arrive. Then I resigned from my full-time job, planning to return to the work force when all of the children were in school. I loved being at home; our days were full with the usual cooking and cleaning, taking the children on walks, play dates, swimming lessons, skating, and T-ball. We read stories, colored and painted; played with Duplo, cars and dolls.

But eventually, it became warring. I recognized that I was overworked, underpaid, and felt like I received little support from my spouse. Peter may have brought home the paychecks, but I never seemed to get a break from this routine, as much as I loved the children. I slowly began to resent Peter and his freedom. We were both hurting. Maybe, accepting a transfer and leaving the security of old friends behind, we'd be forced to talk to each other more.

But at least I had my parents close by. My dad's father had passed away when he was eighteen months old. He grew up in a home in Saskatchewan with three girls and his Mom, and very near the RCMP training facility in Regina. Dad dreamed of becoming a police officer and was accepted into the Royal Canadian Mounted Police in 1948 when he was just twenty years old.

Mom grew up in New Amsterdam, British Guiana (now Guyana). Her father was an ophthalmologist, and her mom was the daughter of a very wealthy merchant family. Her family immigrated to Canada when she was nineteen, and mom went to nursing school at St. Michaels in Toronto, Ontario. Shortly after graduation, she accepted a job in remote Kitimat, B.C. where she met my dad. They were married in 1955.

Both of my parents instilled their strong work ethic in me; I can still hear their words "When you do something, always give 100%." Dad earned his GED when I was seven years old in order to advance in rank within the Royal Canadian Mounted Police. My dad was very well respected wherever we lived, and he was especially known for his sense of fairness in both his job and dealings with his family.

We had always been a close-knit family. Growing up our home was always full of love. My parents were strict but very fair, both disciplined us and I do not recall ever hearing "just wait until your father gets home." We were provided a Catholic school elementary education and I grew up with my fair share of "guilt". I was more adventurous than my sister and showed little fear. As a result I got into more trouble than she ever did.

I often took our children to my parents' home, and when we were not at their house, my parents sometimes made the trek to Hope to spend time with us. They came up to babysit, allowing Peter and I the freedom to go out for dinner or to an RCMP party. They stayed on when one of the children was sick, and gave me a hand when Peter was away, whether at work or on course. They stayed with the two older children who were in school, while I made the frequent trips to medical appointments with Jarad. Sometimes they would show up and stay with all three children while I went off to run errands or so that I could spend the day sewing. The children loved Gran and Poppa so much. Dad had retired in 1988, the year that Jarad was born, in hopes that he could spend more time with all of his grandchildren.

The tears began to fall again. "How am I going to survive with my parents five hours away?" I asked myself. My parents meant so much to me; they were always there to help us out, and were great sounding boards allowing me to vent my mounting frustrations. They were there every step of the way when I was at the hospital with Jarad, or at one of his countless doctor appointments or when, on occasion, Peter and I had a date night. Without my parents around, Peter did not feel comfortable staying home with all three children, so I seldom got a break.

I stopped for lunch at the A & W in Princeton. I always felt guilty going to a fast-food restaurant without the kids; if I was heading home to them, I would've brought French fries. When I stepped outside, there was a noticeable chill in the air; the further I drove north from the coast, the colder it got. This was no doubt a sign of things to come.

I had to remind myself again to shift my thinking, "This is a new beginning—a fresh start in many ways." Our new home, being renovated as I drove, would welcome the children in another week. I loved spring in B.C., when snow drops and crocus begin to push their way through the frozen ground. Spring—a time when everything grows, flourishes and bright colors dot the landscape.

I thought, "How I want to see Jarad flourish too! Would Jarad ever enjoy good health? Would he ever have a good appetite? Would he ever grow normally? What was preventing him from doing so?" These were the questions that I constantly asked myself.

It was March 15, a week before the official start of spring. What a great time for personal rebirth! We were moving to a much larger city with more opportunities. Hope's population somewhere around 2500; Penticton, a ski resort community, boasted a winter population of 25,000, and a summer population of 250,000 (with its two lakes and the channel cruise between them). I was looking forward to spring coming, especially with Penticton's dryer, sunnier days, and I knew I would be inspired by the fabulous lake view from the deck of our new home. Of late my life had been so stressful, and I found myself constantly coming in last in terms of priority. Watching Jarad for potential new infections and Tyler for diabetic lows was a constant concern, while giving Ashley as much attention as I could to balance out what the boys got. This all was wearing me down. Frustration was mounting and at times I felt like I was going to explode. It was the "not knowing" about Jarad that was destroying me. Every doctor that I took him to had assured me that they could find nothing wrong with him. Yet my gut instinct screamed at me that he was not well. Daily vomiting for my little man had become the norm, and how normal was that for a six year old?

In the fourteen years that Peter and I had been together, our relationship had been overwhelmed with unanticipated circumstances. I wanted to believe that this new beginning, this fresh start, was a chance to put the past behind us. For Jarad, the past was always stalking him. While the doctors said they couldn't find anything wrong, he continued to be diagnosed at every appointment as "a failure to thrive," but now I realized that, with my weight ballooning, I too was not thriving. I did nothing more than attend his appointments and read everything I could to uncover to find the root cause of Jarad's health problems. My life was dedicated to serving my children, and I had nothing left to give my husband or myself.

I had become obsessed with trying to find out why Jarad was not growing and developing like his older siblings did. His life so far had been nothing more than a series of hospitalizations and doctor appointments and so had mine. At times even Tyler and Ashley were dragged along while I desperately searched for answers.

In part, I could understand how painful it was for Peter to see his two boys facing potential life-threatening situations. I recalled the telephone calls when Peter proudly told his parents they had namesake grandsons—the only two in his entire family of five siblings. Now these young lives struggled with serious health issues.

As I rounded the bend in the highway, Penticton and its two beautiful lakes were stretched out in front of me. The sun was glistening on the water as I arrived at the Skaha Lake viewpoint. I pulled over to admire the breathtaking scenery, and once again set aside all of my concerns. The airport and city separate the two lakes. As I looked to the north, Okanagan Lake spanned beyond my field of vision to where, halfway down the lake, my sister and her family resided in nearby Kelowna. So we weren't totally without family, but I knew between her family and career she would be no substitute for my parents and all of their help.

I reminded myself that our new home and fresh start was just seven miles down the highway. I could actually see our new home from my vantage point. I climbed back in the car and drove off. For the next week I trusted that my parents would be able to handle any crisis that arose with any of our three children.

Right now, I needed to go see my husband and be assured we would be okay.

CHAPTER TWO

A Failure to Thrive?

As I pulled into the driveway, I was relieved to see that Peter was at home, not out at a hardware store. I rushed in the door to find Dan, the plumbing/air conditioning guy, and Peter hard at work. They had been converting the houses' electric baseboard heat to gas, ripping out the ceilings to prepare for the installation of the duct work, removing bathroom fixtures, and pulling up the carpets.

I could instantly see that Peter was preoccupied with the tasks at hand, and that he didn't have time for a reunion. He and Dan had even been sleeping at the house amidst the debris and dust to maximize their renovation time. Both men appeared exhausted, but not deterred.

"Wow, it looks so different in here. You two have been busy." I walked over and gave Peter a peck on the cheek. "Well, I'm ready to work so let me know what you want me to do." Peter asked me to drive to the General Paint store on Main Street to pick up wallpaper stripping materials, brushes and a five gallon pail of paint, so I could get started with that task. "And while you are out, can you pick up some groceries?" he added

Our house was tucked away on the bluff above Skaha Lake amid the vineyards, overlooking the lake and the airport. I traveled down the windy, steep Crescent Hill Road to town. I was so upbeat; the sun was shining and it felt like spring. I followed Main Street past the strip malls until I reached the heart of the downtown core. This was about ten minutes from our new home. Penticton is a quaint city with its 25,000 population, but it was so much larger than Hope. There were even a few traffic lights along the way, but I soon found General Paint and pulled into the parking lot. I ran in with my list, and the clerk explained the best way to tackle the wallpaper removal job. She showed me the cutter and demonstrated how it would "score" the wallpaper by cutting small lines in it, and that I must rub the cut paper with a solution that would cause the paper to lift. She told me it really cleaned it off the walls, so a base coat of primer could be applied once the sheet rock had dried. She made sure I had everything I needed, including a handful of stir sticks, before I drove off to the grocery store.

As soon as I got home, I changed into grubby clothes. I took out the wallpaper cutter and prepared the bucket with the remover solution and water. I am not a fan of ladders but realized that this job would not get done without one. The kitchen ceiling was fifteen feet high on one side, and the vaulted ceiling angled down to eight feet on the other side of the room. I decided that I might as well get this over with and started on the highest wall in the room.

Peter had already removed the entry carpet and exposed the bare plywood sub floors. I set up the ladder and immediately got to work. I wanted to get as much done as possible, before the moving truck arrived with all of our possessions.

Up the ladder I went and used the cutter as instructed. I found a sponge to soak the remover onto it. I used my nails to tug off the little strips of stubborn wallpaper.

After three tedious hours on the ladder, I was tired and wet. My arms ached. The water mixture had run down from my hands and soaked my clothes. Everything I touched was sticky, including me, and I was not even close to finishing one wall. How disheartening!

The men asked if I was ready for dinner and I realized just how tired I was. We cleaned up a bit, and headed out to Peggy Sue's Diner for dinner.

All through dinner we talked "house repair." Peter began to tell about how our plan to convert from electric to gas heat and air conditioning was coming together. He filled me in on the status of the duct work and shared how easy the fireplace had been to remove. He explained how he planned to change the entire layout of the main bathroom, to give it more space.

I asked him why he had already pulled up all of the carpet, and he said that it was so nasty he just wanted it out of the house. They had already filled an entire dumpster with debris and had only been at work for a few days. Peter had contacted the movers and asked them to hold the delivery until the end of the week, giving us a little more time to complete the renovation.

He really seemed to be in his element, and I was happy for him. I hadn't recalled seeing him this enthusiastic for a long time. I was amazed at just how "handy" Peter had become, and I guess having Dan around to bounce his ideas off of helped too.

On my way home, I stopped and checked in at the Penticton Lakeside Resort. The RCMP would pay for our meals and accommodations for only a week, so we really had to make the most of the next four days.

The guys went back to the house and back to work. I knew that I had lots to do too, but I was exhausted and decided to shower and go to bed so I could get an early start the next morning. The long, emotional drive, the shopping and the wallpaper removal, had all taken its toll on me. Peter chose to spend the night at the house with Dan. So much for our romantic reunion!

I spent the better part of the next four days and evenings climbing up and down the ladder. The night before our furniture was to arrive I was finally getting close to finishing the entire wallpaper removal. The sky was getting darker but that didn't deter me. We had to get these renovations done as quickly as possible. With all the kitchen lights turned on, I went to work scoring, soaking, and tearing the wallpaper from the last wall. This was the end of it, almost finished I rejoiced! I continued to soak and peel. Water ran down the walls and onto the floor, and I hadn't noticed how slippery it had gotten.

A few minutes later, I thought that I felt the ladder start to slide, but I carried on wetting and ripping thinking it was just my imagination. All of a sudden the ladder gave way on the wet, slippery plywood, and I hung on for dear life as it crashed fifteen feet to the floor. The wild ride down stunned me. As the ladder hit the floor, my head bounced forward and slammed into the metal rungs. My arm and leg screamed out in pain as I lay on the floor calling for my husband. He had gone upstairs to bed, exhausted after his week of backbreaking work. There was no response; Pete was a heavy sleeper. I dragged myself up the stairs on my knees, since putting pressure on my foot was just too painful. At the bedroom door, I called out, "Peter... Peter, get up; the ladder collapsed, and I think I broke some bones."

"Can't this wait until tomorrow?" he asked groggily.

"No," I yelled back. I could feel myself going into shock and starting to tremble.

Peter seemed angry that I had awakened him up and asked him to take me to the hospital. I know he felt pressured to finish up before the movers arrived in the morning, but his response to my medical emergency was really cold-hearted.

We drove there in silence. I got the impression that he felt I had done this intentionally. I said I was sorry, but that did not stir a response. Peter walked me into the hospital's emergency entrance. He waited until I was safely on a gurney and asked me to call him when I was released knowing that visits to the emergency room could take hours. I was shaking and freezing, and I knew that I was in shock. My ankle and my wrist were throbbing and swelling. My eyebrow was bleeding.

As he turned to go, I felt abandoned and angry. I was counting on us making a fresh start, and this certainly was not how I had imagined it!

The x-rays revealed broken bones in my ankle, so a cast was placed on my lower left leg; my wrist was also sprained, and a bandage was placed above my eye. I was given crutches and pain killers. I called Peter for a ride. He arrived and helped me into the car. On the way to the hotel, he said little and listened intently as I explained what the doctor had said—I was supposed to elevate and rest my leg and arm. I thought he might join me in the room, but he just dropped me back at the hotel. Peter kissed me goodbye as I got myself and my crutches out of the car. I walked through the hotel doors again wondering about our future. I cautiously made my way to the elevator and into my room. There was little I could do in my condition, so I sat and cried. I hurt everywhere, physically and emotionally, and I just didn't want to be left alone, especially tonight.

Since I arrived in Penticton, there had not been any time for intimacy. We had both been so distracted by our long list of things to do and the time constraint we were under. First Dan was at the house 24/7, and now I had really done a number on my body. We were both working at the house all day and until late every night. I knew we were unlikely to experience any closeness in the near future with me all banged up, so I did not object when he told me he would be spending the next few nights at the house, so he and Dan could maximize their time. Torn between what needed to be done and what I needed, disappointment collapsed in on me as I spent another painful, restless night alone.

I arrived at the house just before the moving truck the next morning. The rain was gently falling and there was a definite chill in the air. The moving guys were great and brought in our recliner first, so I had a comfortable place to sit. Pete found me a pillow and a blanket in one of the boxes. My job became director of the moving men and the furniture and boxes that they were bringing in. Our home was a three-level back-split over 3000 square feet. The entire back of the house on both floors were sun decks. Sitting in my chair, I was happy to point the movers upstairs to one of the three bedrooms, to set up the dining room and living room furniture on the main floor, or to take storage boxes to the basement.

My injuries only slowed me down slightly. Knowing how much remained to be done I set up service on the gas and electric companies, the cable TV, and the telephone. Then I focused on preparing for the children's arrival and their first days at their new school. I visited the school and signed them up for classes and picked up all the teacher/class information. I made sure they had all the school supply requirements for their first day.

In the meantime, Peter and Dan were chugging right along. New fixtures had been installed in the two bathrooms, and the ducting was almost complete; the gas company had run a line to the house, the fireplace was dismantled and replaced with sheet rock walls, the new railings were up on the stairs and the upstairs carpets were laid. The furniture was in all of the bedrooms, so we all had a familiar place to lay our heads at the end of the day. We still had plywood floors on the main level, but we had purchased beautiful oak laminate and the boxes were stacked in the corner of the living room.

As evening set in around us, I noticed it was getting colder. I put on a sweater and hobbled out onto the balcony, wanting to get some fresh air and to enjoy the view. I loved how the moon shimmered across the lake, and as I glanced over the railing, I saw our picturesque city laid out before me. I wished Peter would come and sit by my side for a few minutes. Lights from the park illuminated the walkways and the folks out for an evening stroll. In the distance the blinking runway lights at the city's international airport announced an incoming plane. Having an airport just minutes away was wonderful! My thoughts then turned to Jarad and the many 1 ½ hour long drives we had taken to the children's hospital for appointments or testing or emergencies. I briefly wondered if we would ever have to use this airport to get him to the children's hospital in a hurry. I could not imagine driving 4 ½ hours from Penticton with me stressing all the way. He had been through so much these past seven years: a traumatic birth, open- and closed-heart surgeries, heart catheterization, second- and third-degree burns, allergic reactions, and he was still labeled with the onerous tag of: failure to thrive, which seemed to describe both of us.

At this point it was very obvious that my life was on hold, while we awaited a diagnosis that would explain six-year-old Jarad's deteriorating condition. Until I could make sense of what was happening to him, there was no way I could do anything to help myself. For a split second I was flooded with the feeling of helplessness and hopelessness from dealing with both Tyler's diabetes and Jarad's daily illness. I was under great pressure, feeling alone and overwhelmed, when I recalled a decisive moment on my recent drive to Hunter Creek, just outside of Hope. As I perched myself on a boulder in the middle of the swollen creek, I thought about ending my life by jumping into the icy rapids. In my mind's eye, I saw the reassuring faces of my three angels and climbed carefully across to the other side of the creek. On my drive home, I realized I had to fight, not give up, and that I had the courage and strength to deal with anything that came my way.

My eating was out of control, and my growing size only made me more frustrated. Nothing seemed to be going well, and this broken ankle was just another confirmation.

My life was moving too fast and I really needed to take a break. Maybe this cast was intended to slow me down, at least for the next few weeks. My thoughts turned back to Jarad and all that we had been through together and the apparent mystery surrounding his ill-health. In truth his "failure to thrive" totally baffled me; I'd always believed there was some underlying condition causing his lack of appetite, and I had sought a diagnosis from almost every department at the children's hospital—from cardiology, to infectious disease, to allergies and gastroenterology. None of the doctors could find a reason for his slow growth, although it was a concern for all of them. This made me feel like the least competent parent on the face of the earth, that I was somehow responsible and that it must be the result of parental neglect. We were just three months away from Jarad's seventh birthday, and he still had more sick days than good days. Surely by now he should have outgrown whatever was impeding him.

I reflected back to Jarad's arrival in the world: the nurses telling me to push—saying my baby was in fetal distress, and then to immediately following Jarad's birth when he was whisked away to the nursery and placed in an incubator. I recalled having a quick shower, and then heading straight for the nursery and being confused and sad. Standing beside the incubator, I asked the nurse caring for Jarad, "Please, tell me what's happening here."

I was so afraid it was something serious, but after what seemed an eternity she said, "He's doing better: his skin color is normal now and his breath sounds are good. His oxygen saturation levels are normal now too." I reached my hands inside the incubator to gently touch his soft skin. As we connected, the tears silently dripped down my cheeks. Despite her assurances, I was confused and afraid for him. Earlier I thought he may have suffered from brain damage during the delivery.

The nurse explained that Jarad was born with 'two true knots' in his umbilical cord, and that his cord was also wrapped snuggly around his neck. "And this would explain his low Apgar score, or his inability to pink up, immediately following his birth."

She added, "I feel confident that Jarad will be just fine, and there is no chance he suffered brain damage." However, I was not convinced. As I observed him through the glass, I silently prayed for Jarad.

I believed that if I could just hold my precious baby boy that somehow he would be fine. If he continued to "pink up," his nurse assured me that in twelve hours she could take him out of the oxygen and I hold him, at least briefly.

Just then I longed to hold my other two children, Tyler and Ashley. Their hugs have always had a way of taking away my pain and making everything feel so much better. I wanted so much to be a part of their simplistic lives right now.

But what could I have said to them about their little brother. Would they worry about him, locked inside the small box, as I was?

As I dreamily looked across the lake, I realized that here I was again, alone, only this time all three of my children were away from me when I needed them the most. Peter was too engrossed in the renovations – he gave his all. He had always been so committed to his career. All just excuses for his inability to nurture his family, I believed. A tear trickled down my cheek. I was feeling sorry for my self being all banged up and feeling alone!

At the hospital that first night after Jarad's birth, I was overcome with fear. The guilt was crippling, as I wondered if smoking throughout my pregnancy was at the root of Jarad's traumatic birth. I stayed in the nursery all night, not daring to leave his side. Sleep eluded me.

The nurses were monitoring Jarad's blood gases. This meant regular heel pokes and blood draws. It was on his first day that I heard, "Your son is a very poor bleeder." His tiny feet required more squeezing to just get a few drops of blood out resulting in terrible bruises.

Jarad had only been out of the isolette a few hours when we were told it was time for us to leave the hospital. I felt panic grip me, and began to beg the nurses to allow us to stay longer. "We need the beds," I was told. "New moms and their babies are lining the hallways."

Despite reassurances from the medical staff, my maternal instincts continued to warn me that something was seriously wrong with my newborn son.

We spent those first few days after our release from the hospital at my parents' home in North Delta. On the second day, my mom alerted me to Jarad's labored breathing. My untrained eyes and ears did not comprehend what she was explaining. But I did call the doctor and repeated mom's description of my infant son's breathing.

The first two times I had brought babies home from the hospital, everything flowed smoothly. I confidently looked after the house and the children. Now it seemed like I was constantly distracted, and whenever I started something, I'd run to check on my newborn. I didn't feel comfortable if I could not see, or hear him. If I had had a medical background, perhaps I might have identified what my heart was telling me was wrong with my baby. All I knew was that my gut instincts were definitely saying, "Something is seriously wrong."

A few days later we left the comfort and safety of Mom and Dad's house and made the 1 ½ hour drive home to Hope with tears gently slipping down my cheeks the whole way. I loved this baby with all of my heart, and I surprised myself by the depth of love for him already. Jarad may have only entered our lives, but I could not imagine our lives without him.

Once home we all slipped into our daily routine. When the public health nurse came for our first home visit, I was surprised to hear that my baby had actually gained almost a pound in weight and that she believed all else appeared to be normal. However, only hours later Jarad began to vomit after each feeding. This was unusual and alarmed me.

At my regular White Rock doctor's office, I told our general practitioner that I believed something was wrong with Jarad. We had seen her just two weeks ago, before returning to Hope. "I don't know what's wrong with him;

I just know he doesn't behave like either of my two other babies. He sleeps but seems lethargic and he vomits after almost every feeding." I told her I had not gotten over the trauma from his difficult birth.

She assured me, "He looks and sounds good, and time will heal and fade the memories." After the appointment we drove to my parents' home for a visit and dinner, before we made the 1 ½ hour drive back to Hope.

When Jarad was three weeks old, I decided it is time to see a local Hope doctor—the drive to our old White Rock doctor was too long, especially if there was an emergency. So after asking around, I made an appointment for the whole family to be seen. The new general practitioner in Hope quickly examined Tyler, Ashley and me. I watched as the doctor listened to Jarad's heart, checked his joints and measured his tiny body. He said everything looked good. I told him about Jarad's persistent vomiting, but he seemed to downplay my concern and simply told me all babies spit up. My other two never did, I wanted to say, but decided to bite my tongue and not to argue with him. The doctor did tell me that Jarad's skin appeared jaundiced, and he suggested he may have breast-milk jaundice. (I simply thought Jarad had inherited my golden-toned skin!) The doctor ordered a blood test, and again there was an ordeal as the lab technician tried to squeeze out enough blood to test.

A week later the vomiting escalated to violent projectile vomiting. My baby had also begun losing weight. I was relieved when the Hope general practitioner referred me back to our pediatrician. At our appointment, I could see by the worried look on her face that she was puzzled by Jarad's symptoms. She asked us to take Jarad immediately to the children's hospital.

Once at the hospital, we were quickly introduced to the teaching hospital's hierarchy, and something told me my medical education was about to begin. First Jarad was examined by a nurse clinician, then an intern wearing a short white coat, and then by a resident doctor in a long white coat. Two emergency room pediatricians told us that Jarad appeared to have pyloric stenosis and that he would be scheduled for surgery in the morning. The procedure was explained, and we were told they would keep him in the hospital for a few days following his surgery. But first they would confirm the diagnosis with ultrasound.

The lights were dimmed in the diagnostic room. The ultrasound technician looked puzzled as he pointed to the screen. The emergency room pediatrician confirmed my suspicion: ultrasound did not reveal pyloric stenosis but offered no hint as to what may be plaguing Jarad. I began to panic. Both Peter and I were confused and exhausted. I wished that my nagging feelings of an impending crisis would just go away.

The emergency room pediatrician suggested that Jarad should be admitted to the children's hospital for observation immediately. This first hospitalization would last five days and reveal nothing new—except my exposure to the hospital world: its many wards, illnesses and diseases, and a growing list of potential tests and procedures. It was overwhelming. Finally we were told that they couldn't find anything wrong with Jarad "from a surgical standpoint." The upper GI series, chest x-ray, and the ultrasound showed no abnormalities with any of his major organs.

However, I (with the help of a lactation consultant) came up with a reasonable and plausible explanation for his vomiting: a case of overactive letdown reflex that was causing him to get too much breast milk too quickly. This diagnosis gave the stumped doctor a reason to allow our discharge—if I promised to bring Jarad back if symptoms persisted.

I became obsessed, the focus of my existence turned to getting my baby baptized; I began to think Jarad's vomiting was spiritually based—maybe he was possessed? As I walked out of the Rosemary Heights chapel, I felt relieved to have had this sacrament performed just in case his illness was more serious than we were being told. But those feelings were short-lived, when just minutes later on our way home he vomited all over his baptism outfit and the backseat of the car.

My husband and my parents questioned me about Jarad. No one spent as much time with him as I did. Maybe it was just me? I wondered. Was I making this out to be bigger deal than it was, exaggerating his symptoms? After reviewing the reports from the children's hospital, even the general practitioner had suggested I see a psychologist!

Two and a half weeks later, I was back in the doctor's office. Jarad seemed to have a cold with thick mucus choking him. He was still vomiting and his bowel movements were frothy. This time, the general practitioner ordered another bilirubin test; again he did suspect there is a problem and he called the children's hospital to set up another ultrasound.

The next day at the local Health Unit, Jarad started to choke and gasp for air. In desperation I looked up at the nurse for an explanation. The panic on my face met horror on hers. She seized the opportunity to call our doctor and relay what she just witnessed. For the first time I felt like I had someone on my side, and that gave me strength to make a call that I believe saved my tiny sons' life—the first time.

Even though it was 9:00 P.M., I called our pediatrician at home. Thank goodness she had given me her home number at our last visit. I described the health-unit incident; I told her how scared I was and that a friend had suggested Jarad may have cystic fibrosis. I told her I was desperately afraid my tiny son was going to die.

She called me the following morning to say the testing was all lined up for Monday morning. As it was only Friday she asked if I thought he would be okay until then. She said if at any time I felt things were not going well, to get him to the hospital as soon as possible. I told her I would. I told her I was taking him back to see the general practitioner today.

At the appointment, the general practitioner carefully examined our tiny baby then he gently suggested, again, that I should seek the services of a psychiatrist. "I can recommend a good one," he added. I told him that I would let the pediatrician conduct her recommended series of tests first. "After that, if there is nothing wrong with my baby, I will be happy to follow through with your advice," I told him as I got up to leave his office.

Jarad was not quite two month old when we headed to Vancouver for the pediatrician arranged appointment at the children's hospital. The pediatrician had told me that she would proceed slowly and cautiously. Only some blood work and the sweat test today. "There is no need to come prepared to stay; we will look at the results and then decide what our next step will be. You can go home right after the tests are complete." I just wanted answers. I truly believed that my baby was close to death's door. I was so scared. What they would discover, however, would involve life-saving surgery on one of Jarad's major organs and would keep us all at the children's hospital for many weeks.

Two days later I checked out of the Penticton hotel and drove to our new home to drop off my belongings. When I arrived, Dan had finished all of the conversion and installation work on the house and was heading back to Hope. Mom and dad had brought the children up to my sister's home in Kelowna. I was excited as I headed there to finally pick them up. At last, I thought, we were going to be a whole family again.

I had not told anyone about my injury, and my family was shocked to see my battered body. We all laughed over my clumsiness, and I didn't tell them how harrowing it really was. I was in a hurry to return to Penticton and to show the children their new home. As I stood beside the car saying goodbye, I was balancing on one leg with my hand on the top of the door frame. Jarad grabbed the door handle and slammed the car door shut, squeezing the fingers on my good hand in the door jam. I let out a shriek as Dad ran over and opened the car door. My fingers were bruised but not broken. I drove back to Penticton, the fingers on my hand pulsating and throbbing.

The kids loved the house, most especially the view and the yard. They raced through the three floors in search of their daddy, bursting to tell him about their week away. Unfortunately he was in the middle of finishing a project and could not leave it, so I gave them all their baths and a last minute pep talk about their new school and what to expect in the morning. Once they were all tucked away for the night, I went out to the deck. I relaxed with my cast propped up on the stool. I really was blessed to have such doting parents. Looking out over the lake and the city lights, I realized that this wasn't the fresh start I had been hoping for. While I wasn't *really* feeling very romantic, what I was feeling was uneasy and I wondered what that was telling me.

CHAPTER THREE

The I.C.U.

Monday morning was here before we knew it. My children's excitement was high on what would be the first day at their new school in Penticton. We headed off down the hill to Snowdon Elementary School, discussing the new friends they would likely meet as they wondered out loud about their teachers. I was relieved that all three children would still be in the same school. I knew Tyler and Ashley would keep an eye on their little brother in my absence.

Suddenly I heard the familiar sound of Jarad gagging, one that alerted us to grab a barf bag and hand it to him quickly. We all knew the drill. There was never enough time to discuss what was about to happen—only time to act! My heart went out once again to my precious boy. Our enthusiasm was instantly dampened by the sadness reflected on his face. "Could this be a simple case of nerves?" I asked myself. Ashley was always the quickest to respond; she handed the bag to him. Almost on cue, Jarad began a gut-wrenching course of vomiting. I watched him in the rearview mirror. His skin was so pale, and he looked weak, almost faint.

"We will all get through this," I kept telling myself, only half believing it. I parked the car and escorted each of the children to their new classrooms. As I dropped them off, we were introduced to their respective teachers. Tyler was the first—at eleven years old, it is not cool to be walked into your new classroom by your Mom. He cheerfully said, "See you later," and made his way inside.

Ashley was next. Her teacher, Barb Parliament, was so sweet. She immediately took Ashley under her wing as a newcomer, and introduced her to a group of girls talking near the door. I was confident that both Tyler and Ashley would be fine, but my real concern was Jarad, who was obviously feeling sick again and clung to my side.

When we got to his classroom, we found his teacher yelling at a little boy. Jarad held tighter to my leg. I could feel his apprehension and almost hear him wondering if she would yell at him too if he got sick in her classroom. I wanted to pick him up and run away from this mean teacher, away from this unsettling experience, but I persevered. After timidly knocking and not being heard, I walked him through the door. The teacher had a group of first-grade children surrounding her desk, each of them demanding her attention. She was so preoccupied that she did not even notice us standing there.

I called out her name as I stepped up to the side of the desk, towering above the children. Finally she glanced over and somewhat impatiently asked if she could help me. Spotting Jarad, she said, "Oh, the new boy," and nodded toward a desk at the front of the classroom. I wanted to explain all that Jarad had been through his short life and how sick he had been on the way here and beg her to be kind and gentle—two traits she appeared to lack.

I just stared at her for a moment gauging her impatience, then simply told her that Jarad was not feeling well and we would return tomorrow if he felt better. I bolted out of the classroom with him clutching tightly to my hand. We headed straight for the car and were silent on our ride home. The color was slowly beginning to return to Jarad's cheeks by the time we walked safely through our kitchen door. Maybe it was just nerves after all.

He asked for some ginger-ale to drink and wanted to lie down. I took him upstairs to my room. Peter had stopped off at home briefly, and he shot me a contemptuous look. My husband believed that I coddled Jarad and would not like my explanation for keeping him home on his first day at school. He claimed that I made too many excuses for his myriad of illnesses, and he was not happy that I dismissed his simplistic diagnoses like car sickness for Jarad's vomiting fits.

After Peter left, I cleaned up the breakfast plates, wondering, "Is it me? Am I suffering from separation anxiety now that all three children are in school? Was I responsible for holding my darling little boy back?"

"No," I answered myself. "This has nothing to do with me and everything to do with Jarad. He cannot possibly fake vomiting, nor can what affects him simply be car sickness. That is crazy! What about the numerous times he throws up when we are just at home all day?"

As we lay on the bed, I saw that Jarad was already asleep. "He must feel so miserable," I told myself. Again I wondered what was happening to him, to us, as I thought back to the evening of September 12, 1988—six and a half years ago. I had returned to the hospital, from my parents' home, and was prepared to spend the night at the children's hospital with Jarad, but he was not in his crib on the second floor where I had left him.

As my parents and I walked through the door to his empty room, my heart leapt into my throat. I feared that he had died after the exhausting day of testing we had been through. But his nurse was walking close behind us, saying Jarad had been moved to 3G and asked me, "Do you know how to get there?" I knew where it was. He had been admitted to the unit 3 weeks prior. I did not answer her question, but asked instead: "Why was he moved?" He was asleep when I had left the hospital not three hours earlier. "What happened?" The nurse simply pointed us in the direction of the cardiology unit and watched us leave.

Why cardiology? I asked myself, and then turned to my parents as we hurried down the corridor. "This is where Jarad spent his first night when we were here three weeks ago." At the moment that thought actually calmed me down. Why should I be worried; the report from the children's hospital to our doctor in Hope clearly stated: "There is nothing wrong with any of his major organs." I told myself that, if there was something seriously wrong with my baby, he would have been moved to the Intensive Care Unit, so deduced it was not too serious. I was familiar with 3G, and I understood that the observation room had one nurse for every two patients, so I felt confident that whatever happened, he was being closely monitored. I lead the way with my Mom and Dad in tow, up one floor in the elevator, but as we silently walked past the oncology playroom, I realized that I was unconsciously rushing through the maze of hallways to get to the 3G cardiology unit.

When we got to the blue doors of the module, I could hear my baby's weak cry, one that was distinctly his. There was no mistake now; something was definitely wrong with my tiny baby. A feeling of dread simmered throughout my entire body.

When we passed through the doors of the observation room, I stared in horror and disbelief. In the middle of the room, at least fifteen doctors and nurses surrounded his crib. They were all busy but talking in hushed voices—controlled chaos, I thought. The room was incredibly bright, but I could not take my eyes off the teeny baby who was at the center of all of their attention.

Suddenly I screamed out, "What are you doing to my baby?" Someone blurted out, "His heart is enlarged." I was paralyzed for an instant, feeling as if I had been kicked. I felt a tightening grip in the pit of my stomach, and vomit had begun to rise to my throat. Someone gently nudged me, but at first I could not move, and then finally I allowed them to push me gently forward and out of the room. I looked back over my shoulder as the door swung closed.

Mom, Dad and I were corralled into the tiny office across the hall from the observation room. Although the door was closed I could still hear Jarad's cries. We were joined immediately by a doctor in a long white coat. She basically told us, "At this time, all we know is that a chest x-ray has revealed that Jarad's heart is grossly enlarged, and we are doing everything we can to stabilize him." The doctor then hurried off.

Then we were joined by a nurse, Mary. She appeared relaxed, kind, and understanding. She asked if we wanted anything, or if she could do anything for us. Solemnly we shook our heads. Mary told us that the pediatric intensivist was examining Jarad right now and that he would be in to speak to us shortly.

I felt disconnected from the scene, as I asked Mom and Dad, "How did this happen?" This was so unbelievable—his heart? They also shook their heads in disbelief; none of us had an answer, nor could we recall any medical history in either family to account for this development in my baby.

The pediatric intensivist finally walked into the small, stuffy room. He reiterated what the previous doctor had said, and then added, "An echocardiogram has been ordered and a cardiologist is on his way. Right now Jarad is experiencing heart failure. He's receiving oxygen and an intravenous line is feeding him a diuretic to pull the fluid off his heart and he is being administered a heart drug to help him to cope."

I could still hear Jarad's weak cries. I asked the doctor, "Is he in pain?"

The pediatric intensivist assured me, "No, not real pain, but he is uncomfortable as he struggles." He went on to explain that, "Jarad is having difficulty breathing, and unfortunately he does not like the oxygen mask." I felt as if I was going to explode. Tears began to run down my cheeks. I was shaking and suddenly my entire body was wracked with sobs. I felt the desolate pain of utter helplessness. Then panic suddenly struck me.

I had no medical training, but when I thought about Jarad's enlarged heart, the image of a balloon came to mind: if it got too large, it would burst. Would the same happen with a heart? Suddenly everything was so bleak. I was shaking, crying, and felt like throwing up. I was too overwhelmed to ask more questions as the pediatric intensivist left us alone with our grief.

It had been my intention to drive back to the hospital alone that night, but now I was so grateful Mom and Dad had returned to be here with me. I could not imagine having to walk into this crisis situation by myself.

The pediatric cardiologist was the next to stop by our waiting room. He told us that unfortunately, at this time, he only knew, ". . . for sure, that Jarad is a critically ill baby." He went on to say, "The technician had started an echocardiogram and hopefully they would know more in about thirty minutes." He explained the procedure then ran out to watch as it was being performed.

The absolutely hardest part of having a sick child is the "not knowing" part: once you know, you can get on with your life, adapt and change your lifestyle to cope with any situation, if necessary. Finally, it appeared—or at least at that moment—we were about to get answers to the questions that had been haunting me for the past eight weeks. Although scared, I began to feel empowered, at last.

So many questions flew through my mind: "What happened? What caused this?" Most importantly was, "Will Jarad die?" I had to get out of this stuffy little office and distance myself from Jarad's helpless cries.

I needed a cigarette. This was too much to endure without one. But the thought of all of the cigarettes that I had consumed while I was pregnant brought on a new wave of guilt: Maybe smoking caused this heart defect. I would have to ask the doctor, even thought I was afraid of my own reaction to his possible verification. Nonetheless, my urge for a cigarette won out, and Mom and I walked in to the parents lounge to wait while they finished up Jarad's echocardiogram.

I looked at the phone on the wall. "I really should call my husband but what will I say to him?" I thought to myself and decided to wait until we had received some concrete answers. For now I just sat, smoked, and cried. I was overwhelmed in disbelief.

Dad was drinking a glass of juice when we got back to the little office. I noticed a plate of sandwiches sitting on the desk. The nurse came in to ask if she could get Mom and me anything. I said no, but mom asked for a coffee. Mary returned a few minutes later with a cup and some packets of coffee creamer. Everything seemed to move in slow motion around me. "Why aren't they finished yet? What is taking them so long? Why is Jarad still crying?"

Shortly thereafter the pediatric cardiologist came in to talk to us. I braced myself for what the he was about to tell us. The gentle man picked up a little red book called *Your Heart Matters*, and opened it to the diagram of a heart. He told us that the echocardiogram had, "Revealed a pretty clear picture of Jarad's defect. His condition is known as 'total anomalous pulmonary venous return' (or T.A.P.V.R. for short)." He described this heart defect and drew a picture to show how the normal heart worked and then one to show how Jarad's heart was currently pumping. He went on to explain that surgery must be performed immediately to correct this problem. I interrupted him to ask the question that was heavy on my heart. "Is it possible that my smoking caused this?" The doctor was very quick to say that the causes for this type of heart defect were unknown and went on to assure me that it was nothing more than a fluke of nature. Although I felt some relief at his explanation, I still couldn't help but feel horribly guilty about my smoking habit.

He continued, "Hopefully the ICU staff will be able to stabilize your son, which will give us the remainder of the night to assemble an alert surgical team to perform early-morning surgery on Jarad." The doctor said that Jarad would be first in the main operating room, and due to the seriousness of his condition, he would bump any previously scheduled surgeries. He also told us that Jarad being eight weeks of age was definitely in his favor. He explained that, "Jarad's heart should be the size of his little fist, but one side is as small as a peanut, while the other is stretched to more than twice its normal size."

He briefly went over the open-heart surgery plan and then went on to tell us that they were preparing Jarad to be transferred to the intensive care unit as he spoke. He said that we were welcome to see Jarad once more in the observation room before they transferred him downstairs to the ICU. I eagerly joined my tiny son in the brightly lit room. He appeared somewhat calmer as the sedatives had taken effect. They had also stopped fighting to keep the oxygen mask on his face and were running oxygen into a 14-by-14 inch Plexiglas box, in which his entire head had been placed. As soon as everything was in order, they asked us to step aside so they could get him to the ICU.

Later Mary returned to say that if we would like to say goodnight, we could go down to the ICU now. She accompanied us to the closed doors and showed us how to open them. Once inside, we donned surgical gowns and washed our hands in the big stainless steel sinks. We were then escorted to "cubicle nine," which would become Jarad's new home for the time being. We were told that he would have two ICU nurses monitoring him throughout the night and most likely for the next day or two. As I stood there helplessly watching my son, I did not even realize that I was crying and shaking. I was completely focused on my precious baby. As I bent to touch his tiny hands, I quietly told him, "Be good for the nurses." I called Jarad by Ashley's nickname for him, "Big Guy, have a good sleep, I love you so much," I said with tears streaming down my cheeks. I kissed his tiny hand. With one last look back, I said that we all loved him and that I would return in the morning. As I walked away, I was calmed by the fact that Jarad finally looked peaceful. He had stopped crying and was almost asleep. I prayed that God would keep him safe until morning, and knew Jarad would be getting the best possible care tonight. I could see that he was in experienced, capable and loving hands. Despite my objections, the doctors and nurses had convinced my parents to take me home. I would definitely need my strength in the days to come, they told my parents.

On the long drive home, I said it seemed like we had been at the hospital forever, but Dad told me it had only been fourteen hours. I sat and tried to relax, but it felt like everything was moving in slow motion. The time away from the hospital, when they are unable to reach me, was the most torturous. We got back to my Mom and Dad's home by 2:00 A.M., and I ran inside to see if the hospital had called. In my heart I knew that I should call my husband, but I did not have the strength or the presence of mind to pick up the phone. Besides, I did not want to tie up the line if the hospital was trying to reach me. This was torture! Dad poured us all a drink. I just sat there and stared off into space, lost in my jumbled thoughts.

Then I heard Dad talking on the telephone and explaining the events of this evening. I correctly guessed that he had called Peter, who then asked to speak with me. I reluctantly answered his questions in monosyllables. I did not give him any further details and wanted to end the call. When my husband said, "I'm relieved," I was instantly enraged. What did he mean—relieved? Peter obviously did not comprehend the severity of this crisis. (Weeks later I would discover that he was "relieved" that we finally knew what was wrong with our baby and that it was a defect that could be repaired.) For me, Peter earlier doubting my concerns about Jarad had taken a serious toll on our relationship. We said our goodnights.

As I finished my second drink, I realized that I was mentally and physically exhausted. I worked my way up the stairs to my old bedroom, once again totally alone—a very uncomfortable feeling for a woman with a husband, two toddlers and a newborn baby. I needed my family to help me feel whole again. I noticed the clock read 4:30 A.M.

The next morning I received a call from the pediatric cardiac surgeon, he had reviewed Jarad's case and carefully explained the plan for Jarad's heart surgery. He asked for my verbal authorization to proceed with it. We were given only 25% odds that Jarad would survive the impending open-heart surgery. I told the pediatric cardiac surgeon that I wanted to be at the hospital before they took Jarad into the operating room, and I asked if I could donate my own blood rather than utilize the Canadian Red Cross's donor blood. We knew that Jarad would require blood and blood products for this surgery. He explained that the Red Cross diligently screened all of their blood and blood products, and he informed me there was more risk that I would infect him with something at this late date. So, Jarad Matthew Gibbenhuck would be transfused with donor blood despite my request. Testing the blood for HIV had only been implemented two years earlier and I was afraid of everything that could go wrong and all that remained unknown in the disease world.

The pediatric cardiac surgeon asked us to meet him in the ICU parents lounge around noon. Jarad would not be going to the recovery room; instead, he would go directly from the operating room back to the intensive care unit. He asked me for my oral consent for the surgery, and it was recorded over the phone.

I telephoned Peter to let him know that Jarad would be going to the operating room at 10:00 A.M., and I assured the worried daddy I would call him as soon as I had something to report. I told him that the pediatric cardiac surgeon had said that, if all went well, Jarad should be back in the ICU between 12:00 and 1:00 P.M.

Later that morning the cardiology nurse clinician, Karen, called my parents' home and said that Jarad was still in surgery, but she said he should be out shortly. She also wanted to meet us but before we saw the pediatric cardiac surgeon in the ICU.

After I spoke to her, I announced, "Okay, let's go now." I just wanted to get to the hospital to see my baby. My dad called my sister Susan to let her know that we were ready to leave the house. My mind was racing as Mom, Dad and I drove to the hospital. I heard my parents talking, but I was totally absorbed in my own thoughts. "What news will meet us when we get there? Would Jarad be one among the 25% who do not survive the surgery?" Questions; questions. Although the odds were in our favor, I sure did not like them.

Nurse Karen met us at the intensive care unit within minutes of our arrival. Again, I was happy to be greeted by a friendly and understanding face. The time was now 1:15 P.M., and Jarad was still in the operating room. We had expected to briefly speak with Karen and the pediatric cardiac surgeon, and then make our way to my baby's bedside.

Karen asked me, "How are you doing?"

How do you think I am doing right now? I wanted to snap at her, but I said nothing. She encouraged me to talk about anything: Jarad, Peter, Tyler or Ashley, or even my parents—just to keep me engaged. She was extremely compassionate as I sat beside her and wiped away my tears. I needed to get control of my emotions. Karen told me what to expect when I saw my baby. She carefully explained the reasons for the intravenous tubes, bags of fluids, the medicines and the monitors. She told me that for the next few days Jarad would be on a stretcher, not in a crib. Karen described the sounds and the brightness of the room, and talked about how Jarad would look. He would be naked, covered only by a small blanket, but it was only for my benefit. She told me that Jarad would have two nurses beside him for the next few days. They would be monitoring his progress, charting his vital statistics, but also making adjustments to his medications. She described the ventilator that would be breathing for him. The nurses would have to chart his progress every fifteen minutes around the clock.

In mid-sentence, Karen's pager went off. She went to a phone and called in. She came back and explained that the team was having difficulty getting Jarad off of the heart/lung machine; for some reason his heart was not beating on its own. Tears began to drip from my swollen eyes again. This was not the news I was praying to hear! At 2:30 P.M. we all jumped as Karen's pager went off again. While she made the call, I rested my head on my mom's shoulder and sobbed. I wanted to think more positively at the moment, but I had been prepared for the worst. As Karen returned, we breathed a sigh of relief seeing her smiling at us! Jarad had survived the surgery, and he was finally being transferred back to the ICU. They would have him settled soon, and we would be able to see him within the hour.

I smiled through my tears, as I felt a wave of relief wash over me. I knew this was just the beginning of our journey, but it was our first big step toward recovery. The pediatric cardiac surgeon poked his head in the door of the waiting room and simply said, "Technically, the surgery went well, and the rest will be up to Jarad." It was not as encouraging as it could be, but it was certainly better than the alternative. I cried tears of relief now, as the surgeon turned and walked away.

Dad suggested that I call Peter to give him the update, especially since we were two hours late. I told Peter Jarad had made it through the surgery, but that was all I could say for now.

I decided that, since it would take at least another thirty minutes to get him back to the ICU that now was a good time to go to the parents lounge and have a cigarette. After that I went to the Lactation room and used their pump on my swollen breasts to draw out the accumulating breast milk and relieve my discomfort. There I noticed that the front of my shirt was soaked.

When the time to see Jarad finally arrived, Mom went in with me because now only two family members were allowed at Jarad's bedside. We carefully washed our hands and gowned up in preparation for entering the intensive care unit. We had gotten this far, and I was certainly not taking any chances of bringing infectious germs in to my baby.

One of the nurses came to meet us and escorted us in to Jarad's bedside. Karen brought up the rear. I could not look at anything except the floor ahead of me. I was acutely aware of the lights, the noises and the smells. I was shaking and crying. I stepped forward, on legs that felt like rubber. My steps were slow and cautious. Although Karen had carefully described the layout of his area, I really had no way to imagine the intensity of the scene.

But I must have been well prepared, since I was not at all surprised. My tiny baby was laying on a long black stretcher about ten times his size. The ventilator—with its rhythmic air sucking in and then whooshing out—was breathing for him, and he had a large tube in one nostril. The other nostril contained an NG feeding tube and was somewhat smaller than the ventilator tube. He had stitches on the right side of his face, close to his hairline that was securing a triangular-shaped plastic object. This was connected to a "mainline," positioned in the jugular vein of his neck. Jarad had an arterial line in his hand (for blood tests), and another intravenous in his foot. There was a red light sensor attached to his toe (to monitor his oxygen saturation levels), a drainage tube sticking out of the side of his tummy (draining into a large box at the foot of the stretcher), a temperature probe in his rectum (measuring his core temperature), and a catheter in his penis (draining into a bag at the side of the stretcher). They had only covered his incision with the tiny blanket and it was amazing to see that very little of his tiny exposed body was untouched by medical technology.

I did not want to get too close, just in case I disturbed the carefully placed equipment. I looked to my Mom for strength and support. She held me tightly in her arms as sobs wracked my body. It was so difficult for me to watch my baby laid out this way, more than I could possibly ever have imagined. At that moment I could not believe how much I loved him! I vaguely remember hearing someone ask my Mom if I was okay. I wanted to turn and punch the mouth that uttered those insensitive words! "Look at my baby lying there; would you be okay if he were your child?" I wanted to yell. Besides, I felt I had no right to be okay; somehow it was my fault that my precious baby was in this condition right now. I was filled with guilt. I would do anything to trade places with him. I meekly responded, "Fine," and turned my attention back to my helpless baby.

I pulled myself together, and Mom said that she would go now and send my Dad right in. I do recall being truly in awe of the technology that was surrounding us and keeping my baby alive. I didn't ask any questions, just stared blankly at the machines. I was studying them, willing them to reassure me. I suppose this whole experience was just too overwhelming, and guess that I really was scared to death in these unfamiliar surroundings. My main concern was that Jarad was not suffering. I was assured repeatedly, that he was "comfortable."

I noticed the bag of blood hanging just behind the head of the bed, but I did not ask why he was still getting it. I had reluctantly agreed earlier to their use, but hardly imagined it would still need to be administered blood hours later. I noticed Dad walking toward the stretcher, and I was at once stung by the grief and sadness displayed on his face. I was hurting so much I couldn't believe that I could feel his pain too. Once again, I felt the pressure that builds up just before I break down in tears. My Dad stepped over and put his arm lovingly around me. We both sobbed in each other's arms. After a while we turned to go, and I softly told Jarad I will be back shortly.

My Dad was truly a social butterfly. He easily made friends wherever he went, and the intensive care unit of children's hospital was no exception. It turned out that while I was with Jarad, he had introduced himself to the other parents in the waiting room and was quickly becoming friends with Steve and Linda Boe.

When I finally stopped crying, Dad introduced me to the young couple. They have two children. He explained to me that Jarad had bumped their youngest son, Patrick, who was scheduled for closed-heart surgery earlier this morning. I could see the worry on their faces and I automatically felt I should apologize. I would certainly not have appreciated it if some emergency case had come in and bumped Jarad's scheduled surgery. There had been so much mental preparation that such a setback must have been devastating. But they were so gracious and explained that Patrick was now in the operating room, and that they were waiting to hear when he would be transported back to the intensive care unit. I telephoned Peter again to let him know I'd seen our baby. I didn't go into any details. As soon as we were finished our call, I knew I needed to go back into the intensive care unit to be by Jarad's side again.

As I washed up to prepare for the visit, I could feel myself slowly gaining strength. What I really wanted to do was to pick him up and hold him close to me. Instead, I settled for just being able to touch his free hand and stroke his soft cheek. For the first time I leaned over and talked to him; my voice cracked with the love that was spilling from my broken heart. "Mommy's here. I love you so much. Jarad, you have to fight now. I know that you can do it." These words were more than I could bear as the tears flooded down my cheeks. All of a sudden one of the monitors started to alarm. My heart stopped; I held my breath. I was asked to leave right away. The nurses were scurrying around him, and I did not understand what was happening. When I got to the lounge, Karen attempted to explain what had just happened. Whatever she said, the words did not register; they simply went in one ear and back out of the other.

When the nurses finally got everything under control and Jarad was settled down, Karen asked if I would like to go back in to see him. She wanted to reassure me that he was okay. "Yes, I do," I said with a nod. This time I managed to get closer to Jarad. I spoke quietly to him, telling him that his Daddy, Tyler and Ashley would be here tomorrow to see him. Tears brimmed over as I gently stroked his tiny hand. I yearned to just pick him up and hold him tightly against my body. His nurse, must have read my mind; she explained that it would be far too risky to move him at this time because his sternum had been cut and his ribs were pulled back in order to get at his tiny heart. The pain would be too intense for him if he were to be moved, and also the risk of moving the ribs could seriously impede his healing. She went on to say that as soon as he got rid of some of his IV lines, I could hold him. I was hopeful it wouldn't be too long, since the doctors had said Jarad's stay in the ICU would only be a few days. I thought I could handle this short stay!

In the present I was suddenly aware that Jarad was beginning to stir on the bed beside me. This snapped me back to reality, and yet Jarad was still sickly, if not in a life-threatening situation. Sadness overwhelmed me as I realized neither of us was doing very well. Jarad was physically sick almost every day and still carried the onerous "failure to thrive" label. I was getting heavier, my bones broken, my face cut and my heart sick in so many ways. I too shared his "failure" diagnosis. Nothing was going well, but I needed to press on and discover the root cause of Jarad's maladies and my own.

CHAPTER FOUR

Is It Just Me?

Although he was still pale and claimed to be sick, Jarad was up, dressed, and ready to go to school the next morning. Just as we were headed out the door, Peter appeared, claiming he needed a break from work. He was dressed in his RCMP uniform and seized the opportunity to take the children to school.

"I'm here to take the kids to school," he said, matter-of-factly. "Maybe if I take him, Jarad will stay all day," he added. I felt he shot me a withering look. I could see his point. "You give in too easy and should make him stay at school. The doctors say there is nothing wrong, but you think you know better. He just gets car sick . . ." It was the same conversation we had bantered back and forth since arriving in Hope.

"Yes and the same doctors say he's not . . . thriving," I replied, while thinking my maternal instincts were still telling me something was seriously wrong.

Part of the conflict between us was that we viewed Jarad differently. I had heard Peter, on a few occasions, scolding him for faking his symptoms. This broke my heart. After spending the last six and a half years by our sons' side, I knew his symptoms were very real.

After kissing my children goodbye, I assured them I would be at the school by three o'clock to pick them up. I busied myself cleaning up the breakfast dishes, and started doing the laundry. My house project for the day was to begin the arduous task of removing sheetrock dust from all surfaces that had not been covered when the walls were being sanded. I simply did not want to think about Jarad and how his day was going. My gut told me that he was certainly not faking his lingering illness, but at times I questioned myself. "Is this about me? Was it time for the psychiatric visit my doctor had suggested six years ago?"

I sat down for a moment over a cup of tea. Every time the subject of Jarad not thriving came up, my thoughts slipped back to our days in the intensive care unit at the children's hospital. My subconscious mind was trying to tell me something.

The morning after Jarad's heart surgery, I met the doctors in the hallway as I returned to the ICU. Knowing they had just examined my baby, I asked, "How is Jarad doing today?"

The pediatric cardiologist said, "You'll have to ask him," motioning toward the pediatric cardiac surgeon.

I looked to him hoping for good news. "Not too bad; he had a pretty good night."

I was 'buzzed' into the unit. Jarad lay naked on the bed and totally still. I gasped when I saw the five-inch incision on his tiny chest. I was frightened by the green-and-blue pacer wires that were sticking out of his chest, and the large chest tube draining a bloody substance through it. His tiny body was smeared with blood and disinfectant. The nurses explained the effects of the paralyzing drug Pavulon that was being administered. "He can hear but not move", they said. "You can tell by his heart rate increasing when you touch or speak to him." All of a sudden my attention turned to one of the machines as the alarm shrieked.

"What is happening?" I asked. One of the nurses shuffled me away from his bedside and asked me to wait in the parents lounge.

As I sat in the room, I agonized over what my baby was going through. I was so scared for him. My throat and neck ached. I was too stressed to even cry, but felt that if I suppressed my tears, I would explode. Like Jarad, I now realized I was brokenhearted too.

Linda walked into the lounge and sat down beside me. "Patrick's surgery went well. We should be out of here in two or three days," she said. I tried to smile but couldn't; she grasped my hands—I did not have to talk; we shared a silent understanding. Her day was going so well, mine was horrible. Finally, one of Jarad's nurses appeared at the doorway. We were invited back in to his bedside. On our way to his bedside, she explained that mucous had built up and that he had needed to be suctioned immediately. She explained, "It is a very traumatic procedure for parents new to the ICU to watch." His nurses wanted to spare me the additional pain.

Standing there, I looked around and counted fourteen intravenous bags. I did notice that the blood bag was gone. I stared at the machine breathing for him. I took in all the monitors and their constantly changing numbers. I was overwhelmed.

I gently held my baby's hand and tenderly stroked his forehead. Suddenly I noticed a new sound like raindrops falling on a plastic sheet. Puzzled, I looked around and asked, "Where is that dripping sound coming from?" I felt so silly when one of the nurses explained it was my own tears landing on the bed sheet. I was so focused on my baby, I hadn't even noticed.

I did see Jarad's lips were parched and cracking so I mentioned it to the nurses. One of them handed me a pink lollipop-looking sponge to dip in water and explained how to softly rub it on his lips. I finally felt that I was, in some small way, able to participate in my baby's care.

I headed home knowing sometime today my husband and healthy children would arrive. I was so excited to see them but was torn between my need to be with Jarad at the hospital and at my parent's home with the rest of my family. I hoped to be able to draw on Peter for the strength, support and understanding I so desperately needed.

I was upstairs when I heard the door open and heard the welcomed sound of my children's beautiful voices. They called my name as they ran into the house, then flew up the stairs and hugged my legs. Tyler was the first to reach me and sincerely exclaimed, "I missed you so much Mommy." Ashley joined in, "I missed you more," reminiscent of a game we played regularly. Ashley looked up at me puzzled, sensing something was wrong. She looked around then she asked, "Where's Big Guy?" I crumbled to the floor in tears. They both sat down on the floor beside me staring in horror. It must have been the first time either had seen me cry. I managed to get a temporary grip on my emotions and explained that Jarad was a very sick baby; the doctors had to fix his heart and now he needed lots of rest so he could heal and come home. I held them both in my arms kissing and hugging my children telling them how much I had missed them, as my tears rolled down my face.

I had only brief glimpses of Peter. He was in and out of the house. He was so focused trying to get the children's belongings out of the car. He emptied the truck, set up the trampoline, and put away all of the things I had asked him to bring from home. I went out in the backyard to say hello. He gave me a quick hug, told me they were all hungry, and then silently walked away.

I stared in disbelief. He had not attempted even small talk, let alone asked about Jarad's condition today.

After they ate lunch, I called Karen. I had told her that hospitals made Peter squeamish, and she had told me the ICU staff had prepared a "faint" space for him. There were wet face cloths on a table and a rocking chair beside Jarad's bed. But surprisingly Peter was as tough as nails. He did not even waver as he saw his son for the first time. He had chosen to hold onto his belief: "Jarad will be fine." I could only wish that I had his confidence at that point. On the way out of the ICU I briefly introduced Peter to my new friends Linda and Steve.

The next forty eight hours were grueling. We were warned Jarad was "on the edge of the knife." The nurses worked tirelessly making critical adjustments to Jarad's life support drugs, as they attempted to balance the large combination needed for his immediate survival. They looked to Jarad for signs that he was starting to fight for his life, but unfortunately they saw none. He simply lay on the stretcher totally paralyzed.

Peter had to return to Hope, for a court appearance, for the next day and a half. "How can you leave your family at a time like this?" I wanted to scream at him. "How important is your stupid court case?" I could see that I would have to stand on my own two feet and not expect anyone to bolster me.

Bobby McFerrin's "Don't Worry, Be Happy" had become my theme song. I played it over and over on the way to and from the hospital. For some reason it seemed to give me strength when I was at my lowest.

I was jolted from my thoughts by the ringing telephone. It was Snowden School calling to tell me that Jarad was sick and needed to be picked up as soon as possible. I glanced over at the clock on the range; it was not even 10:00 A.M.

I got in the car and drove down the hill, arriving at school and finding Jarad all alone in the school's front office. The expression on his face was pure sadness. He did not even crack a smile when he saw me. We walked out to the car hand in hand. He told me that he felt like he was going to throw up. "What is going on?" I said aloud but had no clue what the answer could be. I wished he could better verbalize how he felt.

At home Jarad had no desire to play; he collected "Sleepy Bear" off his bed and crawled into my bed. He drifted off to sleep immediately so I lay down beside him and recalled the day I purchased "Sleepy Bear" for him while he was still in the ICU.

I had woken up very early that morning and had actually mustered the strength to pick up the phone and call the hospital on my own. I was told that Jarad had a rough night and decided I needed to get to the hospital as soon as possible. I wanted to see the heart specialists before they completed morning rounds in the ICU. "Why now? What had changed?" I was not prepared for my baby's appearance when I got there. His face was very pale his eyes were bulging to the size of golf balls. I noticed that there was a large syringe full of blood being fed through a regulator box and administered to my baby. "Another transfusion? More blood?" I questioned. I instantly felt the increased tension around his bedside. The nurses were far more serious and their attention fixed on their tiny patient much more than they were yesterday.

They explained this was typical for the third day post-op. I needed to get away from his bedside, and so I stepped out into the hallway. I kept walking until I came to the hospital Gift Shop. Almost instinctively I looked for something soft and cuddly, and then I saw Sleepy. He was a tired-looking brown bear, dressed in a miniature hospital gown. He was obviously a "sick patient" who needed love. I bought him more for me, I realized, than for my baby. I hugged him tightly as I mustered the strength to walk back in to the ICU and Jarad's bedside. I maneuvered my way to his stretcher through the maze of machinery, the poles, the wires and tubes. I introduced my new friend to Jarad and told him Sleepy will keep me company when I am not with him. There was no room on the stretcher for toys.

Jarad struggled for air and I knew this meant suctioning. This was a good time to return to my parents' home and my two healthy little ones. Jarad needed rest and I had to believe that he was in the most capable of hands.

As I walked down the hallway, Sleepy tucked under my arm, I noticed all of the people in the waiting areas. Families here were dealing with so much—from preemie births, to birth defects, to cancer and even death. It was all around me but unlike so many of the patients who had out-of-town families, at least I could go home to my family at the end of each day.

A hammock hung between my parents' two cherry trees in the backyard. It was a fabulous place to relax, but today that was a challenge as Tyler and Ashley took turns climbing all over me. They were not used to having me home from the hospital for very long and were taking full advantage of this opportunity. Once they tired of our horseplay and saw a new distraction, I was finally left alone. It was an "Indian summer" day, unseasonably warm, and I fell off to sleep. When I opened my eyes later, I realized I was being called to supper. I had no idea what time it was, only that I felt more rested than I had in days.

That evening when I went back to the hospital, I was shocked when one of Jarad's new nurses asked me, "Is there any truth to the rumor you didn't take Jarad to a doctor, and simply relied on phone calls?"

I was horrified beyond words. Were they questioning my being a responsible parent? They obviously had no idea how hard I had searched for answers or how many doctors and specialists had checked him over. I told his nurse, "He was admitted here three-and-a-half weeks ago. In fact, it was documented on an x-ray when we were here, that Jarad's heart was grossly enlarged. Unfortunately, the radiologist here missed it."

I was back at the hospital early the next morning and something appeared horribly different. The parking lot was empty and so were the halls. The hustle and bustle we had seen every day was gone. The cafeteria and gift shop were closed. "Where is everyone?" I felt anxiety rising up from the pit of my stomach, so I headed directly to the ICU. I asked the intensivist on duty what had changed at the hospital since yesterday. She explained that it was a weekend. Of course, I told myself, feeling foolish. She added, "Most of the people you see in the waiting rooms are taking their children to various clinics—there are no clinics on the weekend." She reminded me to focus on my baby. "Last night was terrible for Jarad. Can you see how swollen he is and how is color is deteriorating?" she asked. "Jarad is on the edge of the knife. His life is hanging in the fragile balance of these machines and medications. We even had to restart the blood transfusions." This was alarming, and I put my hand to my mouth.

"Prepare yourself. The odds of him living are now fifty-fifty. Jarad could go either way, at any time," she added.

When we returned to the hospital later that evening, we were told that they were decreasing Jarad's Pavulon; this was the drug that had kept his body paralyzed, unable to move or cry, for the past five days. As we stood over him, we could see him moving ever so slightly. His face now reflected the pain he clearly felt, for the first time. And although it appeared he was crying, no sound could escape his ventilated throat. Jarad had begun to squirm, and when he did the machine alarms shrieked. Now that Jarad was no longer paralyzed and was visibly in pain and showing it, I could not bring myself to leave his side until he was settled and sound asleep.

The next day I was met with encouraging news when I arrived at the ICU. "Jarad's condition had been upgraded from critical to stable," his nurse beamed. Our first truly good report since he had survived the surgery. When I went to share our news with Linda, they had just been informed that genetic testing revealed baby Patrick had DiGeorges syndrome. Poor little Patrick, he seemed to take one step forward and two steps back. At least all of my baby's steps, although painfully slow, had progressed in one direction.

"Just cherish that," I told myself as I headed out into the parking lot. At the eight-day post-op mark, I was told Jarad had "done well." He was now free of Pavulon, nitroglycerin, and dopamine. The next step was to eliminate the adrenalin. I was thrilled to see that the catheter and the rectal probe had also been removed, as well as the backup pacemaker but not the accompanying wires. The heat lamp was gone now and his body was fighting to retain its temperature. The central line and drainage tube had been removed, and he had an IV in his arm instead of his jugular vein. Despite all of these improvements, I was reminded, "He is not out of the woods yet."

"If only he would breathe on his own," I sighed, "then we could get rid of the ventilator, the large tube in his nose and the tape marring up his beautiful face." His nurse explained they had started to wean him from the ventilator. They would periodically turn it off and were pleased that Jarad would take a few shallow breaths of his own, although he tired very easily. I still winced and held my breath when his nurses suctioned the mucous from the tubing. The suctioning took his breath away, and I would hold mine! During this procedure, they had to bag him with a bag valve oxygen mask (manual resuscitator) that he hated. With no Pavulon left in his system, he squirmed to get away from it. Still no sound could escape his ventilated throat.

Jarad's body was refusing to digest the breast milk that was being fed into his stomach through his NG (nasal gastric) tube. With each attempt to feed him, his nurses would end up suctioning the milk back out. This puzzled all of his support staff. They were unable to offer an explanation. I interpreted this strange turn as my baby rejecting me.

But without the Pavulon Jarad had become more active, so much so that he had to be transferred to a crib. His body was also beginning to resume normal functions, like urinating and bowel movements. This created a need for diapers.

I was warned that the monitors were telling the story about how Jarad was really doing, and I was encouraged to pay close attention. His heart rate was still far from regular, and the moment he heard my voice his heart rate would raise, and when I touched him and talked to him, he reacted causing the alarms to be triggered. I was asked to "restrain" myself and to watch the machines carefully in order to prevent the increased stress on his recovering heart.

Peter was still at our home in Hope. He needed to sort some issues out with his boss and put in a medical leave request. I headed to my Mom and Dad's home midday and spend some quality time with Tyler, Ashley and my parents. I felt so torn - whether I was at the hospital or my parents' home it did not matter. All three of our children needed me.

When I walked into the ICU later that evening Jarad was unattended and choking. "Help. . . Jarad's choking!" I screamed. The nurse came running and suctioned him immediately. She had to repeat the procedure in order to finally clear all of the mucous so he would settle down.

When my heart had calmed down, I was told some more good news. Although the medical teams had attempted to remove Jarad's ventilator, this was not successful; but he was taking more breaths, and those breaths were a little deeper. "This," they told me, "is definite progress."

The plan was to turn off Jarad's ventilator at 8:00 A.M. the next morning for two hours. I wanted to be there for this monumental event, so I decided to return to my parents' home and to bed earlier than normal. But Jarad had other plans for me. He was very fussy, and now that he was capable of showing different emotions, I couldn't leave the hospital until he was settled and asleep.

On the drive home my thoughts turned to Linda and the emotional roller coaster she had been riding with Patrick. She had seen a doctor at a nearby hospital because she was experiencing heavy bleeding (after giving birth to Patrick a little over six weeks ago), as well as to address her insomnia and blinding headaches. The doctor wrote her a prescription and asked her to work toward lowering her stress. "Was he kidding?" she laughed. She was mentally and physically exhausted and missed her family terribly, especially her young son, Bradley. They were all at home in Nanaimo on Vancouver Island waiting for Linda and Patrick to return.

I had been watching little Patrick for signs that he would be ventilator-free, after what now had been four attempts, but sadly he would gain a bit of ground and then lose a little more. Besides talking with each other, Linda and I had gotten into the habit of checking in on each other's babies when we entered the ICU.

It occurred to me, again, how lucky I was to have my parents, sister and children so close; they were such a "normal" and welcomed distraction from the stress I faced when at the hospital. Linda only had her room at Easter Seal House and the company of other families going through similar trauma. "Maybe she would like to spend the afternoon at my parent's home and meet my other two children," I thought to myself. I would ask my parents if it was okay to ask her to dinner at their home, and afterward we could go back to the hospital together. All of a sudden I felt a little happier, hoping she would like the idea.

When I got to the hospital the next morning, I was pleasantly surprised that the ventilator was gone. The machine had been rolled in to the corner but was still near Jarad's bed. He looked almost normal except for the tape glue stuck to his cheeks and nose. I wanted to clean it off but his nurse cautioned, "The solvent we use here has a very strong smell. There will be plenty of time for you to clean him up down the road."

I took a really good look at Jarad. I was shocked by the amount of skin hanging in folds on his legs and arms. When I asked, his nurse told me the nutrition he was receiving was only 70% of what he needed to maintain his weight. It was imperative at this point that no extra strain be put on his heart while it healed.

It was hard for me to believe when the nurse explained, "Breathing on his own is tiring Jarad out; initially it requires a lot of effort after ten days on the ventilator. It appears your son will be sleeping better now." Funny thing, I had never really thought about it and had always taken breathing for granted until this point!

His breaths continued to be a little more frequent and shallower than they would have liked. He was back inside the familiar Plexiglas "doghouse," receiving oxygen as he had his first night here ten long days ago. It was obvious that Jarad was improving when his nurse asked, "Would you like to hold your baby?"

As I watched him sleep my immediate response was, "No"—I quickly realized that I was terrified at the thought of it. I could not believe my reaction. "Wasn't this exactly what I have been waiting to do for so long?" I asked myself. Knowing all Jarad had been through and that his body was still healing, and how stimulating my holding him would be, I told myself it was too soon. I left him sleeping soundly.

I went to find Linda to invite her out to my parents' home for the afternoon and evening. She was having another rough day, but the outing gave her something to look forward to, and like me she was encouraged by Jarad's progress. We decided to take a short walk around the hospital grounds. Afterward we wanted to get on the road to avoid the rush hour traffic, but I needed to return to the ICU and quickly say goodbye to my son.

When we got to the door of the ICU, I could hear loud talking and laughter from Jarad's corner. I quickly headed over. Peter smiled as he saw me approaching. I stared back in horror seeing him sitting in the rocking chair beside Jarad's bed and holding my frail baby. He was smiling proudly. I wanted to scream, "How could you?" I was furious. And yes, I was incredibly jealous. Peter didn't have a clue of all that we had been through while he was at home in Hope—and now he was experiencing the "reward" before me. I suddenly turned and stormed out of the hospital, tears streaming down my cheeks as I ranted on to Linda about my absent husband who only showed up when things were going well.

At my parents' home, Linda and I sat out in the yard enjoying the sun as we watched the children play without a care in the world. This was a heartwarming break from the stress that had consumed our days and nights since we met. I was so happy that she had come home with me. When Peter returned from the hospital, he wanted to know why I left so abruptly. I did not want to talk to him about it. He saw that I was upset, so Peter quickly said that he had better head back to Hope. He had agreed to work for another week before his month-long vacation.

There was a flurry of activity around Jarad's bed when Linda and I returned to the ICU later that evening. My heart skipped a beat, and I was immediately filled with fear and anxiety. The pediatric intensivist on duty quickly came over and explained that Jarad was facing a new problem, and he would perform a flexible bronchoscopy in the morning to determine its cause. My knees immediately went weak, and I held onto the bed to prevent myself from falling. He went on to explain, "An x-ray has shown what appears to be a problem with air entry to Jarad's left lung." The procedure would be done in the ICU and that "If all goes well, it should only take about an hour and a half." I was stunned.

"Is he strong enough for this?" I said out loud, worried half to death.

The pediatric intensivist assured me, "Your son is in very capable hands, and we need to know what is going on so that he can get better." I blindly signed another consent form, again not bothering to read the fine print, but too overwhelmed to understand it anyway.

Linda met me in the parents' lounge, after watching all of the hustle and bustle around my son's crib. She too was worried that he had taken a turn for the worse. This fear was fueled by us learning that three babies in the Unit had passed away in the last twenty-four hours. "Why didn't I hold him yesterday?" I scolded myself. "Now, I might not get another chance," I cried.

The nurse came in shortly afterward and told me Jarad was asleep, and I should go home and get some rest. I agreed. In the morning I waited in the parents' lounge with my sister while the bronchoscopy was performed. Two hours later his nurse came in to say the doctor was pleased with the results of the operation, but warned me that Jarad was still "high" from the cocktail of cocaine, valium, and morphine they gave him prior to the procedure. "Do you have any extra "cocktail" mix for his super stressed, Mommy?" I asked as I smiled at her through my tears of relief.

Since Jarad would spend the remainder of the day sleeping off the effects of the potent drugs, my sister and I headed off to the Toy Box store. I celebrated by purchasing a 90th Anniversary Gund teddy bear and a soothing-sounds cassette tape for my baby, and a few small toys for Tyler and Ashley. After a while we both had splitting headaches, and decided we had time for lunch before going back to the hospital.

When were arrived at his bedside, his nurse scurried off to find a tape player. We said our hellos, and I held Jarad's tiny hand and stroked the soft curls on his head. He was still very groggy, but the heart monitor did acknowledge my presence there. The nurse returned, set the cassette player at the head of his bed, and pressed play—the new soothing sounds seemed to settle Jarad immediately. The monitors reflected he was fast asleep, so we headed home for dinner.

At four and a half, Tyler seemed more interested in meeting new friends and playing with toys then how his little brother was doing. Ashley at two, however, seemed totally consumed with questions about her baby brother. I was beginning to notice and understand how everyone dealt or coped differently with life's stressful situations, including my two young children.

Dad and I went back to the hospital after dinner. Jarad was awake, and I finally I jumped at the chance to ask if I could hold him. There was a rocking chair beside his crib, so I sat down and made myself comfortable. How could I begin to describe my feelings at this moment? The anticipation simply overwhelmed me as I watched the nurse adjusted Jarad's many tubes and monitor wires, and then gently picked my frail baby up off the bed. I was totally elated, but frightened all at the same time. As Jarad was placed in my arms, I felt totally awkward taking my baby; I did not want to hurt him. It had been eleven days since I had last held him. He still had IV lines, his NG tube, oxygen via nasal prongs, and he was still hooked up to the oxygen saturation monitor. I was very careful not to disturb anything.

My first reaction was at "how light he is now." I noticed that his bones were sticking out of his saggy skin. His nurse explained that while Jarad remained in ICU, he would only receive 75% of the nutrition required to maintain his weight. She added, "He is still not tolerating the breast milk, and we continue to suction the milk out so gaining weight will be a challenge for him." He had also developed tachycardia (rapid heartbeat), which contributed to him burning more calories. Although this bothered me, I really tried to focus on all his little improvements over the past few days.

As I gently rocked my baby, I began to feel myself relax. I felt so complete with him once again in my arms. He began to search for a breast, nuzzling at my shirt. I asked, "When I will be able to start nursing him?" I was told probably not for at least a week. Although I was temporarily disappointed, I trusted they knew what was best for my baby right now.

I looked up at my Dad and asked if he would like to hold him. I knew he wanted to but felt as nervous as I was about it. He just smiled and said, "I'm enjoying watching you hold him."

The next day when I got to the hospital, it was suggested that I try breastfeeding Jarad. "Do you think he is strong enough?" I asked.

One of his doctors said, "This will be a test," and added, "there is no guarantee but let's give it a try. Are you ready?" To no one's surprise, Jarad rooted around and latched on to my breast. He sucked hard, as I felt my milk let down. He tolerated the entire feeding! He was not winded; in fact, he settled down for a well-deserved nap and for the first time, he was able to digest the entire feeding.

I jumped as the kitchen door slammed shut. I was snapped out of my reflection as I saw Peter standing in front of me. I could instantly tell that he was upset when he saw that Jarad was already at home from school. I felt his frustration was directed at me once again. I told him I was sorry and asked, "What do you expect me to do? The school called to tell me Jarad was sick and asked me to come pick him up. They didn't give me a choice." I angrily added, "What kind of a parent would tell the school their child was faking it and that he needed to stay until the final bell?"

I assured Peter I would call the doctor that afternoon and make an appointment for me to see the psychologist. After taking Jarad to so many doctor appointments and being told there was nothing wrong with him, the time had come for me to follow through on the promise I had made to my husband almost seven years earlier. If our marriage was to survive, I believed I needed help now. Maybe Peter and the doctors were right, and I really was guilty of allowing my precious boy to manipulate me. Maybe so, but my heart told me differently as I dialed the number.

CHAPTER FIVE

Crisis

It was a beautiful, sunny spring day. I had driven the children to school and once again, Jarad did not want to go inside. Although he said he was sick, I wondered if his reluctance to attend school had something to do with his teacher. I knew she made him nervous and picked on him. She scolded him, and me, for the number of school days he had missed in his first month since starting school in Penticton.

Later that morning, I was folding laundry and Jarad was coloring at the dining room table. Suddenly the TV caught my attention. The noon news was broadcasting a press conference from the children's hospital. Their announcement was directed to the parents of any child who may have had a blood transfusion at the hospital between the years 1980 and 1990. They asked parents to bring the children back to the hospital for blood tests. The hospital spokeswoman added that, "It is believed that these children may have been exposed to blood or blood products containing the Human immunodeficiency virus (HIV)."

I was alarmed, but in the past two years since HIV had been identified, we had visited almost every department of the children's hospital and Jarad was seen by doctors from almost every specialty. With his variety of symptoms, I had a hard time believing that in light of his transfusion history, that one of the doctors hadn't ordered Jarad be tested for HIV. Bringing up the need for yet another blood test would surely cause an argument with Peter about me being a surrogate hypochondriac. I just didn't have the energy for another fight so I decided that I would not follow through on their request and hold to my belief he had been tested and the HIV test must have been negative. Besides, they said that they "Have sent out letters to all parents" and we had not received one.

Thinking back to those days in ICU, I recalled watching the blood drip from the bag hanging over Jarad's bed after I expressed my opposition to my baby receiving donor blood. I clearly remember the hospitals' reassurances that the Canadian Red Cross blood was screened for all diseases. That was exactly my point, "What about the diseases that were not yet identified, like HIV was two years ago?" My gut had told me back then that **my blood** was Jarad's safest option.

But as Jarad continued to vomit and complain of tummy aches and headaches, the children's hospital press conference haunted me. I was in a battle with myself to believe he was not affected, yet I knew in my heart that something was making him very sick. As I watched Jarad closely, I wrestled with the obvious and finally about a month later, I called the hospital and at their recommendation I made an appointment to see our doctor; "To, at least, rule HIV out," I told myself. Our local general practitioner encouraged us to go next door right away and get the blood drawn for the test. I did not even look at the box ticked off on the requisition. I had no reason to suspect that our doctor would test Jarad for anything else.

Two days later I couldn't stand the suspense any longer and I called the doctor's office. The receptionist asked, "Can you hold on a minute, please? I think some results were just delivered." I held tightly to the telephone receiver. I heard her pick up her end of the phone and held my breath. "The HIV test is negative."

I breathed a heavy sigh of relief, thanked her, and quickly dialed Peter at work. "The HIV test was negative," I said.

He assured me, "I knew it would be." How I wished that I shared his optimism!

"Well, I am so relieved. I think this calls for a celebration," I told Peter.

"Okay. I'll leave work early and meet you guys at (the children's favorite restaurant) White Spot at 5:00," he said,

Just before five o'clock, the three children and I got in the car and drove to the restaurant. The children ordered their favorite Pirate Packs—chicken strips and fries. They loved the chocolate gold coins and ice cream that came in the ship that held their dinner. I felt a need to splurge and ordered old English fish and chips. The children were oblivious to the cause of our celebration but were thrilled their daddy had joined us.

But no sooner were we home, than Jarad was in the bathroom vomiting and the nagging question returned: "Then why is our little boy so sick? And why do doctors continue to refer to his condition as simply a failure to thrive?"

Imagine my shock when two days later I received an unexpected call from our general practitioner. He said, "There is no easy way to say this." My heart sunk and I was overcome by a wave of nausea. I immediately assumed the lab had made an error, and my little boy was, in fact, infected with HIV. I sat down, as he said, "Sorry to be calling you with this news, but I wanted you to know as soon as possible."

"Know what?" I gulped.

He continued, "The good news is that Jarad does not have HIV. The bad news is that I just spoke with the infectious disease people, and Jarad has tested positive for hepatitis C." I was stunned into silence.

I asked, "What is that?"

"It is an infectious disease primarily affecting the liver." He went on to say, "Chronic infection can lead to scarring of the liver and possibly cirrhosis. In some cases hepatitis C patients may go on to develop liver cancer or experience liver failure." But he went on to explain that, "There is very little known about it, especially in children."

I asked him, "Is Jarad going to die?" There was hesitation and the silence was deafening on the other end of the phone. "So what is next?" I asked.

He said, "I will refer Jarad to the specialists in the gastroenterology department, at the children's hospital."

"Wait a minute," I said. "We have already been there twice and one was recently. Jarad has been seen by their specialists. They ran a myriad of tests on him. They knew he had a blood transfusion, but said he was suffering from irritable bowel syndrome—they had never said anything about hepatitis C. There has to be a mistake!"

Our general practitioner had no response. "I knew it," I said to myself. "I knew something was wrong with him," I said again, shaking my head. Although my gut instinct was right, I took no pleasure in that now. I was panicked! My heart was racing. I called Peter at work, and simply told him we needed to talk. He came home as soon as he could. He could see

I was visibly shaken and had been crying. Pete asked me to repeat the conversation that had just taken place with our doctor. I could tell by his facial expression that he was certainly not prepared for this devastating news either.

Peter instantly sprang into action. He called the Public Health Unit in Penticton. They offered us a few pamphlets. They suggested he see their Infectious Disease specialist in Kelowna. Peter got her number, called and spoke briefly with her. They set up an appointment for us to meet with her the following week. For once, when we faced a crisis, Peter had taken control. He called his boss and told him that would be taking his next two shifts off.

We drove to the Health Unit to get a copy of a "Fact File" information sheet on hepatitis C. It didn't say much. The prospect of possibly losing Jarad after all we had gone through had left me feeling totally empty and incredibly sad. Why had this diagnosis taken almost 7 years to discover?

We both tried to act as if nothing was wrong around the children. The nurse we spoke with at the Health Unit asked us, "Please, do not tell anyone about Jarad's infection until you have met with the Infectious disease nurse."

I wrestled with my sadness while not trying to show it. I was quiet and reflective as the memories of all Jarad's tests and surgeries flooded back, as if it were only yesterday. I remembered the moment of Jarad's birth and his Total Anomalous Pulmonary Venous Return diagnosis, and his surgeries and everything else he had been through in his short life. I remembered how Linda had fought for Patrick's life: through all of the appointments, hospitalizations and surgeries—only for him to die him following open heart surgery the day after Jarad's first birthday. With all that we had been through, I knew I could not bear to lose my child now or at any time, for that matter.

Right now there was little either of us could do. Peter had to keep busy. While he went downstairs and immersed himself in our renovation project, the children asked if we could go to the beach. "Sure," I said. I numbly walked through the house, gathering beach towels and extra clothes, a small cooler, some snacks and a beach ball. As we drove the short distance down our street to Skaha Beach, the children talked about their plans for their afternoon at the beach. While I drove, I felt paralyzed by the depths of an impending doom and gloom that churned in my head and stomach.

Once there I sat alone on the warm sand as I pondered what was in store for our family. I did not want to talk to anyone. I had nothing to say.

It was great to watch my three children being children—excited and carefree, playing in the sand and the water, laughing and really having fun. Today, Jarad even kept up with his sister. Tyler had already made his way out to the dock just off shore to meet up with some of his classmates. I sat alone with my hidden feelings and secret hurt. It suddenly occurred to me that all of the symptoms of hepatitis C had been staring me and the doctors in the face, and for a very long time. "Why did no one ever put them all together?" I asked. But I was still hopeful and praying that someone had made a mistake. I desperately wanted for this to be simply coincidental.

I telephoned the children's hospital as soon as the children were off to school on Monday morning. I asked to speak to someone in public relations. I was told that I needed to speak with someone in public relations. She worked for the Vice President of Clinical and Strategic Services. Despite leaving a lengthy message, no one returned my call. Maybe I had blurted out too much! I just wanted answers!

Tuesday morning the Infectious disease nurse from Kelowna arrived at our home amid one of the worst summer storms we had seen in a long time. I was about to burst. I had never kept a big secret this long. I wanted desperately to share Jarad's diagnosis with all of my children. I wanted them to know that their brother really was sick and could potentially infect them, and that he might die as a result of this viral infection. I wanted to tell Jarad, too. But what would I say? I carefully listened as the nurse explained what she knew about hepatitis C and cautioned us, again, to not tell anyone. She recounted the Ryan White story and how the townspeople raised up against this little boy, infected with HIV, as he engaged in activities with their "healthy" children.

The more the nurse described hepatitis C, the more I realized my sons' symptoms were no coincidence. I sat at the table and cried, as did Peter. "The hepatitis C virus was only identified five years ago," she explained. "HCV is the 'new' kid on the block; information is vague and conflicted and it is changing all of the time." I recounted to the nurse the conversations I had had with both the cardiologist and cardiac surgeon, on two separate occasions, asking if I could donate my own blood for Jarad's open heart surgery. "That is not necessary. The blood used by the children's hospital is screened. There is no chance your son can contract any diseases from it," they had reassured me.

When the hospital's representative finally did return my call, she appeared to be on the defensive. She demanded to know what I wanted and asked what my specific request actually was. I told her, "I responded to your request to have my son tested, and I would like to know what the children's hospital has lined up to support the parents and their children when a positive diagnosis is made?" I went on to explain, "Jarad has been seen in the gastroenterology department on two separate occasions within the past year. They are liver specialists. Can you find out if they ever did liver function tests? And lastly, who is responsible for my son's hepatitis C infection?"

Genevieve said she would, "Follow up on my questions," and then added, "from now on deal directly with me when making inquiries or searching for any answers from the hospital." She assured me that she would do her best to get some answers and would call me back in the next few days.

Both Peter and I accompanied Jarad to his first post-diagnosis doctor appointment. Our general practitioner gently checked Jarad and palpated his liver and spleen. Jarad was a good sport. I had taken him to so many different doctors over the past 6½ years that he had become quite the trooper. He never objected, possibly because he felt so miserable. He did not understand what was going on because we had not said anything to any of our children yet. It was heartbreaking for me knowing that the cause of his suffering resulted from infected blood that had found its way into Jarad's tiny body during his open heart surgery.

Our general practitioner did not have any more information to share with us but suggested we take Jarad to see a pediatrician. When he named the pediatrician, I was surprised to learn that she was the same doctor who had delivered Jarad almost seven years ago in White Rock and that she had also relocated to Penticton with her family. "In the meantime, while we wait for an appointment the pediatrician, Jarad needs to have some liver function tests performed as soon as possible. They will tell us whether his liver has been impacted by the virus." He assured us that we would have these answers by noon on Friday if we got the blood drawn today. Even though Jarad was petrified of needles, we hurried down the hallway to the lab. I promised him a treat when this was done.

I began to physically manifest the stress I had internalized for so long in the form of splitting headaches, and I was worried how I could possibly survive another two days of waiting for answers.

Our general practitioner called to explain the results of the liver function tests. He said that three of five liver function tests were within normal range, but two of them were more than three times the upper limit. Numbers swarmed in my head. "What does this tell us?" I asked.

He said, "The purpose of liver function tests is to check the levels of certain enzymes and proteins in the blood. They can be used to monitor the progression of a liver disease, or the effects of certain medicines on the liver and as a way to measure the severity of the disease." He added, "That the numbers can also be affected by certain foods and medications." This seemed rather inconclusive, and I was becoming more confused by the day.

As promised, we received the return call from the children's hospital. I was not really surprised that, although she said this was a "regrettable situation," she was definitely not going to offer any form of an apology on behalf of the hospital. My intuition told me that, although it was at their request that Jarad got tested, the ONLY thing they had in place was their lawyers. I was sure every word I was hearing was carefully orchestrated by the hospital's lawyers. I was shocked that the children's hospital had nothing in place to help our children, or for the parents just learning of this tragedy. As much as the request was to have our children tested for HIV, I believe the biggest surprise was how many little ones were testing positive for hepatitis C. Didn't the children's hospital consider parents learning of their child's infection would be desperate for information?

That evening we attended an *Up with People* concert at the Penticton High School auditorium. As the lights went down and the show started, I began to cry. As I watched these talented young people singing, dancing and acting their hearts out, I wondered if Jarad would ever have a chance to grow up and pursue his passion—whatever it might be. I cried throughout the entire performance.

The next day we shared our "news" with Tyler and Ashley, mostly because we all needed to go for blood tests to insure none of us was inadvertently infected with hepatitis C through casual contact with Jarad. The siblings showed little reaction—they were too young to understand the magnitude of the health crisis we all faced. For once Jarad wanted to go to the lab; his excitement was palatable because on this visit he got to watch everyone else get poked! We were honest with the children as we explained the disease was a relatively new virus and the prognosis for children had not been well studied or documented.

Over the next few days word had gotten out of Jarad's infection, and family and very close friends were calling and offering their help. My parents arrived from North Delta to help me deal with this crisis. Peter had returned to work, and I spent so much of my time on the telephone. **This was at a time when computer's had not yet made their way in to family homes and the internet was out of reach in many areas.**

I realized that this was just the start of my search for *a cure, at any cost!*

I was advised to speak with the Canadian Liver Foundation. The representative offered to send us a package of information. She also gave me contact information for the Hepatitis C Survivors Society in Toronto, Ontario and encouraged me to call them next. When I called the number, I spoke with Teresa. She had lots of information but sadly explained that none of it pertained to children. I felt like a pioneer. Teresa said there was a judge investigating what had triggered this disaster. She also said there were many people needlessly infected with hepatitis C. Teresa explained they had a branch office in Victoria and recommended I speak with June who managed that office.

My brain was on overload as all this information swirled through my head. I realized there actually were a few resources in place, although it appeared that Children's Hospital was unaware of any of them [or were they hiding them from us]. Maybe, just maybe, I was going to get to speak to another parent in a similar situation.

I was referred by the Hepatitis C Society of Canada (HeCSC) to Greg Clifford, a lawyer in Victoria. They explained that he was interviewing infected individuals and was appalled by the shabby treatment some of the victims were receiving. At this point the connection between the hospitals and the blood supply was sketchy, and infected individuals were being drilled over other possible sources of infection. HeCSC believed Mr. Clifford was very knowledgeable on the subject and was researching the possibility of a lawsuit.

The next day I received another phone call from the children's hospital A nurse there asked me if she could fax me twenty-one pages of information. She included on it the names and numbers of support people at the children's hospital. There was a cardiology nurse clinician, a G.I. clinic nurse, the HIV clinic nurse at the Oak tree clinic, and an infectious control nurse. Funny I thought; as resources, neither the Canadian Liver Foundation nor Hepatitis C Society was listed!

A few days later the children's hospital representative called again. She suggested I speak with the G.I. clinic nurse and gave me her direct line. I called her. I asked her to please check the results from the blood tests from Jarad's last two G.I. clinic visits. She explained, "They always do liver function tests." She asked if she could fax me the latest information from the American Liver Foundation. The only treatment available, interferon, did not show favorable results and caused detrimental effects to growing children, stating the risk/benefit ratio was unfavorable.

My last call that day was to the Canadian Red Cross. I could picture this building, located right next door to the children's hospital. I requested they contact the donors of Jarad's blood. I recounted Jarad's history and told them at least one of the units of blood that Jarad received must have contained hepatitis C, since he had no other risk factors and no one else in his family had the disease. They assured me they would conduct a trace back and let me know when they received the results.

That night I slept better than I had since learning of Jarad's infection, and restful sleep was well deserved after a very productive day. Instead of simply feeling sorry for myself, my son and his siblings, I was focused on learning everything I could about this insidious disease and finding him a cure. Despite the fact that Jarad was still vomiting on a daily basis, the diagnosis had finally given me a focus and I knew that I was now headed in the right direction.

Walking into the pediatrician's office was like déjà vu. This was the same doctor who had whisked Jarad away moments after his birth. I arrived at this appointment totally prepared with copies of all the information I had gathered to date to give her. She explained that Jarad was her first patient with hepatitis C, and she explained to us that the pathology in children was not well documented. She suggested that we get more blood work done and ordered an ultrasound of Jarad's liver. She brought up doing a liver biopsy as a diagnostic tool. I was opposed to this invasive procedure as it was not risk-free. She said she would refer us back to the children's hospital gastroenterology clinic, so that Jarad could be seen by the gastroenterologist/liver specialists.

Jarad stayed very still while the pediatrician performed her physical exam. When she was finished, she said, "Physically Jarad appears well, although he is very skinny and he does experience some pain when I palpate his liver region." She appeared surprised that his height and weight barely registered at the 2nd percentile on the boy's growth chart, since she had treated his brother and sister when we lived in White Rock. Again it was confirmed that one of my son's diagnosis' remained "a failure to thrive," even at seven years of age.

A few days later I received a phone call from the mother of a 12-year-old who had tested positive for hepatitis C last October. Although her son showed no symptoms and had normal liver function, she told me he had three open-heart surgeries at the same children's hospital and he received blood transfusions each time. I had been so overwhelmed these past two weeks, talking to people and collecting and reading as much information as I could, that I realized I had begun to believe that my son was the only child infected at the children's hospital. At least that was what I thought they wanted me to think! The woman also informed me that our sons were not the only two either! She was aware of two other hepatitis C infected children that also lived on Vancouver Island, not far from her home. That made four children and all of them cardiac patients. After our conversation, I knew I was not alone, and as we said our goodbyes, she told me she would send me everything she had collected on the virus—but of course, none of it related to children.

I immediately dialed the children's hospital and spoke with both the cardiac nurse and the gastroenterology nurse clinicians. I wanted to let them know that I was aware other cardiac patients had also been identified. They denied any knowledge of anyone else infected other than Jarad. I began to suspect the hospital was not being totally honest with me, and they were possibly embarking on a cover-up. During this conversation, I was told his gastroenterology testing would have included liver function tests. I had asked for the results two days ago and I had heard nothing. I could do little else than leave more messages. I was outraged by the long delays in returning my phone calls and answering what seemed to me to be questions with easy answers. Jarad had now been sick almost every day for the past four months.

The attorney in Victoria returned my call four days later. He apologized and explained that his firm was involved in serious discussions regarding the viability of a class action lawsuit on behalf of the victims who received hepatitis C transfusions. "Victims?" I asked. It had not occurred to me that my son was a victim. I was grateful that the children's hospital had saved Jarad's life more than six years ago, and it was difficult to believe that they would have intentionally given him infected blood. He spoke briefly about the Krever Inquiry and went on to explain some of the findings and the

Class action potential from the information that had emerged. He went on to say, "We are hopeful our firm will reach a decision and decide to proceed in the next four to six weeks."

The Krever Inquiry was, I learned, hearing testimony into tainted blood products supplied by the Canadian Red Cross. He warned, "If we chose to take this [hepatitis C] case on, it will be a very long and very painful class action suit. It is believed there are thousands of innocent Canadians infected with the disease." He asked me to provide him a brief history of all that Jarad had experienced. He liked that Jarad was only eight weeks old when he was transfused and that he had no other risk factors. Many of the infected adults were being blamed for contracting the disease through poor lifestyle choices. "With Jarad," he went on, "they cannot factor in anything except receiving the tainted blood transfusion."

I took Jarad to see a naturopath. I carefully watched and listened while she tested him for sensitivities. The tests indicated he had liver damage. She told me that she believed she could repair the damage and reverse the hepatitis C through a change in Jarad's diet and with the help of supplements. These included acidophilus, B12, and the homeopathic preparation Hepeel. For the next two weeks, Jarad's diet was severely restricted. He was not allowed alfalfa, avocado, eggs, hops, dairy products, cashew nuts, salt, sesame seeds, turkey, watermelon, yeast (bread and buns), potassium sorbate, sodium nitrate, and sodium metabisulfite or anything that contained any of these ingredients. I told her I was skeptical about her claim. I explained that I had only just begun to learn about hepatitis C, and from all that I have read there remained no documented cure for this disease in any of the medical journals.

The naturopath told me that she would try these steps, and if they didn't work she would try others, at no additional charge. I paid $222.53 for this visit and left her office wondering what Jarad would eat now that he would have to give up so many of the foods he liked. I remained hopeful Jarad would be cured but after trying her suggestions and the recommended supplements with no improvement – we never went back.

It had been two weeks since I had first contacted the children's hospital, to inform them of Jarad's hepatitis C diagnosis, when I received an early morning phone call from the department head of pediatric gastroenterology. I was shocked; I knew that the specialists rarely, if ever, called the patient or parent at home. And I thought that this was less believable because he had only seen Jarad twice.

After he introduced himself, he asked, "Has Jarad had a PCR test?"

I told him, "I don't know. He has had so many tests lately, and I am stumped by all of the new vocabulary." I added, "Understandably, I am overwhelmed right now." He explained that this test would tell us whether the results could possibly be a false-positive reading on the hepatitis C test.

"Is there a chance that Jarad is not infected with the hepatitis C virus?" I asked innocently.

"Not likely," he flatly told me.

He asked me to **decide** whether we would stay with our local pediatrician, or whether we would come to the pediatric gastroenterology department at the children's hospital. "Decide?" I asked. "I have to choose?" I was confused; I saw the two doctors working together, and never an either/or situation. He simply said that he was not willing to work with Dr. Gross.

Something was not right. Finally, he explained, "Jarad was tested a year ago for all hepatitis viruses here." He went on to say that "Jarad tested positive for hepatitis C then."

I was dumbfounded. "A year ago?" I asked. I could not believe what I heard. "Why were we not told?" I asked. I thought for a second then said, "What are you saying? You knew he was infected and did not tell us?" No reply. "This is considered an infectious disease," I continued, "and not only have we, as a family, never been told, but neither was our general practitioner, or Jarad's dentist. I am so angry that you have needlessly put us all at risk!"

The gastroenterologist said, "It's your fault; you did not bring Jarad back to the clinic." He went on to say that, "Jarad's liver function was elevated on tests in May 1994 and again in July 1994, and our records indicate numbers even higher in 1991. In fact, the day following his open heart surgery his liver enzymes had skyrocketed." As if any of this new information made me feel better! It just seemed to me that he was attempting to pass the buck!

I thought about his accusation and recalled being asked to contact the clinic two to three weeks following our July 1994 appointment at the children's hospital to see if anything had shown up in the blood work. I <u>had</u> called and was told by the lady I spoke with that "everything appears normal."

When I had reviewed Jarad's medical file, a May 25, 1994 letter from the gastroenterology clinic revealed that Jarad's problem was "irritable bowel syndrome." It was noted in the pediatric gastroenterologist's correspondence that "there is little we can offer except for relaxation therapy with the help of a psychotherapist."

Both my husband and I had attended the follow-up appointment in July 1994. Irritable bowel syndrome (a condition which there was no definitive test) was discussed again, and we were told this would be a lifelong disease for Jarad. "Give Jarad *Cisipride*," we were told. I didn't buy the diagnosis and after giving it to him for a period of time, with no signs of improvement, I felt strongly the drug was causing Jarad's additional vomiting. "More drugs," I thought angrily. "Drugs that could further damage his liver." Neither Peter nor I recalled the suggestion that Jarad seek psychotherapy. Certainly we would have been told if they suspected there was a possibility that Jarad was infected with hepatitis, or would they?

I did just as I was instructed following that appointment, including giving Jarad the medication again. As I believed, it had absolutely no effect on his symptoms, and he vomited up almost every dose I gave him. After three months I stopped giving it to him, believing that was a long enough test period to show results. In light of what we had been told, including normal blood tests, I had decided not to return to the clinic when they called in March of 1995. "What more can the children's hospital offer Jarad when every test appears normal and you keep telling us that Jarad is plagued by nothing more than irritable bowel syndrome," I asked. I told the receptionist that we were moving to Penticton in two weeks and that at this time we felt there was no real urgency to make the long trek to the children's hospital. She did not attempt to convince me to make an appointment nor suggest we bring Jarad in for a follow-up consultation. Certainly no one told us of his elevated liver function results.

I had not, until now, given any thought to what would happen should our whole family test positive for hepatitis C. We had all been subjected to Jarad's blood and body fluids, from simple actions like kissing scraped knees to burn care, to stitches in the chin, to cleaning up buckets of vomit. Although the diagnosis was new to us, I had to keep reminding myself that Jarad's transfusions had happened almost seven years ago. And the possibility of one of us contracting his infectious disease was very real . . .

A month later I was still processing all of the new information I had collected on hepatitis C. I was unable to sleep one night so I picked up the book "Sweet Reprieve" by Frank Maier and his wife Ginny and began reading. When I took this book out of the library, I had taken it out of the "inspirational" section. To my amazement on page nineteen, I discovered it was a gut-wrenching but candid account of Frank's journey with hepatitis C and his subsequent liver transplant.

I learned a lot from this book about strength, a strength that I could only wish to have one day facing our life with this disease. For Frank, hepatitis C symptoms started with a condition called labyrinth vertigo it progressed to general fatigue, lapses of concentration, episodes of confusion and tinnitus (ringing in the ears). He was diagnosed in 1984, transplanted in 1988, and died in 1990. His symptoms of hepatitis C came on too suddenly—yet, at times, not fast enough. On more than one occasion, he wished for death to end his suffering. He faced life-threatening hemorrhages and a slow but steady deterioration of all his vital organs in his body, including his brain. Weight loss of twenty-five pounds was followed by a weight gain of forty as swelling and fluid retention threatened to take his life. He developed varices in his esophagus that ruptured and caused the loss of an incredible amount of blood. Four procedures of endoscopic sclerotherapy caused irreparable damage to his liver, allowing it to barely recover from the Demerol/Valium anesthetic. Itching, fatigue, nausea and swelling of the belly followed, as the next symptoms of liver disease began to set in.

Hepatic encephalopathy was the final stage of his liver failure; "constructional apraxia" was the liver's inability to clear the ammonia from the system, which caused confusion and physical impairments—slurred speech and writing difficulty. The fluid accumulation in the belly was agonizingly painful; for Frank, a gain of eight inches and forty pounds occurred in just two weeks. Sleep became impossible as fluid pressed on the lungs making it hard for him to breath. It also made walking almost impossible because of severe back pain. Another symptom bradycardia (or slowing of the heart) was caused by blood loss and a malfunctioning liver. Potassium levels were so high in his body fluids that they caused Frank's heart to slow and eventually stop beating.

After reading this book, I no longer wondered why I was depressed. I knew what was bothering me. It appeared that when you had hepatitis C eventually you could die a long, slow, painful death. Not only did the patient suffer but I could only imagine the agony that the family would endure as they stood by helplessly watching their loved one fade away. The thought of going through such an ordeal with Jarad was unfathomable.

Jarad and I had another appointment to visit our pediatrician. She said the ultrasound revealed his liver was 7 cm and normal size for his age. He had managed to gain one pound since last month. Otherwise everything else appeared to be okay. I told her that last night he complained of a very sore throat and that he had a low grade fever.

I explained to her that I had received a phone call from the gastroenterology department at the children's hospital and how confused I know was. I told her that the pediatric gastroenterologist expected me to choose between coming to the gastroenterology clinic at the children's hospital or seeing our local pediatrician - but not both. She listened intently but offered nothing in response, although I could see she was visibly upset by the demand being made by doctor.

Our old general practitioner, from White Rock, called to discuss Jarad's new diagnosis. She suggested that a liver biopsy, no matter how painful, was a necessary diagnostic tool. I was not convinced, or was it that maybe I was just not ready to face the results?

Despite everything that we had been through the past month and a half, our whole family gathered on July 17th to celebrate Jarad's seventh birthday. Mom and Dad took us all out for dinner, and then we went back to our home for cake and gifts. It was a bittersweet celebration. I knew Jarad's future should have been the furthest thing from my mind, but I found myself questioning just how many more birthdays he might have.

The infectious disease nurse from the public health department called to ask if we would be willing to participate in a study. She made another appointment to come see us. During the visit, we completed the questionnaire. I caught her up on all that had happened while she was away on vacation. She was appalled by the apparent runaround I was getting from the children's hospital. She did not understand how or why we were not told about Jarad's hepatitis C infection the previous year when they received the hepatitis C positive diagnosis confirmation.

Our pediatrician commented at our next appointment that she ". . . had words with the children's hospital pediatric gastroenterologist." She said he had told her off and threatened to file a complaint against her with the medical ethics board. She had evidently tried to defend us. He questioned her harsh criticism of the gastroenterology department not telling us of Jarad's infection. The department head told her said that as long as she remained involved in Jarad's care that "Jarad would not be welcome in his department. However, he could not prevent Jarad from being seen in the Infectious disease or other departments of the children's hospital. "This is ludicrous," I said. Jarad needed the expertise of a pediatric gastroenterologist. I was incredibly confused and angry. Neither our pediatrician nor I could understand what had caused this reaction by the gastroenterology department head. Was this about someone's ego? Guilt? I wondered.

In a nutshell I had taken my sick baby to the children's hospital at five weeks of age, then again at eight weeks of age. On the latter visit he was admitted and went into massive heart failure. They performed open heart surgery, and sometime during the surgery and ICU stay Jarad was transfused with blood containing hepatitis C. After we left the hospital he continued to be sick; I took him back for a heart catheterization and closed heart surgery four months later. He continued to be labeled a failure to thrive, and for six years he got increasingly sicker. I took him to see many different doctors in a desperate attempt to find out what might be going on in my tiny boy's body. On July 21, 1994 at a gastroenterology clinic appointment Jarad was tested for hepatitis C. The department received the positive test results and for some reason they did not convey the results to us. Almost an entire year later we stumbled across the diagnosis, thanks to the thoroughness of our new general practitioner in Penticton. He called us as soon as he received the results, not waiting to make an appointment and tell us face to face. And now this pediatric gastroenterologist expected me to shoulder the blame for a hepatitis C diagnosis that he failed to convey and for his assistant who told me "all tests were normal." I could only believe that the defensiveness of the children's hospital was about them covering their butts, perhaps worried about a lawsuit?

A few weeks later with appointments arranged for both boys, we had packed up the car and all three children by two A.M. to make the five-hour journey to the children's hospital. Jarad had the first appointment of our day, at 8:00 A.M., in cardiology. This entailed an EKG, a physical exam by his cardiologist, and then an echocardiogram. His cardiologist told us that the right side of Jarad's body was not draining effectively. He believed that it could have something to do with his hepatitis C infection and said we should follow up with him in a month to see if there was any change. Our next appointment of the day was also for Jarad, with an infectious disease specialist. We were none the wiser when we left that appointment, still being told there was very little known about the effects of hepatitis C in children. Tyler's diabetes clinic took up the remainder of our day, where he was seen by the endocrinologist, a nurse clinician, a psychologist, and a dietician. There were no surprises for him as we had worked at maintaining his diet and documenting everything.

Over the summer vacation, we had decided to transfer the children to a new school. In September we made Jarad go to school for the first nine days despite him complaining about feeling 'sick'. To make things worse, he cried every morning when I dropped him off.

Peter and I went to see his pediatrician and get advice on how to handle this situation. She suggested that Jarad had learned how to manipulate me. I vehemently disagreed. It was now evident that he was indeed sick from the hepatitis C infection and that he was not faking it. However, she was not the only doctor to suggest this scenario. For me it was too simple of a scenario.

She recommended that he might benefit from antidepressants; I said "no." It had become so important to me to protect his liver, and I knew most medications were metabolized through the liver and this might further damage his already compromised organ. She also recommended that Jarad have a mental health assessment, to which we both agreed.

On the tenth day of school, he began vomiting again. The school called to say he had thrown up, and since they were aware that his body fluids posed a risk, they didn't want to take any chances with the other students or the staff. I agreed to pick him up. As we walked through the door of our home, he promptly threw-up on the floor. I noticed that he had thick mucus in his throat and nose, and when I checked he was running a fever. For the next four days, I kept him home while he continued to vomit and feel crummy and feverish.

I made another appointment to see the pediatrician. He had an ear infection and had lost 2 ½ pounds since we visited the doctor almost a month ago. For the past three days, Jarad had also been limping and complaining of pain in his right leg. "See," I told her, "he really is sick." This time she agreed.

I was asked to give another talk at the children's new school; the first one had been to inform the staff of what I knew about Jarad's hepatitis C infection, and this one was to address the PTA and concerned parents. It did not take long to see the results of the latter talk when a boy approached Jarad on his first day back to school. The boys were at the playground when the little boy told Jarad his parents told him that he couldn't be his friend. Jarad told him, "That is okay! You weren't my friend before my Mom's talk."

I had arranged a Saturday seminar for people diagnosed with hepatitis C and their families. We were all grateful to Herb Moeller when he brought two experts to present the latest information on the disease and to introduce the Hepatitis C Society of Canada. I had reserved space for fifty people at the Kelowna General hospital and arranged the refreshments. My family had joined me at the hospital to set up the room an hour before the meeting. Jarad and I then went to the airport to pick up Herb and his guest speakers. As we left I noted the room had already begun to fill up. I was pleasantly surprised that it was standing room only upon our return. But I was even more shocked by how far some had driven in search of information!

It was great to finally meet Herb; we had talked on the telephone so many times. His expertise was clearly evident when he opened the meeting, spoke for over an hour, and could answer every question that was asked. He shared his wealth of knowledge about the disease, as well as gave the latest update on the Krever Inquiry. [On September 16, 1993 the Canadian federal, provincial and most territorial ministers of health, recommended a public inquiry into the reasons why the Canadian blood system, "Did not respond to the HIV/AIDS challenge as quickly as it might have." They wanted answers to two questions: 1) regarding the introduction of a test for the HIV antibody to screen blood donations for HIV and 2) the introduction of blood products that had been heat-treated to inactivate HIV in order to reduce the risk of infection. It was believed that by examining these issues it could clarify the tragic events of the 1980s, to reaffirm public confidence in the blood supply system, and to ensure the current Canadian blood system would be able to deal with future challenges as well as those of its day-to-day operations. Chief Justice Horace Krever was appointed, "To review and report on the mandate, organization, management, operations, financing and regulation of all activities of the blood system in Canada, including the events surrounding the contamination of the blood system in the early 1980s."]

Herb described how this inquiry was originally conducted to look into why HIV had gotten into the blood supply and infected just over 1200 persons. But the bigger story became how similar errors in testing blood had resulted in as many as 40,000 Canadians being potentially infected with hepatitis C. Sadly it was discovered that many of the hemophiliacs who received blood products were needlessly infected with both HIV and hepatitis C. He explained that just this week it was discovered that the Canadian Blood Committee had shredded documents key to the

Commission of Inquiry, when it appeared their attorneys had gotten close to uncovering what had actually happened.

Herb struck me as a generous man, sharing his own personal story on how he had received serious burns in a chemical explosion and had unfortunately received hepatitis C-tainted blood. He shared the information that he had gathered since learning of his own infection. Herb had paid for the group's airfare and for all of the handouts he had brought for us. By the end of the meeting almost every one of the seventy plus attendees had joined the national support group—the Hepatitis C Society of Canada. Jarad met many other people with hepatitis C, and appeared relieved that so many shared his ongoing symptoms and that he was not alone in his struggle to get well.

This gave him renewed energy, and the Monday following the meeting he went to go back to school but unfortunately he did not last half a day. We had an appointment to see the pediatrician right after school that day for his pre-vacation physical exam. He was still nauseated, in pain, and had continued to lose weight. However, the *Make a Wish Foundation* had gifted us a trip to Disneyland, and we were all very excited about the trip. We were supposed to be leaving in two days, but we weren't sure if Jarad would be well enough to fly.

Our entire family needed this get away so much. The constant strain of our day-to-day living with a chronically sick child was taking a toll on all of us, and most especially on my marriage. His pediatrician agreed that a holiday was in order. As she examined Jarad and completed the required paperwork, she smiled and gave us the green light to go. From that moment forward, we treated Jarad like a celebrity—even Tyler and Ashley! The excitement and anticipation grew as we boarded the airplane two days later. We were met at Vancouver International Airport by a limousine and whisked off to a nearby airport hotel. There we were met by an official from the *Make a Wish Foundation*, who presented Jarad a gift package containing park passes for Disneyland, Knott's Berry farm, Medieval Dinner Theater, and spending money. He was very excited, even though he was not feeling his best. Over the past two weeks his weight had dropped more than five pounds, and he was really looking thin and gaunt.

The family landed in Los Angeles to bright sunny skies and wonderfully warm temperatures. We were shuttled to our hotel, and although Jarad was still a little nauseous, he wore a huge smile as he saw the Magic Kingdom entrance across the street. That night we decided to lay low: take the children down for a swim in the pool, have an early dinner, and settle them into bed so that we would be among the first in line when Disneyland opened in the morning.

Although Jarad was not feeling great, he did muster up some excitement as we arrived at Disneyland Park the next day. He was thrilled to meet the Disney characters he had only seen on TV and in the movies or read about in books. Jarad posed beside them for pictures in the wheelchair Disneyland had provided for our frail son to move around their enormous park. When Jarad thought his tummy would not tolerate a ride, he was okay just watching his siblings enjoy it and strained to keep track of them as they rode along. Disneyland had given the family a "handicap pass" that allowed us to skip the long lines for the park rides. With the help of all of their conscientious employees, we truly enjoyed three wonderful, carefree days in their Magic Kingdom. We were all proud of Jarad, who wasn't feeling well but didn't complain, not wanting to spoil everyone's fun and to make the most of our family vacation. Sadly each night in the hotel room, the nausea took hold of him and he would fall asleep in my arms with the garbage bucket filled with vomit beside him.

The next three days we were at Knott's Berry Farm. Our favorite ride was the Bigfoot Rapids Rafting, and we all laughed so hard when the kids figured out how to steer our raft and rotate so that either Peter or me landed directly under the waterfall! After our first ride down the rapids, we were soaked to the skin and had to buy new clothes at the gift shop for all of us. For the next two days, we packed a change of clothing for our return trip to Knott's. None of us recalled ever laughing so hard and having so much fun. While we were there, Jarad smiled or laughed the whole time, and all three children slept on the ride back to the hotel.

While Jarad was fairly symptom free on the first couple days of our family vacation, the last few days were hampered by his nausea, vomiting and diarrhea. Unfortunately this lasted throughout our plane ride and after our return home.

CHAPTER SIX

It's Complicated

My excitement peaked with every packet of new hepatitis C information that came to my mail box. I eagerly ripped open the large brown envelopes, hopeful that they would shed some light on my young son's future and possible cure. I read every word on those printed pages. I traced the history of hepatitis C, learning that in 1974 a new strain of hepatitis was identified. At that time it was labeled nonA nonB for what it was: neither hepatitis A nor hepatitis B. I discovered that following years of research the hepatitis C virus was finally identified in 1988 (the year Jarad was born), but also that it was not named until a year later.

All of the information was fascinating. But it did cause me to wonder if the surrogate testing was well documented and if so much was known by then, why was my son infected in 1988? How had this disease gotten into the blood supply and why wasn't everything possible being done to filter it out? I also quickly learned that almost none of the research pertained to children who were infected with the disease; there was not enough of them to conduct comprehensive research. As I learned about the importance of the liver and its five hundred functions within the body, I became deeply concerned about how I would protect Jarad's. Among others, the liver's function is to metabolize proteins and fats in to substances required for life and growth, and store glycogen (the blood sugar regulator), vitamins, and minerals. It also produces the enzymes and bile required for digestion.

"I must protect Jarad's liver from harm; this is one organ the body cannot survive without," I kept telling myself. "Especially after all of the harmful drugs he had taken since his heart surgeries."

I became acutely aware of all of the threats to the liver—toxic foods and drugs, viral and bacterial infections, and environmental contaminants. I read about the possible routes of transmission of hepatitis C, the symptoms, and the numbers of people infected. Although I had heard the term 'Universal Precautions' brandied about, it now took on a somber meaning for our family, especially when I would have to explain it to doctors, dentists, teachers and others who had contact with Jarad and had possibly been exposed to his body fluids. We simply could not risk him innocently infecting anyone. When I thought about Jarad's health in the future and the impact this disease could have on it, my number one mission became FINDING A CURE.

Further testing on Jarad conducted at our next pediatrician appointment determined that he had the most difficult genotype to treat: type 1b. "Genotyping is a classification of a virus based on the genetic material in the RNA (Ribonucleic acid) strands of the virus," I read, "and generally, patients are only infected with one genotype, but each genotype is actually a mixture of closely related viruses called quasi-species. These quasi-species have the ability to mutate very quickly and become immune to current treatments."

"Well that explains why chronic hepatitis C, in general, is so difficult to treat," I thought. I learned that although there were six different subtypes; I had read repeatedly that Genotype 1 was the most common genotype of hepatitis C in North America, but again it was also the most challenging to treat.

My mind flashed back to all of the major body fluid exposures that I had been subjected to—from Jarad spitting up on me in the very early days, to his open heart surgery, heart catheterization, and closed heart procedures. I recalled when at three him standing on a chair that tipped over, and he fell off splitting his tiny chin open, and my immediate cleansing of the cut. This resulted in a large amount of bleeding and four stitches. When he was four years old, Jarad and I collided in front of the stove. Unfortunately I was turning from the burner with a frying pan of boiling water as Jarad was running toward me ready to give my legs a morning hug. To my horror our collision resulted in deep second- and third-degree burns to a large portion of his upper body and open wounds for almost six months. These biggies—in addition to all of the scrapes and cuts Mommies kiss better on a daily basis—put me directly in the line of fire. I had become his full-time nurse, doing everything that was recommended by everyone who recommended it. I shook my head contemplating how many times I was exposed to his blood and body fluids.

After the follow-up blood testing for the whole family, I considered it very fortunate that Peter, Tyler, Ashley or I had not contracted the virus in those first seven years of our exposure. In the meantime, I became obsessed and totally focused on my number two priority: FINDING SOMETHING TO COMFORT JARAD WHILE WE WAITED FOR THE CURE—one that did not include drugs, which could further damage his liver or alter his mind. It was important that we allowed him a quality of life that was worth living. So it was, in those early days, that I learned there was no medical treatment for children (at least in Canada) for the disease. The adult treatment of interferon severely damaged growth hormones, and so if children took the medication they would have stunted growth. All the doctors could tell me was that they were not sure the impact hepatitis C would have on Jarad's growing body. However, they believed the side effects of interferon would be worse on a growing child than the damage it would cause by letting the disease run its course.

I soon began to seek out every possible alternative approach: from simple supplements like milk thistle, to treatments from Pranic healers, Native Indian medicine men, naturopaths, Filipino faith healers, and even some snake oil salesmen or other wacky folks who could not explain what they did. All came with a price tag, a promise of a cure, and some form of treatment that I would have to administer to my son. Both Tyler and Ashley loved the little leather medicine bag Jarad was required to wear by the medicine man; they said "he is lucky" and they wanted one too.

I felt the mounting nurturing demands on my time and my mental health. I tried everything that was suggested and felt defeated as one by one these treatments made no difference at all to his declining health.

Our bank accounts were also being drained, but when faced with the possibility I might deny Jarad the one treatment that worked, I forged ahead turning over every possible rock to expose potential opportunities for restoring his health. In addition to my self-education and "doctoring," I felt torn between tending to the needs of all three of my children. Each made different demands: Jarad—whom I understood could now have a shortened life span due to the hepatitis C infection—to Tyler who had developed Type 1 diabetes eleven years earlier, to Ashley—my healthy happy figure skater.

I was also attuned to the larger global issues of Jarad's disease. In the documents I received, I had read references to submissions made to Justice Horace Krever during his inquiry. Although this Commission of Inquiry had been front and center in the news since it was commissioned two years earlier, it was all "news" to me that I struggled to understand. Although I was totally absorbed in caring for Jarad since his hepatitis C diagnosis, I was definitely paying closer attention to this unfolding story. While this Inquiry had begun as a look back as to how and why just over 1200 individuals received HIV-infected blood from the Canadian Red Cross, it had been quickly expanded when Dr. Alan Powell and others testified and provided evidence of a much larger issue. In addition to the HIV infections transmitted through the blood supply, it was believed that tens of thousands of innocent Canadians had also been transfused with hepatitis C-tainted blood. I was relieved that this investigation was ongoing, and that a non-biased judge was hearing testimony from all sides about this escalating crisis. I had no idea how big nor how serious it would become—nor the impact it would have on the Canadian blood supply or on our country's medical history.

I considered myself an intelligent woman, yet all of this medical maneuvering was too much to fathom. Was there really sufficient evidence to prove there was deliberate exposure? When I read about Dr. Blajchman and Dr. Fineman's grant application to conduct a study, in multiple medical centers, to examine the efficacy of ALT and anti-HBc as surrogate tests for post-transfusion hepatitis (and its subsequent approval in September 1989 by the National Health Research and Development program and the Canadian Blood committee), I was shocked. "A study?" I questioned. "But the U.S. FDA had made recommendations for the implementation of surrogate testing in February 1986 over three years before Canada did. This was despite the fact that many large US medical centers, including some in New York, had begun conducting surrogate testing in 1981?" My heart sunk; it was unbelievable that innocent Canadians were being used as human guinea pigs.

I now had a new focus and embarked on a quest. I was compelled to learn all I could as quickly as possible, and was put in touch with David Smith, president of the Hepatitis C Society of Canada's Victoria, B.C chapter. We talked at length, and he was able to connect me with the mother of a 13-year-old boy who also had open heart surgery and had received hepatitis C from blood transfusions at that time. The boy's mother and I eagerly compared notes, and she told me about the upcoming monthly meeting in Victoria and asked if I would be willing to come there and share my experience and all that I had learned so far. At this point I was the only affected person to request that the Canadian Red Cross research Jarad's donors. I had received a positive confirmation of an infected donor. I encouraged others infected with hepatitis C to call the Red Cross and request a similar trace back.

I was unsure how everything would come together, but within a few days I received a phone call from David Smith to come to Victoria and tell Jarad's story. "Can you attend the meeting next Tuesday?" he asked. "We will provide you with an airline ticket, and you can stay with my family."

I was very excited; I was actually going to meet more people in the same situation as us, but at the same time I was absolutely terrified at the thought of speaking in public.

Little did I know this would be the first time I would become acquainted with the "routes of transmission" division among those infected: there were those who could prove infection through blood transfusions, others who were more likely infected through drug use, and those that did not know how, when or where they were infected.

The group that attended was diverse—more than fifty people of all ages and socioeconomic backgrounds were at this my first official Hepatitis C meeting. It was as if a St. Bernard had come to their rescue. To date the medical profession had done their best to discredit everybody's claims of non-culpability, in most cases blaming assorted life experiences and age on the route of infection.

But when a 7-year-old boy walked in, never having used IV drugs, with no piercings or tattoos and certainly not sexually promiscuous and armed with a letter identifying a hepatitis C-positive blood donor, the liability of the medical profession was clearly evident. Jarad immediately became the poster boy of hepatitis C in Canada, and other infected people and their family's related instantly to his story and his suffering.

My talk went very well, once I calmed down; I told our story from the beginning and spoke from my heart about our struggle. Before I knew the meeting was over, and I had captivated my audience for over three hours.

So when Teresa mentioned the upcoming annual general meeting of the Hepatitis C Society of Canada in a few months in Toronto, I knew that

I had to find a way to attend. Peter, I believed, was quietly in denial and still in shock following Jarad's diagnosis, but he could no longer claim that our boy was simply car sick. Peter made it clear he did not want to attend the meeting, but he strongly encouraged me to attend and to take Jarad with me. He assured me he would take care of the Tyler and Ashley and the house in our absence. I quickly applied for a Hepatitis C Society of Canada scholarship to attend the Annual General Meeting in Toronto. Soon after Theresa call to say we had both been approved and she sent us our airline tickets.

This was so exciting. Our trip entailed first flying from our home in Penticton to Vancouver. Jarad and I were thrilled to be able to sneak in a quick stay over at my parents' home before flying to Toronto. We had all missed Mom and Dad so much since our move to Penticton. We had only seen them twice since Jarad's diagnosis.

But that was about to change, too. On their first trip to our new home months earlier, they had announced, "With both our girls in the Okanagan valley, we have decided to sell our home and move to Penticton. We know you can probably use all the help you can get."

I had shared with them all that I had learned since Jarad was diagnosed, and told them that I would get involved at whatever level was necessary. I also explained the results of phone calls from the children's hospital and outlined our ongoing struggles with them. And after I had put Jarad to bed, I brought up my ongoing marital issues. More importantly, after our conversation I believed I had gained credibility in their eyes as well, proving that I was right about Jarad's "failure to thrive" having an underlying cause and then diligently learning as much as possible about his hepatitis C.

The next morning Dad, Jarad and I left for the airport and were immediately stuck in rush-hour traffic. I got anxious and worried that we would miss our flight even though we had left more than three hours before our flight's check-in time. The airport was a short forty five minutes away in normal traffic. "I am so excited, something tells me I am going to return with a better understanding of this disease and answers to my growing list of questions," I said. Dad and I both cried as he dropped us at the Canadian Airlines departure doors; since Jarad's hospitalizations Dad and I always cried when we parted. We appreciated each other more and had become very close since I had settled down, married Pete, and had a family. The time we spent at the hospital with Jarad had strengthened our bond and made us both realize how precious life really was.

I was nervous travelling with Jarad. His vomiting was unpredictable, and I was concerned the travel might be too much for his frail body. This was going to be a long flight with a sick child in tow. I was also solely responsible for him, as well as retrieving our suitcases and keeping track of our travel documents. As promised Peter had taken the time off from work to be home with Tyler and Ashley while we were away on our eight-day trip. It felt weird to be leaving home, my family, and our doctors. Toronto was so far away.

Jarad and I were called to pre-board the plane bound for Toronto, Ontario. We settled in our economy seats, and as we waited for everyone else to board, Jarad said, "I feel sick, Suki." I checked his forehead for a fever and was relieved he was not burning up. At least that was positive; a fever usually was a sign of a virus or bacterial infection. I was still hopeful that when the plane took off and "fresh" air began to circulate throughout the plane, Jarad would begin to feel better. I attempted to distract him with thoughts about how much fun we would have in the Toronto. We had a few extra days so depending on how he was feeling, I told him about some of my favorite tourist attractions—The CN Tower, The Ontario Science Center, the subway system and Niagara Falls. He appeared to brighten up, if only slightly.

Unfortunately, just as we reached our cruising altitude Jarad began to throw up. The flight attendants were so attentive to his needs and kept checking in with us, removing full "barf bags" and keeping us supplied with empty ones. Sadly he was either throwing up, or feeling like he would, the entire time the plane was in the air. By the time our flight landed, it was evident from the glares and stares that people around us were not happy I brought a sick child on the plane. I wanted to tell them that he had hepatitis C, and unless they touched his body fluids, it was not contagious. We may have been among the first on the plane, but people got out of our way to make sure we were *also first to get off.* As we slowly maneuvered our way to baggage claim, I thought, "Jarad ate nothing and drank only small sips of ginger ale on the six hour flight—what could possibly be left in my poor baby's stomach?" At the baggage claim, we were met by my cousin, Tommy, who had offered to pick us up. He would take us to Auntie Carmen's where we would stay while we were here in Toronto. I had removed some barf bags from the plane just in case, and explained to Tommy that Jarad had a rough flight and he still felt horrible. The idea of car sickness briefly crossed my mind despite me believing hepatitis C was truly at the root of his vomiting.

As we drove away from the airport, before we even reached the freeway, Jarad had begun to wretch again. When we got to my Auntie's home, Jarad ate a little bit of the dinner she had prepared and then promptly threw up again. I was beginning to think this trip was a horrible mistake, but something continued to nag at me that it could also be life-changing. This was a pivotal national conference, and I had been urged by my family and the B.C. lawyers to attend and bring Jarad with me.

I was told it was important for people to see the "innocent side" of hepatitis C, and everyone who had heard our story believed Jarad to be the perfect poster boy for this disease. [As mentioned, a smear campaign had associated it with unhealthy lifestyles choices like IV drug use.] I was so excited to be attending my first annual general meeting. More importantly I was looking forward to connecting to the people I had only spoken to on the phone and learning more—perhaps about an emerging breakthrough treatment that would end Jarad's and my misery of the past seven years? I was also a little nervous, having never attended such a large and important conference, and I really did not know what to expect. Although little Jarad slept soundly beside me, I tossed and turned as sleep eluded me that first night. As exhausted as we were from our day of travel, I was nervous that I would sleep through my alarm, so I lay awake all night—my body no doubt still on B.C. time.

I was out of bed, showered, and all ready to go when I gently woke Jarad at 7:30. He was slow to stir but that was okay; there was no need to rush him. At this point his wellbeing was my main concern, and although I did not want to be late for the registration, I was going to let him dictate when it was time for us to leave the house.

I had lived in Toronto seventeen years earlier and was very familiar with the transit system. I knew exactly how to get to the University of Toronto on the subway system. Auntie Carmen had generously offered to drive us to the TTC station, not far from her home, eliminating an extra bus ride.

Slowly I watched as Jarad began to stir. He was such a soft-spoken, gentle spirit. "How do you feel this morning, sweet man?" I asked. I could tell by the hesitation in his voice that it was not one hundred percent, but I was relieved when he slowly got up out of bed and asked if he could have a bath. This was a good sign because he usually emerged from the tub feeling better than when he went in. "I have a headache and I'm hungry," he quietly said.

"What do you feel like eating?" I asked. Sometimes he would ask for his food to be brought to him when he was in the tub. With Jarad I had learned to feed him whenever he asked for something, as often him feeling good or comfortable was a fleeting sensation that did not last long. I was happy to go downstairs and bring up anything that might help him feel better.

I had always allowed Jarad to eat whatever he desired and whenever he asked for something. I felt it was better than forcing "healthy" food on him that might make him throw up. Quite often after days of vomiting, and only sips of ginger-ale, a chicken Caesar salad with croutons would be his first choice. If I did not have anything that he was craving, I would rush out to the store to get whatever he asked for before he changed his mind. That was my intent this morning too; we could always pick up something on our way to the meeting as we were not sure of the contents of Auntie's pantry and fridge.

He asked specifically for "a grilled cheese sandwich with sweet pickles, and a ginger-ale." After vomiting all day yesterday, his request was my command. I had once been tempted to buy shares in Canada Dry and Schweppes because most days all he could consume was ginger-ale. I went down to the kitchen and discovered that Auntie had all of the fixings for me to make his sandwich. When I came back upstairs, his color had already improved and I was relieved the warm bath had made him feel better.

Jarad quickly devoured half of the sandwich and was ready to get out of the tub. I noticed he was moving a little faster but I had no intention of pushing him. The subway cars left the station every ten minutes so we did not need to rush.

He walked over to the suitcase and picked out what he wanted to wear. "It is cold out," I told him. "A lot colder than B.C., even if the sun is shining."

We were both dressed warmly as we climbed into Auntie's car. She backed the car out of her garage and in less than fifteen minutes, we were inside the Kennedy station and waiting on the platform for our train. Our adventure was about to begin. Jarad looked so much better than he did yesterday. I just wished there was a way for me to settle his stomach and relieve this nausea. It was severely impeding his enjoyment of life.

Both of us were excited as we boarded the subway train. When I lived here, this was my main mode of transportation but today was Jarad's first trip on a subway. He had difficulty understanding how the train could go underground. I loved the excitement in his eyes and thoroughly enjoyed his interest in our adventure as we rumbled down the tracks. Suddenly the outside went dark and his eyes went wide as he asked, "What happened?" I told him we were under the road going through a tunnel. It was all so new and very magical to him.

We had to transfer to the east/west line at Yonge Street for our short ride to the University of Toronto. When we stepped out of the subway station, it was bitter cold as we made the two-block trek to the campus. Once we were on campus, Jarad watched with amusement as the large black squirrels ran across the grounds and seemed to fly up the trees. He continued to track them with delight as we walked past the brick-and-stone buildings to the small campus church and hall where the AGM was being held. We climbed the stairs to the meeting room as a blast of heat hit our chilled bodies. The old building had a distinct musty smell and it appeared Jarad had a negative reaction to it. He had become very sensitive to smells in the past few years. He turned white and began to gag as we reached the top floor landing. We turned the corner into the large room with its new mix of smells. There were tables covered with table cloths and an assortment of breakfast foods against the far wall. The room was crowded with a real variety of people milling about.

At the registration table, Teresa greeted us with a most pleasant and welcoming smile. I was not at all surprised that this beautiful Irish lassie was wearing a tailored-green dress. The color suited her and accentuated her beautiful dark hair and eyes.

"It is so good to finally meet you," she said.

"I can't thank you enough for all of the information you sent us," I said. "The packet of material and the big yellow book were very informative. It's sure hard to find anything in print about children with hepatitis C," I told her as I introduced Jarad.

She asked him how our trip was and he announced, "I puked all the way!" He smiled as she came around the table to hug us both. Teresa then motioned an older gentleman to come over to the table. She introduced Jarad and me to Dr. Alan Powell, the founder of the Hepatitis C Society of Canada (HeCSC) and its current president. He had been transfused with hepatitis C years before following a surgical procedure. In the early days if it had not been for Dr. Powell and his research, the awareness gained about hepatitis C transfusions would not be documented. He was instrumental in the Hepatitis C Society of Canada being granted standing at the Krever Inquiry, and being represented by their attorneys Philip Tinkler and Ian Blue. I had been privileged to read most of the research this PhD professor had presented to Justice Krever. Dr. Alan Powell was truly a hero to all who were transfused with this deadly disease. His heart shone through as he greeted us both warmly, as if welcoming "family" to his home.

Although we had only ever spoken on the phone, meeting both Teresa and Dr. Powell in person was like reconnecting with old friends. Teresa said, "I am so glad that you both were able to join us." Dr. Powell reintroduced us to another friendly face—Herb Moeller. This kind man- a husband and father of two was also from B.C. and had spoken at our meeting in Kelowna the previous month. He was also one of the national HeCSC board members. Herb had been infected with hepatitis C from one of the 120 units of blood that he received following a workplace explosion resulting in third-degree burns over 75 percent of his body in 1984. Jarad and Herb felt an instant connection. Jarad could see Herb's scarred skin and told him that he had a bad burn too, and showed Herb his scarred shoulder. We met Joanne Manser, also a mother of two, and like Herb currently held a seat on the National board. She, like Jarad, was sick and it was heartwarming to watch the two interact—sharing horror stories about vomiting, headaches, achiness as well as what it was like to feel sick on a daily basis. Joanne introduced us to Dr. Michelle Brill Edwards, a retired high-ranking Health Canada pediatrician. Over the course of the conference, I was overwhelmed with all of her knowledge - about hepatitis C and how this blood disaster had occurred in Canada.

I could see that being here would be a truly a life-changing experience for me. There were so many people from all across the country who all shared so much in common—maybe not how they got the disease, but a bond formed between them as they learned about the full scope of this epidemic. Besides Teresa, I was the only person in the room who was not infected with hepatitis C, but through Jarad I felt a kinship with each of them. What seemed to set the "transfusion" victims apart was that each had very serious health problem requiring a blood transfusion. Some were injured in motor vehicle or industrial accidents; some had serious surgery, while others received transfusions as an adjunct to chemotherapy. With this virus coursing through their veins, it made recovering and healing from their initial illness or injury far more of a challenge. Again I heard how the transfusion victims were prone to attack by the medical profession to transfer the blame to them for poor lifestyle choices. It became obvious everyone needed the confirmation that a blood transfusion trace-back study would provide.

I had felt so alone in Penticton dealing with Jarad's disease. I certainly had no idea that this many people were infected with the hepatitis C virus; the room was full with more than two hundred of them. The first day of lectures went until just after 5:00 P.M. and was immediately followed with an organic vegetarian dinner.

During our breaks I took Jarad outside for fresh air and to walk around the campus. He ran about and chased the squirrels, laughing as they darted away when he got too close. Inside again he stayed right by my side as the sessions went on, either drawing or coloring or sleeping with his head on my lap. Since the first day had run so long, we did not have time to return home for a nap or to dress for dinner, so we simply stayed in the church hall talking with other attendees. It was fascinating to hear the parallels between those who had the disease. It had taken most years to get diagnosed, and like Jarad many whom I spoke with had also been told they had irritable bowel syndrome.

I was engrossed in the daily exchange of information at the meetings. Dr. Powell updated us about the Krever Inquiry, which had now turned into an investigation of epic proportions examining how the health care system had allowed contaminated blood to be used on patients. The Canadian Red Cross and their role as an independent charitable body that supplied donated blood to hospitals were at the focus of this inquiry. We were told that in the late 1970s a management crisis allowed thousands of people to be infected with HIV and hepatitis C. It soon became apparent that inadequately screened blood, often coming from high-risk populations like drug users, had entered their blood supply system.

At the conference lawyers discussed openly the possibility of a class action lawsuit involving all individuals that could prove they received their disease from the blood supply. A gastroenterologist provided the most up-to-date medical information on hepatitis C as well as the available Interferon treatment and the new drug Ribavirin. It was no secret the side effects of the current treatment was horrific and offered very low odds of killing the virus. Some of the infected folks were barely hanging on, having experienced the scourge of chemotherapy including nausea, vomiting, and hair loss. Depression and feelings of isolation and even suicide were prevalent, we learned. There really was a lot of information to absorb. I had completely filled a notebook with my notes, collected every handout, and had many leads to follow-up on when I got home.

The following day Dr. Powell asked me if I would like to speak to the group and tell them of my experiences seeking a diagnosis, conducting the traceback with the Canadian Red Cross, our shabby treatment at the children's hospital since Jarad's diagnosis, and the doctors' hesitancy to deal with us since that point. He also asked me to explain the hepatitis C awareness ribbon campaign that I had helped to create to bring attention to this potentially fatal disease. I was only nervous before I took the stage, but once I started to tell our story, my shaking stopped. What I shared was well received and I even received a standing ovation. Everyone was thrilled to meet Jarad and see the innocent side of the disease.

On the third and last day of the AGM, I was asked if I would join the Board of Directors. Both Jarad and I were viewed as "clean" representatives of the transfused group since I was not infected and had no skeletons hiding in my closet and Jarad had no other risk factors. They saw that I was already a champion of the cause, and as the mother of an infected child, I was like the proverbial mother bear, prepared to fight for my cub at any cost. I was overwhelmed by all I had heard over the weekend, but for Jarad's sake I was committed to learn more. Although I did not feel as informed as some of the board members, I knew my potential and my dedication to do anything and everything to save my son's life, put me in a position to become a board member. I decided that being on the Board would keep me involved with the bigger picture on days when I was hyperfocused on Jarad; plus, being totally healthy gave me the distinct advantage of sustained energy and focus.

I felt I owed it to all who voted for me to take on this new responsibility with one hundred percent dedication. Afterward I was congratulated by everybody there. I believed it was Jarad's innocent face—the poster boy to come—and my connection to him that really helped me get elected. Now I had my work cut out for me.

Four days after we arrived in Toronto, as mysteriously as it appeared, the nausea that had plagued Jarad suddenly disappeared and the vomiting abruptly stopped. Jarad ate all day as if he were starving to death. It was such a welcome relief.

Finally, we were able to enjoy a couple of free days in Toronto. We left the conference an hour before it actually ended to go outside and watch the Santa Claus parade in the bitter cold as it passed down Bloor Street just steps from the campus. The parade was a definite highlight, but one I did not want to discuss with Jarad a few days earlier when he felt so crappy. Before we left the conference, Dr. Powell mentioned that he had a friend, a pediatric gastroenterologist at Toronto's Sick Kids Hospital, and asked if I would willing to take Jarad to see her. This is a great opportunity for Jarad now that the Vancouver gastroenterologists had requested we take Jarad elsewhere. He said he would arrange the appointment. I was surprised when he called me first thing Monday morning to tell me that his friend had agreed to see Jarad that afternoon. During our appointment, she spent an hour with us and ordered every possible test that would possibly give us a better idea of what was happening with Jarad. The appointment ended with her saying that Jarad was actually doing quite well, although he definitely was underweight. She did not readily have an explanation as to why he was nauseated and vomited regularly. "It is perplexing as I have not seen this in any of my other young patients," she said. She promised she would send a detailed report to Jarad's pediatrician and summarize all of the results. We thanked her and also let Dr. Powell know how much we appreciated this opportunity.

There was so much to think about. Toronto was obviously too far to go to attend doctor appointments but what would transpire with the children's hospital gastroenterology clinic in Vancouver? Surely the doctors there would reconsider the wellbeing of their patient. I knew it was time to find him someone closer to home that was knowledgeable and who could assist us with additional testing that might give us some concrete answers. In the meantime, we would have to wait to receive the results of the testing and his friends' subsequent report.

Our flight home was delightfully uneventful. I was catching up reading all of the new hepatitis C information I had been given at the conference, when the flight attendant invited Jarad to tour the cockpit. She had remembered him from our flight six days earlier when he had vomited his way across the country, and I had shared some of my hepatitis C information with her. She was happy to see that he was looking and feeling so much better. She took his hand and walked him to the cockpit door. It opened and he disappeared inside. Almost thirty minutes later I looked up the aisle for my son, finally catching the flight attendants eye. She came over and explained that he was entertaining the flight crew with his stories and asked if I would object to him staying in the cockpit until after the plane had landed in Vancouver. "Oh my goodness, of course not! I am sure Jarad would be thrilled. What an amazing experience for him," I exclaimed. I was really enjoying my alone-time after spending six days on the road with Jarad. It was at this point of our trip, after meeting so many victims struck by this disease, that my thinking had shifted from asking why me, to simply wanting to know why had this disaster occurred for everybody infected? I knew I had my work cut out for me!

In the cockpit the flight attendant prepared Jarad for the landing in Vancouver by strapping him into in his jump seat. He was beaming from ear to ear when the plane had landed, taxied to the jet way and he was escorted back to his seat. His enthusiasm bubbled over as he excitedly told everyone within earshot that he got to "land" the plane.

My parents had hoped to find a new home close to ours, sell theirs, and be living in Penticton before Christmas. Everything fell in to place like clockwork; their house sold and they found a beautiful home on the next street over from us, also with a fabulous view of Skaha Lake. Dad had informed me that the date for their house sale to complete was two days after we returned from Toronto. So on our return trip, I had planned to stay at their home in North Delta, to help with the packing and cleaning. Jarad and I drove back to Penticton with them. This saved us the return airfare back to Penticton!

Jarad was so happy to be back at Gran and Poppas home, and even more enthused to be helping with their move. It was wonderful to watch him when he was feeling good. He was in and out of the back of the big moving truck, helping out where ever he could all day long.

The next day, our caravan left North Delta very early in the morning. We were so lucky to have beautiful, sunny weather for the trek to the Okanagan considering it was November. Winter had set in almost everywhere else in Canada, but the roads were clear and the sun was shining for our entire drive along the Hope-Princeton Highway. My nephew Daniel drove the moving truck; Dad drove his pickup while Mom, Jarad, and I were in their Ford Taurus. We wanted to get to Penticton as early in the day as possible so we could get as much unloaded and put away before dark.

The next few days we were kept busy and distracted while helping my parents get settled in their new home. The children and I spent all of our free time over at my Mom and Dad's during the week emptying boxes and rearranging the furniture. Peter came over and helped whenever his work schedule allowed. My three children were excited to have Mom and Dad living so close. They could just walk down the side of our hill, through the brush, and up the road to get to their house. We had always lived a few miles from my parents' home, so being just five minutes away on foot was going to be a real treat for all of us. I was looking forward to the breaks they could provide me with, and with all that was happening in my life, I would really need them. We both felt so comfortable with Mom and Dad looking after the children that maybe Peter and I would now get to spend some quality time alone together.

Peter chose let me go on with the political fight I was about to embark on but had to keep his distance, because his employer was the federal government. The Royal Canadian Mounted Police was involved in an investigation into possible criminal charges against government officials. I knew he felt pulled in both directions by his decision—family and career. For us it was a no brainer—we needed the paycheck. After hearing all about our trip, Peter was happy to return to work as soon as we got back.

The following week Jarad began to complain of headaches. After we tried all our home remedies and three days had passed, I took him to see our general practitioner. Our general practitioner wrote prescriptions for pain medication and anti-nausea drugs that he believed would help to alleviate Jarad's symptoms. Sadly, the very next day, his vomiting returned with a vengeance. He was all ready to go to school, but by midmorning the school had called and asked me take him home. Once at home, Jarad spent the remainder of the day throwing up.

When I called and told our doctor that Jarad was really sick again, he told me to take him to see his pediatrician. She said the headaches could be migraines and suggested we should consider getting Jarad a CAT scan. She also explained that she thought Jarad would be better off on long-term antibiotics, as he still had fluid in his ear canal from the infection he had the first week of school, some three months ago. She also suggested a new nasal spray might help to clear the fluid in his ear.

I had decided since drugs could have harmful effects on his already compromised liver that I did not want him to go back on long-term antibiotics. I also asked that with all the testing she's had lately, wouldn't it would be best to just wait on the results from the pediatric gastroenterologist in Toronto?

The next day Jarad broke out in a rash from head to toe. Over the next two days his rash got worse. It covered his trunk, his face, his arms, and his legs. His feet and hands swelled. He complained that his wrists hurt. On the third day I noticed that a large lump had formed on his right wrist. His hand and his wrist were swollen, red and sore.

Although he wanted to go to school that day, he actually threw up on the way there, so after dropping Tyler and Ashley off we turned around and headed home.

Four days before Christmas 1995, Jarad had an appointment with our pediatrician. His wrists and hands were still very swollen, but he only had faint rash spots on his legs and trunk now. But, by the time we arrived at her office, he had totally broken out in large, red welts.

She asked, "Has he eaten anything new? Have you switched shampoo, soaps or detergents?"

I told her "No."

Her advice was, "To continue watching him closely and bring him back in if it gets worse."

The next day Jarad was still covered in welts. He did not sleep much and complained that he was very itchy. He was angry when I told him as long as he had the welts, he could not participate in his school's Christmas concert. Jarad did not want to join us the following day for a visit to my sister's home in Kelowna; he just wanted to stay with Mom and Dad and possibly spend the night. They readily agreed, happy to be able to help out. That night Mom filled the bath in oatmeal and it seemed to temporarily sooth the welts. The next day Jarad was grumpy and itchy when he came home. His feet were swollen and visibly painful when he walked. He had spent the entire day having five oatmeal baths and asked for one more as soon as he got home. This time it did nothing to ease his discomfort.

For the first time ever, Jarad asked me to take him to the hospital; he knew they always poked him with needles there. His request scared me so I took him right away. The doctor immediately gave him a shot to stop the itching. It made him sleepy almost immediately. The doctor explained it was quite possible this was a virus and that it could linger for up to six weeks. That posed a new threat; Jarad would scratch the welts in his sleep, opening the skin and causing them to bleed. I became nervous one of my children would inadvertently touch one and be exposed to Jarad's hepatitis C. After all, we knew the virus was transmitted through contact with blood.

Before we left the hospital the doctor gave me a prescription for Atarax liquid to ease the itching when we got home. That night Jarad slept well for the first time in five days—no wonder he was grouchy!

If it was a virus, there was nothing else we could do so we decided to distract ourselves with a visit to my sister's. I did not tell the children that cousin Robin had just arrived from Calgary and was coming to spend a week with us. Everyone's spirits were shored up when we saw her! Jarad called the young adult cousin his "girlfriend" and would grin like a Cheshire cat when she was near him. His crush on her was no secret!

We had a great visit and Peter was in the drivers' seat on the way home. We were on the highway and had alerted the children to engage our "Bambi" patrol (where we all kept a lookout for deer)—this was crucial because the deer were so abundant this time of year and they were easily blinded by oncoming headlights. As we drove along red brake lights suddenly appeared in front of us, and a Honda going the opposite direction swerved and hit the gravel shoulder. A deer had strayed in front of it, and they hit the animal and sent it flying across the road where it hit our front end and bounced up the hood and onto the windshield. Not realizing what had just happened, everybody in our car all screamed as Peter pulled to an abrupt stop on the side of the road. After checking that nobody was hurt, he was able to limp our broken car home—the whole front end was totaled.

Sadly, it appeared this year was going to end in crisis. Jarad not well and the car required major front end repairs. As we toasted the New Year 1996, we all commented "Things can only get better!"

CHAPTER SEVEN

Seeking Truth

A week later we sat in the pediatricians office as she explained the prognosis for hepatitis C. "They are about two years from any in-depth research on hepatitis C in children because the disease was only identified six years ago. In truth there is very little known about it in children, and since the symptoms may take years to manifest, fewer children are identified," said our pediatrician. She suggested I stay away from lawyers. "They can cause grief and anxiety."

"But wait a minute," I reminded her. "I've been suffering from anxiety ever since learning of my son's infection, and what about the tragedy surrounding the Blanjchman-Fineman study that was brought to light at the Krever Inquiry?" Initially all I wanted was for the children's hospital to say, "We are sorry." I desperately needed to hear those three words more than anything else; at that point I would have appreciated an apology from anyone. I anticipated the hospital and doctors would provide us with whatever medical information or treatment was available to get Jarad healthy. I didn't think I was asking for much; I was taught to apologize when I was wrong and to always accept responsibility for my actions, and under the circumstances I expected the doctors and the hospital to simply do the same.

But I was confused: why did our pediatrician not mention the results of the Sick Kids Hospital testing? When I called the nurse clinician in

Toronto, she informed me that the report had been sent some time ago. When I questioned our pediatrican she gave no explanation and simply stated the results, "There are no indicators that there is anything else wrong with Jarad; no irritable bowel syndrome; nothing except hepatitis C. All of Jarad's liver numbers indicate his liver was under siege by the virus from infancy." The numbers were more than four times the normal level. Something felt different on this visit. During the appointment, she was considerably less supportive and friendly than I had experienced in the past.

While the children's hospital and its staff had worked around the clock in September, 1988 to save Jarad's life, I now felt betrayed by the medical establishment. They had given my baby the gifts of life and of death at precisely the same time. Now, instead of feeling welcomed there, I felt hostility from the staff on my visits to the children's hospital. I encountered hospital officials and their attorneys who changed the rules, skirted around my questions, downplayed Jarad's symptoms saying hepatitis C rarely affected children, and then they passed the blame on to me—all of which added to my stress and frustration.

I remembered back in June when we were notified of Jarad's infection and cautioned by Public Health not to tell anyone about it. I questioned their reasoning and was told, "Disclosing the disease serves no purpose and can cause the victim to be ostracized!" The nurse went on to say, "You have been placed on a need-to-know basis. And the truth is no one needs to know, nor do you have a right to know if someone has hepatitis C or AIDS." She added, "What you have to be aware of is that anyone you meet could be infected, and that you should act accordingly."

I learned that hepatitis C was very different from hepatitis A or B—there was no vaccination nor was there a cure for hepatitis C. It had mutated and that made research into cures extremely challenging.

I did not want Jarad to be "victim," and I felt my silence would only perpetuate more misery. I knew me, and being silent and not speaking out would drive me crazy. But for the next few months I went along with them and struggled with our "secret." Initially, we told only our immediate family, but the more "ostrich-like" the medical professionals became when discussing the disease; the more I knew I could not hold my silence much longer.

Was the medical community's callousness responsible for spreading the disease? I had just read that the president of the Canadian Association for the Study of the Liver, Eve Roberts, reported that "300,000 Canadians were infected with the hepatitis C virus," and she added "most of them do not know it." She went on to say that, "It is one of the main health issues facing this country today." At the same time the World Health Organization (WHO) estimated, "A proportion, in the order of 3%, of the world population has been infected with HCV and there are more than 170 million chronic carriers who are at risk of developing liver cirrhosis and/or liver cancer." The World Health Organization added that due to the sheer number of people infected that **"Hepatitis C is emerging as a global health issue** is by all means an understatement." Given its worldwide health threat, the hush-hush cover-up was a little late in the game.

It was at that moment I realized that I was becoming a hepatitis C activist! I was infuriated after hearing a Canadian Red Cross commercial on my favorite radio station, requesting monetary donations for their "Friends for Life" campaign. I called the radio station and asked them if they would consider pulling the Red Cross public service announcement—they were certainly no friend of mine! I briefly recapped to the station manager what I had learned from the preliminary findings of the Krever Inquiry and the Red Cross's culpability in the tainted blood crisis.

Next I called the Canadian Red Cross and asked to speak to the person in charge of advertising and promotions for regional Red Cross fundraising. I carefully explained our story; she appeared genuinely touched by what I told her and agreed the Red Cross should be helping our family, and if my information was correct, probably thousands of others too. She explained that, although the commercials were being run as public service announcements, she would speak to someone about discontinuing them as a show of respect for the victims of this disaster, or at least until after Krever had tabled his final report.

That evening I shared my small, first victory with my family!

After hours spent in family discussions about whether or not to disclose Jarad's hepatitis C infection, I decided to contact a reporter at our local newspaper—the *Penticton Herald*. I was nervous and requested our first encounter "be totally off the record."

The reporter was Gary Symons, and asked for his opinion on how to best present our sensitive story. He wrote copious notes as he carefully listened. I explained about the early days when Jarad was only five weeks old, and told him of the medical report that was sent to our family physician confirming, "There is nothing wrong with any of Jarad's major organs." I walked Gary through my return to the hospital three weeks later for testing, and how Jarad had gone into massive heart failure that day [I still question how a heart is not a major organ?] I then told how the whole experience affected me. I meticulously described his open heart surgery, his painstakingly slow recovery, and all that occurred during the thirteen excruciating days in the intensive care unit, as well as detailing the deterioration of my relationship with my husband due to the stress of living with this illness over the past seven years.

I went on to explain how ill Jarad continued to be sick after his surgeries, and my frustration at the medical professionals' inability to diagnose the cause. "At every appointment, I was crushed at repeatedly hearing the words failure to "thrive"; I blamed myself and, more importantly, I believed there must have been something, anything, I could have done differently. At that time, I was continually assured any illness he was currently suffering from was not related to his heart. I explained that Jarad and I had over four hundred days of hospitalization or medical appointments since his birth—appointments where doctors investigated his confusing symptoms: the nausea, vomiting, chronic infections and unexplained rashes." I continued that our last two clinic visits at the children's hospital—just before Jarad was diagnosed with hepatitis C—both occurred in the gastroenterology department, and for lack of a better diagnosis we were simply told Jarad suffered from irritable bowel syndrome. This conclusion really puzzled me because Jarad endured chronic constipation and was prescribed daily laxatives. "Everyone I knew with irritable bowel syndrome," I told the reporter, "was affected in the exact opposite way: diarrhea within minutes of eating." Over the following weeks of giving the prescribed medication to him, none of his symptoms disappeared; in fact, I believed the medication made him vomit every day, and he showed no signs of improvement. The more research I did, the more I realized his symptoms did not match any definition I could find for the new diagnosis. So after a few months I took him off the irritable bowel medication.

I told Gary that when we received the hepatitis C diagnosis I contacted the children's hospital gastroenterology department to ask if they had ever tested Jarad for hepatitis C ; and then how in a telephone call from department head the next day, I was matter-of-factly told, "Yes, and he tested positive a year ago."

"What? You tested him a year ago? Why were we not told?" I screamed. I was furious! I felt he simply blamed me for not returning with Jarad to the gastroenterology clinic. I sat, horrified, wondering how this could have happened. Upon first hearing the diagnosis just a few months earlier, I was both heartbroken and terrified. But now I felt vindicated knowing after all these years, there really was something wrong with my son—a valid diagnosis for his poor health." I told Gary I no longer felt welcomed in the gastroenterology or in the infectious disease departments at the children's hospital, and how difficult they were making it for me to get answers and how they restricted my access to personnel. I said, "A couple of weeks ago," I asked the children's hospital to request the Red Cross initiate a look back to Jarad's donors and that all of them were from B.C. They said they would call me back on Friday, and unsure of their procedure, I planned to ask them if they had contacted the donors. When they called, the children's hospital reported that the Red Cross would release no personal information about the donors. That was okay with me because I really only wanted to confirm one infected donor and for that infected donor to be informed they had the virus, if they were not already aware. I was told the Red Cross would conduct a trace back and provide me with "official" documentation as soon as they confirmed that the blood Jarad received during his 1988 surgery was contaminated with the hepatitis C virus.

I told Gary that "silence does not sit well with me." In reality it suffocated me. I believed everyone should be talking about hepatitis C! My head was spinning ever since I was first told about this disease. Besides, as far as I could tell, little was being done to educate the public. I had never heard of hepatitis C before Jarad's diagnosis nor had anybody else I knew. The library had no reference material that I could read. Access to the internet to do research was limited at that time in Penticton. I found it incredulous to be told it would "serve no purpose by telling anyone." How were individuals supposed to protect themselves from a disease carried by the blood and other bodily fluids, when they were not even aware it existed? This was a time bomb waiting to explode with a potential devastating and deadly impact on Canada and the world. What recourse would families have when they learned their loved ones were infected? I was even more horrified when Public Health told us we "should be wearing gloves when cleaning up Jarad's body fluids."

"Wear gloves?" I shrieked. "It is kind of late for that! I have been cleaning up his blood, vomit, urine, and spit for seven years now."

In addition to learning about this new deadly disease, the reporter was horrified by the run around treatment we were being subjected to at the children's hospital since learning of our son's infection. He told me that there was so much to consider in going public with our story, but I told him my tendency was towards "a tell-all" that would expose the lies we had been told and the shabby treatment we were receiving. "Disclosure would be a gamble but worth the risk," I said.

A few days later Gary excitedly called and we met again "off the record." He had conducted a preliminary investigation and was astounded by what he had uncovered. Gary had contacted a children's hospital spokeswoman, Pat Evans, who was shocked at our allegation of mistreatment by the children's hospital and of the gastroenterology department's failure to disclose our son's hepatitis C diagnosis. "If that is indeed the case, then that's extremely serious," she told Gary. She promised to research the issue immediately; however, when Evans called Gary back days later, she said the hospital's lawyers had been assigned to the case. "The hospital was now providing "no comment" on the Gibbenhuck child," she said.

Gary went on to say our story had widespread implications. He had spoken to politicians, government officials, hospital officials, doctors, and consumer groups; and he had identified many local people infected by blood transfusions with hepatitis C. He was stunned by their stories that also alluded to a cover-up of epic proportions within our government!

He explained it would likely take him a few weeks to gather all the facts, conduct the interviews, and verify all of the information before he would begin writing a four-to-six part series. In the meantime he asked me to keep on top of any breaking news and to pass everything that transpired along to him. Like me, he believed the public had a definitive need to know about this insidious disease if we were ever going to slow or stop its spread.

In his mind there was no doubt that we had been treated poorly but also that a little boy's life hung in the balance. Gary overwhelmingly encouraged us to "go public with your story." He promised to take every precaution when telling our account, and vowed he would run each installment past the newspaper's lawyers to ensure we could not be held liable for any of the story's content.

Through it all Jarad was still plagued with daily vomiting and there was no end in sight. It was wearing him and me down, so we made another trip to see his pediatrician even though I had sensed a change of heart on her part since our last visit. By the end of the new appointment, I felt like a small, scolded child. Our doctor had been contacted by Gary, and she had serious concerns about him snooping around and wanted to know what we thought could be accomplished by talking to the media. She expressed her concern that we were acting out of anger and that we should be dealing with this whole issue more objectively. She believed I blamed the gastroenterology department for Jarad's hepatitis C infection. "No!" I fumed. "Not for the infection, just for not telling us his diagnosis in a timely manner—a year later is a year too late!"

At the beginning of the school year, I had explained to the school principal that Jarad was infected with hepatitis C. I told him about Public Health's position on the subject, and I felt it was important that we made him aware of Jarad's illness. He then consulted Public Health. Just before the story was to break in the press, the principal and I met again to consider the consequences for Jarad and the school. He asked if I would address the Parent Advisory Committee (PAC) of our children's school to do some damage control before the release. He assured me that someone from Public Health would also be there to answer questions. I thought long and hard about this forum and decided a door was being opened to educate everybody on hepatitis C and the needed precautions.

I was trembling when I walked into the crowded room and could not believe how many parents had showed up to hear my talk. I knew what I would say but I suddenly became terrified of these strangers and feared their overreactions. Would they demand my son leave the school immediately? Or would they possibly run us out of town? I wondered if I should have brought an escort to accompany me home.

I was relieved when the outcome was actually quite the opposite. I began by alerting them to the upcoming newspaper series and explained why we had chosen to tell our side of the story, which was very well received. Then I shared the most compelling evidence on transmission routes. I told my audience over the past seven years, when we did not know about Jarad's infection, none of our family members had been infected despite being exposed Jarad's blood and body fluids on many occasions. I assured them that unless there was direct blood to blood—or with other body fluids—contact, there was little possibility of his peers or teachers being infected. I reminded them, "This is a new world we live in. In our generation, young people chose to engage in a ritual of becoming blood brothers (or sisters) by making a small cut in the skin and touching the open wounds together. This practice is now definitely to be discouraged!"

After hearing my story some of the parents asked probing questions. Like me, they simply wanted to understand as much as they could about this disease. I believed that because they were parents and could feel my pain, they were genuinely sympathetic to our plight. After I had told our story, the Public Health nurse backed me up and confirmed the validity of my information. At the end they gave me a standing ovation. It shook me to the core. I realized that I was now considered somewhat of an expert on this subject and was no longer just Jarad's mom.

A few days later, Gary called to see how the parents had reacted to my presentation. He also shared that his research was complete and he had started to write our story. He wanted photos to run alongside the story and asked if the newspaper's photographer could meet Jarad and me at our doctor's office to take pictures the following week. He said it appeared the Krever Inquiry was forcing the hepatitis C issue out in the open, making it an "accepted" topic of discussion. He informed me that our pediatrician was just alerted to the importance of getting hepatitis C infected patients vaccinated for the A and B strains as soon as possible, and that he would work this tidbit of new information into our story.

Upon learning of Jarad's infection, I had filed amended tax returns to take advantage of a disability tax credit for Jarad that would have brought some much needed income into our cash-strapped lives. In the seven years of Jarad's infection, our bills for trips to medical appointments had added up considerably. But our three requests for the tax credit had all been denied, and eventually out of desperation I took our case to the local Member of Parliament. Jim Hart wrote to Revenue Canada Taxation on our behalf, and after five months and four separate appeals Jarad's hepatitis C infection entitled us to finally collect the disability tax credits and get a tax refund of more than $5000.00. What a wonderful reprieve!

I went down to the *Penticton Herald's* office to tell Gary the disability tax credit was finally approved. I also told him that I had been in contact with a Vancouver attorney, who told me to stick with Gary and the local paper if we trusted him. He went on to explain the value of having at least one trustworthy media person who was on our side.

Gary and I then went over the entire story one last time. When I saw it in writing, I got a really uneasy feeling about its release. Gary shared that two of the doctors in the story had now retained attorneys, and that children's hospital had retained the big Vancouver law firm, Bull, Housser & Tupper, to represent them. As well, he said that the Canadian Medical

Protection Association (C.M.P.A) would represent Dr. Hassall, the pediatric gastroenterologist.

Gary was very excited to tell me what he had learned from Dr. Alan Powell, founder and president of the Hepatitis C Society of Canada. Dr. Powell had been in the gallery at the Krever Inquiry and clearly understood the magnitude of its investigation. Gary went on to say, "You know the sole purpose of the Krever Inquiry was intended only to discover why fourteen hundred-plus people had been transfused with HIV and to explain how it happened." But as a result of this Inquiry, "A much larger picture is materializing revealing an additional ten thousand innocent individuals who were needlessly infected with hepatitis C, and," he added, "some of them intentionally." We discussed the Blajchman-Feinmen study conducted to analyze if additional testing was worthwhile to reduce the frequency of post-transfusion non-A, non-B hepatitis from the donor pool. Most of the world had already been testing for these surrogate markers; New York Blood centers implemented this testing in 1981, and they believed a whopping seven thousand infections per year in New York alone would be eliminated. The Blajchman-Feinman study conclusively revealed some of these innocent victims received infected blood just to see whether they would develop hepatitis! I was glad Gary had done his own follow-up on this study and had come to the same conclusion. It did nothing, however, to mitigate the magnitude of its results. This truly was inconceivable to accept and it made me sick!

Dr. Powell had diligently sat through over a year of the Inquiry's testimony, and initially was the only hepatitis C representative present during the proceedings. He shared with Gary, "Now there are lawyers working for the Hepatitis C Society, and they have just won a case for 'free standing,' enabling them to appear in the Supreme Court on behalf of hepatitis C-transfused."

Dr. Powell told Gary that he had been in close communication with his VP, Herb Moeller, who was setting up a meeting in Vancouver for all of the infected. He went on to explain the importance of Jarad being "the poster boy" for the group, because the Red Cross lawyers had already begun a smear campaign severely trashing those with hepatitis C. He acknowledged that due to Jarad's young age and his lack of exposure to harmful activities, it would be impossible for anyone to pass such judgment on him.

With the minimal research I had done, I shared with Gary that the Saskatchewan government appeared to be the only ethical provincial government involved in this inquiry. They agreed that all who were transfused with hepatitis C were entitled to know the whole truth, and had already gotten involved with look-back/trace back studies at every hospital to identify and notify the recipients of tainted-blood products to be tested immediately.

Dr. Powell added, however, that the province of B.C. had announced its intention to follow Saskatchewan's humane lead regarding treatment of the hepatitis C sufferers. He explained the B.C. government had set aside funds that would provide training and pay staff in order to keep up with the demand for hepatitis C information. He went on to say a $200,000 grant was allocated as the seed money to get the project off the ground. The B.C. government had also offered additional money as the need arose to help set up Hepatitis C Society of Canada chapters in other cities and towns as facilitators stepped forward. It was a proud moment for me.

Our story, it appeared, was really coming together.

For the first time in four months Jarad stayed at school all day. This just happened to coincided on February 14 (Valentine's Day) with a celebration—complete with a carrot cake decorated with 100 candles—marking the hundredth school day for this school year. And carrot cake just happened to be Jarad's favorite!

We were all in celebratory mood the next day when we decided to go visit my sister in Kelowna. Our day included lunch at Red Robin followed by a visit to the Society of Prevention of Cruelty to Animals (SPCA) to see the kittens and puppies. As might be expected, this resulted in us bringing home a puppy! None of us had experienced much happiness in the past few months, but this furry, little fellow made us all laugh and smile. I believed the puppy would be perfect for our family and provide a great distraction. The children all agreed to name him Grizz, as he looked like a small black bear cub. As adorable as he was, I soon realized we all lacked knowledge necessary on how to care for and train him. We immediately went shopping and purchased all of the necessary items for a puppy including gates to contain our fluffy little guy. But within a few weeks the novelty wore off; the puppy created a lot of extra work for me, and Grizz failed to take Jarad's mind off his illness. Instead he kept growing and was soon knocking our frail Jarad over, hurting him and making him cry. It was with heavy hearts that we drove our pup, Grizz to my sister's and gave him to her family.

Herb Moeller had arranged for me to be interviewed on the upcoming hepatitis C litigation meeting in Vancouver. We had been speaking on the phone regularly, and he helped me understand many of the medical details coming from the Krever Inquiry. The interviewer was Debbie Wilson from the Georgia Straight newspaper. She was very interested in the upcoming Vancouver meeting and wanted to know what might be accomplished. I explained it was primarily to disseminate information about the disease and to assess the possibility of bringing a class action lawsuit on behalf of the transfused. She was fascinated by Jarad's story. I did not breathe a word about the upcoming hepatitis C series scheduled to appear in the *Penticton Herald* the following week.

Over the last few days of February, eight months after we learned of Jarad's infection, the front pages of our local newspaper announced our story. Our personal lives became very public. The story stirred emotions and controversy. Even one of our provincial newspapers picked up and ran our story. Headlines announced: "A seven-year-old boy is likely to be a key figure in a lawsuit being launched against the Canadian Red Cross."

CHAPTER EIGHT

Priorities

The day our story went to press, Jarad was sick at home. I bundled him up and took him to the store with me to get us a copy of the *Penticton Herald*. On our way to South Main Market, I had no idea that my life would dramatically change when a few hours later our home phone rang with the first inquiry. Over the next three days, I fielded calls from people infected with hepatitis C, as well as family and friends of those infected who were desperate for answers. Many people simply wanted to say thank you for telling our story, while others just wanted to offer us their support. A few calls were from people angrier than me at what we had been put through, but all in all the feedback we received was very positive. Sadly, I learned most of these people had been living with their "secret," afraid to tell anyone of their hepatitis C infection. I had to wonder if they were worried what people would think or if they were expecting a backlash similar to those infected with HIV had received.

Over the next four days, I faxed the *Penticton Herald*'s newspaper installments of our story to the Hepatitis C Society of Canada in Toronto, Ontario. Their response was to ask me to if I was willing to take on the role of a parent advisor.

At our next appointment I thanked our pediatrician for her support and shared how much it meant to me to be able to tell my story. I also explained the impact the children's hospital pediatric gastroenterologist's accusation had on me. I was grateful that she had conscientiously written a letter to the head of the gastroenterology department to address the issue. Our pediatrician wrote: "To be told that the gastroenterology clinic had positive results of the hepatitis C testing one year ago, and that they [Leslie and Peter] are at fault for not returning for follow up, is devastating." She knew his remarks were detrimental to my already shattered self-esteem. In the pediatric gastroenterologist's response, he chastised our pediatrician for choosing sides, and for even questioning him. He criticized her for writing a letter that simply defended our reactions.

In light of the medical community's response, the fact that the hospital and a few of the doctors had already retained lawyers, we felt it necessary to consult an attorney and possibly retain one to protect us as we ventured into this uncharted medical/legal territory. David Butcher had come very highly recommended as an attorney who had been following the emerging hepatitis C story. We were able to work an appointment with him into a clinic day for our oldest son Tyler at the children's hospital.

Butcher had read about us in the newspaper, and we agreed that I needed legal guidance on my media responses and how to proceed from here. I was bitterly angry at the picture materializing from our history at the children's hospital, and was really furious at the information coming out of the Krever Inquiry explaining what had transpired.

He explained the preliminary findings of the Krever Inquiry, which strongly suggested that the Red Cross needed to get out of the blood business. He added there were surrogate tests available that could have eliminated most of the infected blood from the system, and explained that the government of Canada played a large role in this disaster. He brought to our attention an Ontario attorney's testimony presented at Krever. "You can't help but wonder if another decision would have been made if the Red Cross wasn't on that committee lobbying for its own interests. They saved millions [of dollars] by not using the tests years earlier." He called it, "An unforgiveable gamble with human lives!"

I told Butcher how grateful we were that our son had survived his open heart surgery, and that we had no intention of suing the children's hospital. I went on to say, "It is very likely that if our questions had been met with honest answers, acceptance of responsibility, and a heartfelt apology [instead of blame, denial and lawyers], we would never have needed to consult a lawyer." But after the cruel treatment we had received from them, we were now on a mission to seek the truth about how this tragedy had occurred—both at the hospital level and the government's part.

When I described what had transpired between the children's hospital and our family since Jarad's diagnosis, Butcher explained, "Although the pediatric gastroenterologist stated under no circumstances could the hospital refuse treatment, the doctor is not an employee of the hospital, and the attorney defending the doctor was working with your pediatrician to research an equally trained doctor to treat Jarad illnesses."

This translated that because the doctors and the hospital were treated as separate entities, the doctors did not have to treat Jarad but the hospital had to admit him. The whole mess had gotten so convoluted that we were told, "The children's hospital officials are pitted against the children's hospital doctors, and now they are required to speak to each other only through their lawyers!"

Butcher said it was time to protect our son and ourselves, too. Peter and I agreed that it was in our son's best interest to move forward now and notify the authorities that, based on our history with the children's hospital and Krever's initial findings, of our intention to sue. The writs were filed early the following week. In them Butcher named: the federal government, Canadian blood supply services, Canadian Red Cross, the provincial governments, B.C. Children's Hospital, Dr. Jacques Leblanc, Dr. Michael Patterson, and assorted John Does and Jane Does as liable on Jarad's behalf. He explained that he would include the parties responsible for Jarad's infection, as well as those who did not notify us in a timely manner.

A few days after the writs were filed in court David Butcher called and informed me that the children's hospital had requested a meeting. This was to be held in Vancouver with legal representatives of the hospital, the doctors, and us. It was cancelled the first time and was then rebooked a few weeks later on March 9. The parties explained to Mr. Butcher, "This is your opportunity to let us know how you feel, hear your concerns, and to share your intentions." They had set aside seven hours for us to meet and to reach some kind of agreement. Jarad was too sick to make the nine-hour trip, so I cancelled the first arranged meeting, and although there was talk of potential dates, no meeting was ever rescheduled.

In an interview the week following the issuance of our writs, Peter summed up our position by saying, "These people better know that we won't just take a few dollars for Jarad and go away. It is not about money.

We want answers for everyone. There are indications that the government is going to blame lifestyle choices on the adults and we are prepared to fight to hear the truth."

Two weeks later our family made the trip to Vancouver to attend the brainstorm hepatitis C meeting that was to take place the following day. The drive from Penticton to Vancouver took us five and a half hours. Jarad threw up for the first four hours—all the way to Hope. When we got to Richmond, I called Herb Moeller, the meetings organizer, and he met us at the hotel that he had booked for our stay.

Being a prominent businessman, Herb had called all his media contacts to let them know about the possible litigation meeting. He announced, "This is the first meeting of its kind and who knew B.C. would lead the way in hepatitis C class action?" He went on to say, "The rest of the country is eagerly watching what we are doing, in hopes we pave the way for their province too."

Herb wanted the media to hear our story. He asked if I would be willing to share what David Butcher had been doing on our behalf, talk about my request for a trace back from the Red Cross on my son's donors, as well as introduce Jarad at the meeting. "I can handle talking about the trace back and introducing Jarad, but Mr. Butcher is better qualified to speak to what he has learned and done on our behalf," I told Herb. I felt like someone had my back and I had to admit that it made me feel more confident. What I realized was going public with Jarad's illness and its consequences were really pushing me out of my comfort zone, and lately my stomach had developed a case of chronic butterflies! When speaking to individuals, I was fine, but I had to confront my fear of speaking in front of large groups and do that soon!

The individuals and families who attended the meeting arrived from all over the province. Most of them were recently diagnosed and desperately seeking information and direction. Many attendees got up and shared their personal horror stories of diagnosis, treatment and the subsequent isolation.

One of the attendees, Katherine, had made up ribbons to symbolize hepatitis C—much like the AIDS awareness ribbon. She had laid a yellow ribbon on top of a red one and fastened them together with a straight pin. She handed them out to everyone there. We tossed around some ideas and decided that, since hepatitis C was a blood-borne disease, using straight pins on the ribbons were probably not a good idea. The colors would remain red, to represent the blood that carry's the disease, and yellow because it affected the liver and that a person suffering from liver damage would likely turn yellow. I left the meeting with the seed planted and had every intention to make the hepatitis C awareness-ribbons for the world a reality as soon as I got home! Ribbons offered one way to strike up a conversation and presented a platform from which I could talk about hepatitis C.

Television and print media reporters were present covering the meeting. I was interviewed by every one of them. They asked if they could talk with Jarad, but they could see he really was not feeling good. One of them was freelance reporter, Debbie Wilson, of the Vancouver newspaper the *Georgia Straight*. She had heard snippets of our story from Herb and was very interested in reporting the entire story. So far our coverage was confined to the Okanagan Valley, with the exception of one small feature in the Vancouver Province newspaper, but we hoped that her newspaper would get our story out to the entire country.

During the meeting, a few law firms addressed the pros and cons of a large hepatitis C class action lawsuit, as well provided the eager listeners with a description of how that might proceed. The case would be handled in one of three ways: personal injury, professional liability, and/or inferior product. Each approach carried with it its own statute of limitations. Some were under the impression that there was a six-year statute that started from the date of infection—most of the victims had been transfused more than six years earlier; others believed the clock started ticking from the date the individual learned of their infection. In that case, we had all found out less than a year ago. The attorney's also believed that children had until their nineteenth birthday to file a suit. In any case, the look back/trace back confirmation was a critical component.

We were told, "The minister of health has set up an industry reference group to determine the efficiency of a look back as well as the most cost-effective way of conducting it." This lawyer continued, "When government is involved, timing becomes an issue, and in this case, a limitation that consists of six years passing from the date of delivery of the medical treatment." Many of those who were transfused, including my son, had already passed that mark! At this rate the limitation was likely to run out before any of the innocent victims had the proof of their transfusions in their hands. Should the statute of limitations expire, it was explained, "It would not be possible to proceed with a lawsuit after that date." The urgency to proceed with a class action suit just became more critical.

They explained a suit of this magnitude could cost in the neighborhood of three hundred million to prosecute and that the law firms would have to be prepared to absorb those costs because the victims collectively simply did not have that kind of money. They warned it would likely take years to bring closure to the lawsuit, and many victims may not live long enough to see its outcome. This was a cold dose of reality for all of us.

Herb suggested because of his young age, Jarad would make an excellent representative plaintiff. Our innocent little boy, infected at eight weeks of age, couldn't possibly have the other risk factors; unlike many of the adult victims, he had no history of IV drug use, tattoos, body piercings, or promiscuous sex. We all felt confident that, by portraying him as the face of hepatitis C, we could present a stronger case on behalf of everyone in the court of public opinion.

There was a lot of new information introduced at the meeting, and hearing it all began to overwhelm me. It was difficult to keep up with this new and emerging illness. When I left, my head was reeling. After the meeting our attorney encouraged me to host a "class action clinic" in Kelowna for all of those who had been unable to attend the meeting in Vancouver. I also wanted to share the results of the secret ballot vote taken during this meeting that overwhelmingly recommended that Jarad should be named the representative plaintiff, if a class action lawsuit was to move forward.

Within hours of arriving home from Vancouver, Dr. Powell called. He had already spoken with Herb regarding the meeting and the response of victims to a class action lawsuit, and wanted to let me know we had his support going forward. He asked if I would consider doing national radio and TV interviews now that our story had gone public, and would be willing to appear before Justice Horace Krever. He told me, "The Krever Inquiry is in recess until the end of February, but by the time they resume hearing more testimony, your story would likely have made the national news."

A local TV news personality, Mohini Singh at Kelowna TV, requested an interview for a feature story about hepatitis C. She explained it would spotlight our family and our struggles prior to and since learning of Jarad's infection. I returned her phone call and said I would be happy to be interviewed. I believed the sooner we began a dialogue about hepatitis C the more familiar people would be with it. Mohini arrived at our home the following day with her cameraman in tow.

Spring break finally arrived! It was hard to believe our first year in Penticton had flown by this quickly. Instead of home renovations, this year I busied myself registering a nonprofit geared to raise public awareness to hepatitis C, to provide education to the population, and to begin a legal fund for the Blood Transfused Victims (BTV) with Hepatitis C Foundation. We called a press conference to announce the launch of the BTV Hepatitis C Foundation-B.C., and to unveil the fundraising ribbon campaign. This would be a nonprofit, support agency. I sewed together another 2000 yellow and red ribbons. The first 2000, sewed two weeks earlier, had already been bought up, but the bank account was emptying as fast as the money was rolling in. It became a fulltime job staying ahead of the emerging disease, photocopying and sending out hepatitis C information packages, sewing and distributing awareness ribbons.

I contacted our Member of Parliament, Jim Hart, and asked him if he would put the word out that we needed Canada flag pins to hold the ribbons together. I was amazed how fast we began receiving large envelopes full of pins from many Members of Parliament who wanted to show support for our cause. Peter was helping me with the ribbon program and had become amazingly supportive.

By April Jarad and I were enroute to Toronto where we were interviewed by two influential journalists who had been covering the tainted blood investigation from the beginning. They were Andre Picard from the *Globe and Mail* and the author of *The Gift of Death*, and Vic Parson's author of *Bad Blood*. After speaking to them and seeing their passion for this issue, I came up a new acronym to describe myself—MOM—Mommy on a Mission! I shared their passion but for a totally different reason . . . my infected son Jarad.

Sadly, with all that was happening, I realized Jarad was again sick more days than he was feeling good. After a brief respite, the nausea and vomiting returned with a vengeance. Dr. Gross was doing research to see if Jarad could take either of the hepatitis C treatments. She had even spoken with Schering Canada drug reps to ask if Jarad would benefit from taking Ribavirin alone. At seven years of age Jarad's weight has dropped to only 21.2 kg (47 pounds).

At our next pediatrician appointment, she told us she was still in discussions with the drug company, Schering Canada, to see if Interferon would be suitable for Jarad's hepatitis C infection. It was well known Interferon was a potent chemotherapy drug used to treat adults with hepatitis C, but she was told it should be avoided for growing children because it would stunt their growth. She informed us we did not have to go back to the children's hospital because a pediatric gastroenterologist in Calgary, Alberta, had agreed to see Jarad as a patient. He assured our pediatrician that our medical insurance would cover all of costs for consultation, medical testing, or procedures performed while in Calgary. We agreed to make a decision on Interferon only after Jarad had been examined and tested by the new pediatric gastroenterologist. However, this Calgary appointment meant a twelve-hour drive one way instead of five hours of driving for appointments at the old children's hospital, but whose doctors had all hired or been assigned attorneys.

We finally got the Internet hooked up at our home. I had no previous experience with computers so it was a very frustrating learning curve. Once I had a basic understanding, the Internet opened up a whole new world for me—now I had the latest information available with a click of the mouse. The best online resource was Peppermint Patty's Frequently Asked Questions on hepatitis C and her answers. She had her own website and made it available for everyone. She updated them as frequently as new medical journal papers were published. Through the Internet I was introduced to new people, places, and events, and began to feel less alone and more a part of a larger community with a shared a common bond.

An internet search on the topic of hepatitis C in 1996 resulted in one hundred and sixty four (164) information sites. [In 2015 there are 20,600,000.] I learned there were many differing opinions on hepatitis C treatment in children. I quickly learned to critically examine all of the information, weeding out the medical websites from the experiential or "speculation" sites. I read in an article by an herbalist that hepatitis C affects children very differently. He stated it took the first two years of life for a child's immune system to fully mature. Hepatitis C was very difficult to treat in transfused babies, like Jarad at the time, because the immune system had never been disease-free so the virus could be far more aggressive.

Jarad and I were doing a lot of travelling. We were invited back to Victoria to provide an update on litigation at their next Hepatitis C Society of Canada chapter meeting. It was the middle of May when we made the trip back to Vancouver Island. We were invited to spend the night at the home of our hosts, Ron and Barbara Thiel. I was hesitant to accept their generous offer because how Jarad felt each day was so unpredictable. But they assured me they understood and would give Jarad his space if he was feeling unwell. [Over the years and many visits to Victoria for meetings, rallies, or when gathering with provincial politicians, the Thiel's home became Jarad's favorite place to stay.]

Ron was a feisty character. He was well-spoken and outspoken on the issue of compensation. He and his wife Barbara became close friends over the next few years. Despite Ron's hepatitis C infection and fragile health, he was respected as an active, outspoken member of the Hepatitis C Society. He was lovingly known to us as the Grim Reaper, easily recognized for wearing his costume to every hepatitis C rally he attended across Canada.

Later during the month, Jarad and I boarded a plane bound for Toronto, again. I had a Society board meeting and was asked to prepare a presentation regarding the *potential* class action suit; the plan was for the Board to decide how best to deal with the issue. Obviously this was a touchy subject because not all of the Hepatitis C Society's members were transfused. Most had ended up infected because of their lifestyle choices. This group did not support the national organization's push for legal action. Our board meetings generally lasted three days, but this one covered a very hot topic. Krever had recommended restructuring the blood supply system and removing its distribution from the Canadian Red Cross, which had been decided on April 26, 1996 by the federal and provincial Ministers of Health. There was mounting evidence to support the creation of a new independent blood agency, and the Hepatitis C Society of Canada had been asked to forward their recommendations to the Government. As board members we were entrusted to reach an agreement on the subject so our collective voice could be heard.

As the Krever Inquiry progressed, the Canadian Red Cross became increasingly in the hot seat. It was reported the Red Cross was against the surrogate testing. More importantly in the victims' favor, George Weber, secretary general of the International Federation of Red Cross and Red Crescent Societies, insisted that not only HIV victims but also all hepatitis C victims should be compensated. Cartoons began to appear in national newspapers poking fun at the Red Cross for being negligent and for not offering an apology to the victims of this health disaster. During this time, the Red Cross was forced to recall units of blood because it was believed to contain the fatal Creutzfeldt-Jakob blood-borne disease.

When Jarad and I left Toronto, I was laden with even more emerging hepatitis C information. It was exciting to see that Health Canada was going to get onboard, and the top Canadian gastroenterologists were finally able to pass along much needed information. At the same time, I unfortunately began to see how the government was attempting to silence the media regarding Justice Krever's findings. The Canadian Red Cross and eighty individuals, including former health ministers, federal and provincial governments and their bureaucrats, and pharmaceutical companies, had launched a major legal battle against the scope of the Krever Inquiry. They all argued that Krever didn't have the right to blame anyone for the tainted blood tragedy, one that had already cost hundreds of lives and would likely cost thousands more in time. In response the Hepatitis C Society of Canada organized a picket line to march back and forth in front of the federal court building in Toronto everyday while lawyers argued the case. We believed this legal maneuvering could ensure that those responsible for the hepatitis C disaster would be protected from criminal charges and walk away scot-free. This totally contradicted the intended purpose of the inquiry: to discover how this happened and who in the chain of command were responsible to ensure it will never occur again.

When we returned home from Toronto, there was a "registered letter" waiting for me. I eagerly ripped the May 22nd envelope open to find confirmation that a positive donor had been located from among Jarad's blood bag identifier numbers. Although I knew of no other risk factor for him, I was at the same time both relieved and heartbroken at the same time. There was definitely no chance of an incorrect diagnosis now. I would not be able to forgive myself for allowing the transfusion instead of demanding my blood be used during Jarad's heart surgery and ICU hospital stay. Despite everybody's entreaty to the contrary, a part of me still believed I had allowed Jarad's infection to occur.

At the beginning of June, I flew to Vancouver, met Herb Moeller at the airport, and we flew together to Victoria. We were met there by David Smith—a fellow Board member and friend. We had been invited to attend our long-awaited meeting with our Provincial Health Minister, Penny Priddy. We were able to present our case for provincial funding to help our fledgling hepatitis C support groups to disseminate information. We let her know, "Everything that has been done to date has been paid out of hepatitis C victims' own pockets." We all returned to our homes immediately following the meeting.

A few days later Jarad and I were back on an airplane winging our way back to Toronto. Jarad won the hearts of another flight crew on a

Canadian Airline jet when he explained to a flight attendant why he was wearing the hepatitis C awareness ribbon. He was getting very good at articulating his story. Again he was invited to spend the final hours of the flight in the cockpit and "helped" land the 767 jet as we approached Toronto International Airport.

It seemed people from across the country were hearing about Jarad and our hepatitis C cause. The Toronto-based flight crew put together an impromptu fundraiser at a Toronto nightclub to raise awareness and money for our BTV Hepatitis C Foundation. Jarad and I spent the evening outside the club, at a table, where we greeted the club patrons and explained our cause. The money we raised helped to cover the mounting expenses of sending out information packages.

The purpose of this trip to Toronto was to attend the Federal Court hearing where the federal government, most provinces, the territories, the Canadian Red Cross, four pharmaceutical companies, thirty-four former health ministers and several individuals were presenting their case to prevent Justice Krever from assigning blame in his final report. They contended it would be unfair, insisting that, "Personal reputations, potential lawsuits as well as civil and criminal charges are on the line." They accused Justice Krever of overstepping his authority. How strange—the very federal government that appointed Justice Horace Krever to conduct this Inquiry, costing taxpayers millions of dollars, was now attempting stifle and limit its findings.

"The inquiry's original stated mandate was two pronged: First, it was to investigate what went wrong with the blood system in the 1980s, when thousands of Canadians became infected with viruses causing AIDS and hepatitis C from blood collected and distributed by the Red Cross."

"But Krever was also charged with the task of recommending a restructuring of the blood system so that any future crisis could be dealt with quickly and efficiently." *The Toronto Star* reported on Thursday May 23, 1996 that during the injunction hearings, Harvey Strosberg, a lawyer representing some of the victims, looked around the courtroom and counted thirty-seven attorneys. He said, "The Krever Inquiry is being hijacked by the Red Cross and the governments in an attempt to shade the truth." Strosberg estimated this injunction hearing alone was costing Canadian taxpayers upwards of $6,000.00 per hour!

While we were in Toronto, Jarad and I were flown to Ottawa, Ontario and taken into the House of Commons by our member of parliament,

Jim Hart. He stood up in the house and introduced us. He then accused the "Liberal government of attempting to circumnavigate the inquiry by muzzling it in court, while simultaneously launching a national reform of the blood supply system."

We returned to Toronto on June 28, 1996, just in time to read Justice John Richard's written ruling ". . . that the people directly responsible for tainted blood that left thousands of Canadians infected with AIDS and hepatitis C can be singled out in Justice Horace Krever's final report." His verdict confirmed Krever was permitted to assign blame to fourteen Red Cross officials and three federal government officials; however, the report forbade him from assigning blame against forty-seven other individuals.

Richard's ruling allowed me to take a deep breath, savor the mini victory, and begin to prepare mentally and physically for Krever's long awaited final report.

Unfortunately, as the potential class action lawsuit developed, no replacement doctor was offered by the pediatric gastroenterology department at the children's hospital, and we were forced to look outside of the hospital for one. I explained, "A few weeks ago our pediatrician told us we were no longer 'welcome' in the gastroenterology department. The best she could do, in the meantime, was to recommend an adult gastroenterologist in Vancouver for Jarad to see."

We were up very early the day of our appointment to make the trek to Vancouver. Jarad was to see Dr. Frank Anderson. Although he was an adult gastroenterologist, he had agreed to see Jarad, now that there was a feud between the pediatric gastroenterologists at the children's hospital and us.

When I made the appointment weeks earlier, I had faxed in the required medical release form that would allow Dr. Anderson to obtain all of Jarad's medical records from the children's hospital. As we headed to Vancouver, I was hopeful that he had received Jarad's entire file and that he had time to review all of the test results and notes.

We stopped at Mom and Dad's home to drop off Tyler and Ashley on our way out of town. Five hours later the three of us arrived in Vancouver. At the doctors' office Jarad and I were taken directly to the examination room. It was only a few minutes until Dr. Anderson came through the door and introduced himself. I watched carefully as Dr. Anderson checked out our tiny seven-year-old son. "I will draw my own blood," he explained as he carefully arranged the vials for Jarad's blood on the examination table beside him.

"There won't be any left in him," I weakly joked, staring at the twelve empty containers on the table. As he drew the second to last container, I noticed the color drain from Jarad's cheeks. As the last vial was filling, Jarad's eyes rolled back in his head and his body went limp. Jarad had fainted but was quickly revived.

Dr. Anderson invited the three of us to sit in his office and quickly got to the point. The children's hospital did not send any of Jarad's medical files. While they had acknowledged his request in writing, they refused to hand them over. He was aware of our story from what he had read in the newspaper, and was obviously at a loss to defend their actions and hesitant to continue the appointment without Jarad's medical history.

I was furious. It was one thing if they did not want to treat him, but it was quite another to prevent another doctor from doing his job by withholding all Jarad's medical records. Dr. Anderson suggested we "Rebook the appointment in three weeks. I'll have the results from all the blood tests I ordered today, and hopefully I'll have his medical file by then." He also asked us to complete another medical release of information form on your way out. We thanked him for his time, and although we were both furious and perplexed, we expressed our deepest gratitude for him agreeing to see our son.

I mumbled to myself all the way out of his office. Fuming, I slammed the car door. "Let's stop at the children's hospital," I told Peter. He knew better than to argue with me. I was on the war path. We had driven all the way to Vancouver for nothing. "I'll just go to medical records and pick them up myself and take them to Dr. Anderson's office," I added. It sounded like a great idea and a very simple solution to our problem. I confidently walked through the doors of the hospital and went directly to the Medical Records department. When I was asked how they could help me, I demanded Jarad's complete medical file and impatiently stood waiting for the clerk to hand it over. [I truly had no idea how this worked or the magnitude of the size of his file!]

Instead I was refused his records, and the hospital representative I had spoken with before showed up to escort me off the hospital property. Along the way she calmly told me to contact the hospital's legal firm—Bull, Housser & Tupper—if we wanted any information from the children's hospital in the future about our son.

"Since when can a hospital reject a physician's signed request for the release of medical records?" I asked her as she continued to accompany me to the door. "What are else are you hiding?" I screamed at her. I was visibly shaking, had turned red with anger, and was not going to be thrown out of the hospital peaceably. This had been my "home" for so many years. What had I done to deserve this horrendous treatment?

I was so incredibly infuriated that as I was walked through the automatic doors—a security guard on one side and the representative on the other—I slammed my fist into the brick entrance wall. I was horrified as I looked down at the blood escaping from all four gashed-open knuckles. Never had I ever felt so frustrated and humiliated in my life!

At the car I immediately placed a call to our lawyer David Butcher. He said, "It is obvious the children's hospital has retained the services of a team of very high profile Vancouver attorneys. They have unlimited funds and time—unlike your family whose medical expenses have already wiped out your entire savings account. I understand your main concern is to get your son prompt treatment after the latest delays. I have also noted that you are unsure if your son will survive the year." He said he would do what he could to get the files.

As our next appointment with Dr. Anderson approached, we still had not received a copy of Jarad's medical records but we did receive a letter that basically said: *"I am unable to comply with your written requests [for]clinical records The records are being held in the medical legal file as a* ***"secured chart,"*** *It was signed by a* Release of Information Technician

The same day Dr. Anderson received similar correspondence. His stated: *Although this is a "secured chart," we have decided to release this information to you, so that Jarad can continue to receive ongoing care."*

This letter was also signed by the same person as mine.

This made absolutely no sense! Why would they tell me they could not provide the records but fulfill Dr. Anderson's release of information request the same day? This was driving me crazy!

Two weeks later I received another letter from the lawyers representing the children's hospital. In short, it was a scolding for my unannounced visit to the hospital when I attempted to retrieve Jarad's medical records. The letter was to inform me, in writing, how my "new" relationship with the hospital would work. John Ankenman, attorney for the hospital wrote, "I regret that you chose to approach the hospital directly. You would not have had to undergo the difficulties which flow from such an unannounced visit if you had contacted me directly. The children's hospital does ask that you contact either, Dr. David Matheson, Ms. Georgene Miller or myself, if you have any further concerns or requests of the hospital. Jarad continues to be welcome as a patient at the hospital on referral from a treating physician or for any emergency." They certainly were not going to make access to the hospital easy.

In preparation for the upcoming class action suit, we had to discharge our attorney, David Butcher. It was an amicable parting since his firm was not prepared to front the required money to support the hepatitis C class action. We signed the preliminary paperwork with Camp, Church and Associates giving our permission for Jarad to be named as the representative plaintiff. Another class action attorney, Bruce Lemer, requested I sign a release of medical information form. He went to the children's hospital with these forms to request Jarad's entire medical file. When we finally received the file, the confirmation of his first hepatitis C diagnosis—from blood drawn the year before we were told of his hepatitis C infection—was suspiciously not included. Lemer had me sign another release and specifically requested the confirmation document. After a lengthy delay the children's hospital produced what I believed was Jarad's entire twelve-inch-thick file and all the chart notes on my baby. After almost two years of haggling, I finally possessed all my son's medical records.

Interestingly, exactly a week later, the Canadian Red Cross Secretary General Douglas Lindores finally apologized to the victims of the HIV and hepatitis C victims "... for mistakes made in the 80s" in a speech he gave to more than two hundred business leaders in Toronto. But his speech failed to be more specific or offer the victims any details. We all saw it as just the beginning: soon the Red Cross and federal and provincial governments had opted to compensate the twelve hundred individuals that were infected with HIV in the tainted-blood disaster. The subsequent press release stated the officials were adamant they would **not** provide compensation for the fourteen thousand individuals infected with hepatitis C. The press release made a point to state that this was because "their medical is covered." Federal Health Minister David Dingwall taunted the hepatitis C victims when he said, "If you do not like our decision, then you can seek redress in the courts."

So it was on September 19, 1996 Camp, Church and Associates joined forces with Lemer, Kambas as they filed "A class action lawsuit on behalf of hepatitis C infected victims of Canada's tainted-blood scandal. The representative plaintiffs were seven-year-old Jarad Gibbenhuck from Penticton and Anita Endean, a thirty-three-year-old nurse from Prince George." Little would happen over the next eight months, as the individuals who had contracted hepatitis C from the blood were forced to wait for word on whether the courts would approve the class action lawsuit while they scrambled to get their own medical records.

From the initial discussions of a potential lawsuit, it was impossible to fathom the fallout we might encounter. No one expected the callous backlash we received from the Canadian Red Cross by naming our little boy as the representative plaintiff in the first of many class action hepatitis C suits across the country.

I finally got a chance to sit down with Jarad's complete medical file and read through the whole box of papers. There were over five hundred pages of notes, test results, and correspondence. Reading through and studying the file, I gained a new appreciation for the excellent care the children's hospital had provided my son. I also read some notes that disturbed me. Foremost was that during his open-heart surgery, doctors had removed his thymus gland. The report stated that: "It was in the way, so it got cut out," and removed for good. I couldn't believe my eyes. I asked myself, 'Could this possibly be why he had such a weakened immune system and why he gets sick so often and has such a hard time shaking viruses?' My research revealed that the thymus is a specialized organ of the immune system, which 'educates' T-lymphocytes (T cells)—critical to the adaptive immune system.

My subsequent inquiry of the hospital about removing Jarad's thymus gland was met with more frustrating legal obstacles, and since nothing could be done to put it back, I decided to move forward and pick my battles carefully.

The residents of Penticton came up with a plan to help our family, and *The Friends of Jarad* became our family's saving grace. Donations could be made at any Valley First Credit Union. The fund was administered by three trustees who would assist us to cover all out of pocket expenses for the medical testing necessary to accurately diagnose and treat young Jarad.

Soon after, Jarad and I went to UCLA Pediatric Medical Center for testing. Online research pointed to this center as having the most current information and treatment for children with hepatitis C. I felt strongly that

Jarad was not receiving the best care in B.C., and because of the pending law suits I had lost trust in the Canadian medical system. It appeared they were going to continue with their cover-ups and lies while we sought the truth. So we decided to seek answers from an independent health center with no ties to the Canadian system. UCLA pediatric medical center had a very good reputation, and the *Friends of Jarad* had raised almost $5,000.00 to pay for Jarad's initial medical testing.

We flew to Los Angeles and checked in to the Holiday Inn just down the street from the hospital. Over the next three days, Jarad had an upper GI series, a fluoroscopy and a 24-hour PH monitor. He and I spent all of our free time sitting in our hotel room and watching movies or TV programs. Considering all the invasive testing, Jarad was in unusually good spirits. We did go to the hotel pool once, but the water was too cold for Jarad.

The extensive testing revealed that Jarad could benefit from a procedure called Fundoplication pyloroplasty. The case they made for having it performed at UCLA pointed to a 98 percent success rate, as opposed to a 40 percent success rate if performed in Canada. If it was done at UCLA, costs could run between $35,000 and $50,000—money we certainly did not have nor could we have come up with it. In the days ahead I researched this procedure and eventually rule it out as being beneficial for our son. I still strongly believed the cause of Jarad's vomiting stemmed from his hepatitis C infection not a malformation in his digestive track.

When we arrived in Vancouver, Jarad and I turned around and boarded another airplane headed to the Hepatitis C Society of Canada AGM in Toronto. Jarad had become somewhat of a celebrity, and all of our hepatitis C friends attending the meeting had requested he be in attendance. I was thrilled that Jarad was feeling so much better. At this meeting I was elected to the Board of Directors for a second term.

The Krever Inquiry was told the blood was "filthy" screamed recent newspaper headlines! I was learning more about this inquiry and the connections between the Federal Government, Provincial Governments, and the Red Cross. At the time Prime Minister Jean Chretien refused to hand over some thirty documents, invoking Cabinet secrecy. These were documents that might have helped to explain why thousands of Canadians were infected with the HIV/AIDS virus and hepatitis C from contaminated blood in the 1980s. Victims of the scandal were outraged and accused the government of a cover-up.

But, more than a year after stumbling across the diagnosis, we were no closer to resolving our awkward situation with the children's hospital. We were prepared to be understanding of an honest mistake, but found it very difficult to forget or forgive the children's hospitals' lack of compassion and deceitful behavior.

On December 19, our general practitioner called me in to his office to explain that he had been told he could no longer treat Jarad due to legal tactics being employed by the Red Cross. Despite Jarad's legal situation, our doctor, however, assured the rest of our family that we could stay under his care, but unfortunately Jarad would be left without access to medical attention and treatment. What made matters worse was we faced the possibility of him being turned away from the hospital should a medical emergency arise. Peter and I were forced to discuss options for his future healthcare, and to seriously consider the ramifications that might happen to Jarad's health if this class action took years to settle. Without medical intervention for that long, it was conceivable our chronically ill son could die.

The Canadian Red Cross lawyers named all of Jarad's doctors as third parties in the legal battle. They included all medical doctors: past, present, and future. All of Jarad's doctors began to withdraw their services and announced they had been warned of legal ramifications should they continue to treat him.

The lawyer for the Red Cross defended their actions by saying, "We are naming doctors as third parties in an attempt to demonstrate that the issues are far more complicated than people simply contracting the disease from blood." He went on to say, "In order for the judge to fully understand the issues, he must see that for each of the plaintiffs involved, there may be allegations against their physicians as well. It may well be that in some cases the doctor did not act properly." Reporters commented, "These legal tactics are despicable; this is a disgusting use of the legal system. It's much more akin to emotional blackmail, than it is to any kind of dignified and fair adversarial legal jousting."

What they failed to see at the heart of the matter, in drawing these third parties—past, present, and future—into the court battle, was that it left sick little Jarad to sink or swim on his own. We had no access to medical treatment without significant risk to the medical professionals who were simply trying to help our son. With this looming threat for any doctor becoming involved, the options for healthcare were fast drying up. Peter and I were seriously contemplating where we could move until the class action was over. We both felt that if his condition should serious worsen the Canadian Red Cross would be culpable. Moreover, as a humanitarian organization, we thought the Red Cross should be ashamed of itself for the grief it was inflicting on the victims of the tainted blood crisis.

During a year when so many hepatitis C stories graced the cover of our *Penticton Herald* newspaper, our family received the honor of *1996 Newsmaker of the Year* award. Their stories chronicled every aspect of our involvement with the hepatitis C struggle, litigation, to our travels and speaking engagements. It brought to light the local fundraisers put on to support the BTV Hepatitis C Foundation [our newly formed charitable organization] and *The Friends of Jarad*. For us, being Newsmaker of the Year meant only that we were featured one last time in a collaborative year-end special edition paper to commemorate the honor and remind us of all we had endured that year. But for Gary Symons, the reporter responsible for the top-notch coverage of our family's personal story, a prestigious journalism award awaited him in New York City.

CHAPTER NINE

Stepping It Up

A few days into the New Year, I received a telephone call from a very excited Gary Symons. "Are you going to be home for a while?" he asked. "Can I stop by and share some good news?" Gary had become a trusted friend, and Jarad really liked it when he came to visit so I readily agreed. "Jarad is home sick again, so I'll be here all afternoon," I told him.

When he pulled into the driveway and stepped out of his car, Gary was grinning like a Cheshire cat! He had won the North America-wide Thomson Award for feature newspaper writing and an accompanying $1,000.00 check for his series detailing the struggles of our family. "Symons' stories provided a font of knowledge about the fallout of an institutional problem and personalized a national tragedy," said judge and Pulitzer Prize winner Jacqui Banaszynski, "while offering moments of truly lovely writing."

In response our humble friend was quoted, "This is a family who had a lot of difficulty dealing with the disease, but who went public and took on the medical system, the Red Cross and the federal government. The series was good because the story was good."

In a press conference at the end of January, it was announced that the Federal Court of Appeal, in a unanimous decision, upheld Justice Krever's right to make allegations of misconduct against all but one person. Some of the parties were very afraid this decision would land them in jail. However, the Red Cross and two pharmaceutical companies proceeded with a further appeal to the Supreme Court of Canada. The federal government and the provinces decided not to pursue any further appeals.

At our next appointment, Jarad's growth pattern remained labeled as a *"failure to thrive;"* there had also been no significant improvements in his health, and we felt forced to confront the possibility that he might die. He had more sick than well days and I was at a loss, knowing there was nothing medically we could possibly do to help him. One day it was nausea plaguing him, the next giant welts and rashes, and another upper respiratory problems, bronchitis, and pneumonia. Other days he was limping and complaining of joint pain. Nausea was still his most prevalent ailment, and even faint odors sent him into gagging fits. If Jarad was healthier, these symptoms would have been handled much differently, but all together they painted a pretty bleak picture. In light of his declining health and combined with his compromised immune system, our options seemed very limited.

I was literally at my wits end. I was losing sleep and feeling lousy from constant worry about my limited options. I was sickened knowing that it was just a matter of time before every doctor in B.C. heard about our Jarad Gibbenhuck, and one by one refused to see and or treat him because they were afraid of being dragged into a Canadian Red Cross countersuit. I was relieved that at least Jarad's heart was doing well, and we did not have to return to the cardiology clinic for another two years. I had spoken with his cardiologist, and Dr. Patterson assured me he would continue to treat Jarad. It would have broken my heart to never again be able to see the heart doctors who had saved Jarad's life.

After speaking with my parents and explaining what we were up against, they agreed Jarad's fragile medical condition really left us with few options. The prospect of having to drop out of the lawsuit was maddening, but friends and family totally understood the choice we faced.

I discussed withdrawing Jarad from the class action with colleagues who were furious that we were being bullied and forced to choose between medical attention and our legal rights in a this country.

I set up a conference call with the Hepatitis C Society of Canada's directors to explain our dilemma. The reality and gravity of the situation was met with anger and disbelief. No one could believe with Jarad being as sick as he was that doctors could refuse him care. Can the Red Cross do this? Can the Canadian Medical Protection Agency cancel the doctor's insurance? Yes, yes and yes! And they not only could get away with doing it but they were!

After careful consideration we all agreed we were left with no choice but to remove Jarad as representative plaintiff from the hepatitis C class action lawsuit. While the other representative plaintiff also had to give up her doctor, thankfully she was not sick, and as a nurse by profession, she could manage her few symptoms or possibly consult her colleagues in the hospital where she worked.

I assured the board of directors that no matter what happened I would continue to be an outspoken advocate for all transfused victims and that I would stay involved with the Society. I assured them, "Jarad's face will remain front and center in this fight." Jeremy and Herb immediately began preparations to call a press conference to reveal the despicable actions of the Canadian Red Cross and their impact on our innocent little boy.

I began to second guess many of the decisions I made after learning Jarad had been infected with hepatitis C. I wondered why our attorneys had not warned me these kind of underhanded pressure tactics could be brought to bear against us. Basically, if we withdrew our writs and removed Jarad from the class action lawsuit, life as we knew it should return to normal. But now, in light of the way the Red Cross had retaliated was that even what we wanted? And what about individuals who just wanted to join in the class action? Would they apply the same pressure to every member of the lawsuit?

On January 10, 1997 Jarad was officially removed as Representative Plaintiff from the class action lawsuit, although we kept it from the press until the end of February. The Society had called an emergency board meeting in Toronto to confront our dilemma, so Jarad and I were, once again, on a plane headed east. We were met at the airport by board president Jeremy Beatty. He drove us to his home in Mississauga where we were introduced to his wife Joy. These trips were really showing us the family struggles of those living with a person with hepatitis C—something that we knew all too well but only from our experience with Jarad. As we had been invited to stay in a variety of infected persons' homes, I had really seen firsthand the varying stages of this disease.

Our host sat us down and explained, "The media has been calling. Anne McIlroy would like to interview you and Jarad before the press conference." Initially I said, "No, won't it lighten the impact of our press conference?" But he went on to say, "Anne is a trusted journalist at the Globe and Mail.

Her coverage is thorough and she is respected by her colleagues. She really wants this interview and I would suggest you consider it."

"But what about tomorrow?" I asked. "Won't the other reporters feel slighted when they find out Anne had already conducted an interview and scooped our story?"

"That is a chance we will have to take," Jeremy added. "The news business is fickle. If a bigger story breaks, yours can quickly become insignificant and get pushed aside receiving no coverage at all."

It was with some apprehension that I granted the interview, and the next morning Jeremy drove Jarad and me to the University of Toronto Society offices to meet with Anne and her photographer. It was my first National (*Globe and Mail*) front-page interview. There was no doubt this story was huge, and it had grabbed the media's attention *today*. I was so grateful that I had listened to Jeremy and granted the interview!

The next morning a fierce snowstorm hit Toronto. Jarad was throwing up as we were leaving the house and heading to our big press conference at Queen's Park. Looking pale and frail, Jarad sat in the backseat of the car. I sat beside him, holding the barf bags while he threw up. When we got there, we stopped at the rest room where I was able to wash his face and comb his hair. I gave him a 'spicy' cinnamon breath mint and a hug as I settled him in a chair in the auditorium. There were just a few media people present, but the "big name" reporters were covering the big weather story; the snow had pretty much paralyzed the entire city.

The reporters had read the briefs we distributed and had interviewed both our general practitioner. They were already familiar with what I was about to say, since Anne's story had made the front page of the Globe and Mail before the snow story broke. These reporters were incredibly sympathetic to our plight, and labeled the Canadian Red Cross as a most despicable tyrant. When our press conference began, I was asked to react to the Red Cross's statement, "It was using public money to pay for the legal fight that had forced us out of the lawsuit."

My reaction, "It certainly isn't fair. As a Canadian taxpayer, I am paying for both sides of this dispute." We were digging into our own pockets in search of justice and it was costing us dearly.

There was no doubt in anybody's mind that this Red Cross tactic was unethical, and it would likely set an alarming precedent for all who would choose to get involved in the hepatitis C class-action lawsuit.

I was sickened when I heard the Red Cross lawyer, Jim MacMaster, tell the media, "Physicians were never told to stop treating their patients. They were told it's a balancing act they had to consider." But that was not what we were told. The Canadian Medical Protection Agency, insurer of our general practitioner, warned him to stop treating Jarad or lose his insurance. I could see how that veiled threat left our doctor with no options—lose your insurance, and if you get sued, you lose your practice and everything you have worked so hard for since becoming a doctor. I don't think, if the roles were reversed, that I would take the chance.

Jeremy Beatty commented, "The Red Cross is undermining the basis for Canada's health system by forcing doctor's to quit treating patients. If you were a doctor, would you take on a hepatitis C patient? You'd steer clear of them if you faced being dragged in to a legal battle. We believe the Red Cross is trying to force Canadians to file suit individually, which would be impossibly expensive for most victims."

Although part of our story was told on the front page of the following morning's newspapers, the whole story was relegated to the middle pages of the second section. But it was the front-page picture that truly told the story and won the hearts of every Canadian who picked up a newspaper. During the press conference, I had been watching Jarad constantly, and although I heard the sound of the camera's shutters, I was unaware anyone would defy my request to leave Jarad alone because he was sick. When I saw his picture in the newspaper, I was heartbroken and struck by how pitiful and dejected he looked. It was no secret Jarad had vomited all of the way to the press conference. Was I wrong to have placed him at the center of this mess? On that day I understood that most cameramen were looking for the perfect shot; only a handful actually cared about Jarad and what we might be going through. But they managed to capture a picture that would become the "face" of our story—one that was missed in the previous day's interview. When it was all over, I was so glad to be heading home to our reporter and trusted friend, Gary Symons.

We garnered the sympathy and support of almost every person who had read about or heard our story. Even the Canadian senate decried the Red Cross's tactics. Jarad became the center of debate in Canada's upper house when Senator Richard Doyle demanded, "The government stop the Red Cross from using legal maneuvers that caused the Penticton boy to lose access to medical care. My question is directed to the leader of the government in the Senate; it has to do with an eight-year-old boy," said

Doyle, a Progressive Conservative. "His name is Jarad Gibbenhuck... and to a large extent his life may depend on what we, in this place [the House of Commons] do on his behalf, and on behalf of the 12,000 other Canadians who contracted hepatitis C from blood transfusions in the 1980s." He went on, "We are all aware that the Canadian Health Act assures universal and accessible care for all Canadians. Does the minister not consider that she (Senator Joyce Fairbairn, government leader) and her government have a responsibility in ensuring that this overriding right of all Canadians not be undermined by legal tactics seemingly designed for the sole purpose of discouraging the victims of this tragedy from pursuing their legitimate claims?" He asked, "Is it fair that one of the two parties in this dispute carries a blank cheque supplied by the Canadian taxpayer, while the other party is overwhelmingly disadvantaged financially?"

Although we were immediately able to return Jarad to our general practitioner's care, there remained too many hard feelings between the children's hospital and ourselves. The trust was forever broken, and I was still awaiting the apology John Ankenman said might come one day. For those reasons we chose to seek pediatric specialty care elsewhere.

March was Red Cross awareness month, and the Penticton City hall proudly raised the Canadian Red Cross flag in front of their building to honor the cause. Given the hepatitis C stories of local victims in our newspaper almost daily, and the news of the Krever Inquiry findings, I could not fathom how the mayor and her staff believed raising this flag would be a popular move at this time. As quickly as the workers put up the Red Cross flag, the mayor and city counselors were bombarded with requests to show respect for victims of the disaster and remove it. Its display was in very bad taste at a time when so many residents of Penticton and the Okanagan Valley were just learning of their hepatitis C infection.

At this time the Red Cross was appealing the Court of Appeals decision to allow Justice Krever to lay blame. In addition, it was facing new blood shortages as Canadians became confused and angered by the blood tragedy news headlines. "The sad fact is the Canadian Red Cross' handling of the tainted blood scandal has caused the would-be donors to mistrust the agency," it was reported. "That is too bad. The Red Cross earned a proud reputation throughout this century, pioneering battlefield medicine, rescuing victims of war and disaster, and volunteering its priceless services at the community level." The reporter went on, "The Red Cross' involvement went sour in Canada, when in the 1980s the agency decided not to initiate blood screening for the HIV virus and for the virus now known as hepatitis C. It was believed that decision resulted in approximately 1,200 HIV infections and as many as 14,000 hepatitis C infections in Canada; it was a human tragedy almost impossible to fathom. Unfortunately, the Canadian Red Cross cannot be forgiven, nor can it be trusted, because it refuses to acknowledge it did anything wrong."

The flag coming down was one small victory and showed us that our town was paying attention to the bigger picture and to the residents who elected the City Council.

At the end of March, our whole family headed out in our station wagon destined for Alberta. With minimal stops we would be on the road at least eight hours and had timed our trip to arrive in Calgary for dinner. We needed an early night because we had to be at the doctor's appointments by 9:00 A.M. This was our first trip to Calgary and we were unfamiliar with the city. In addition it was a weekday, and we had no experience with their rush hour traffic situation.

Our pediatrician had appointments lined up for Jarad to see two pediatric liver specialists at Calgary's Foothills Medical Center.

It was spring break, so we had packed light for our trip fully expecting sunshine, blue skies, and warm "spring-like" temperatures. We planned to stay with family and see the sights during our week in Calgary. The weather was beautiful—sunshine and clear skies all the way as we drove through the Rocky Mountains. We rolled into town a little behind schedule but arrived at Jean and Irv's by 4:30. The sun was shining, the grass green, and it really felt like spring. The extended family was all there to meet us, and a great dinner awaited us in the toasty kitchen.

We caught up on each other's activities over dinner. So much had transpired in all of our lives since we were last together. After dinner I gave the children baths and we read stories before we headed downstairs to our respective bedrooms. We were all asleep early. In the morning I was the first one out of bed. I showered, and was dressed before I woke up the children. When I walked up the stairs from the below-ground basement, I was struck by the living room's bright glow. I looked out the windows to see that pristine, white snow had blown high against the patio doors. Outside a blizzard blew the likes of which we had not seen in B.C. We quickly turned on the TV. The weatherman said, "The overnight snow has broken all previous records set, and if you don't have to go out today, make plans to stay home."

We had come all this way for Jarad's appointments, so despite the severe weather warning and reports of bad roads, we needed to go out to the medical center. "Maybe everyone else will stay home and traffic will be fine," I suggested.

More snow had fallen in the past 24 hours—an accumulation of 17 inches—than Calgary had seen so far this winter. The snowfall broke a record that had stood unchallenged for over one hundred years.

Traffic was almost at a standstill as we inched our way across the city in the white-out blizzard. There were deep ruts in the roads left behind by the tires from the brave souls who had ventured out before us. We safely made it to the medical center but were thirty minutes late for Jarad's first appointment of the day.

Although late, we were still able to see the doctors. They were very accommodating but not as knowledgeable about hepatitis C and children as I had hoped. They ran tests and looked at the numbers but offered no explanation for his growing list of complaints. I felt they downplayed the seriousness of the disease, and was disappointed when they failed to acknowledge a possible connection between his symptoms and hepatitis C. I understood they had a full slate of patients and were dealing with many gastrointestinal diseases—many more critical than Jarad's. Since I was spending most of my time reading everything I could on hepatitis C and was plugged in to worldwide organizations that worked with the top liver specialists, their lack of knowledge was discouraging.

They commented how undersized Jarad was and also used the medical terminology "failure to thrive" to describe his current state. "Tell me something I don't know," I almost said out loud. I was disheartened as we walked back out into the storm. I had allowed myself to get my hopes up and expected these doctors would have solutions to improve Jarad's health. I was disappointed and felt as dismal as the dreary weather. I could feel depression oozing its way into my body.

We stopped at a grocery store after we left the medical center. I purchased all of my favorite high-calorie foods in an effort to tempt Jarad, but when he showed no interest in these goodies, I devoured them all! I knew my emotional eating was out of control, and I looked for solace from Jarad's suffering in the quality and quantity of the foods I consumed. My weight had crept up to just over 200 pounds.

It had been almost two years since we learned of Jarad's hepatitis C diagnosis and a year since the Canadian Red Cross confirmed Jarad's positive donor, yet we still received a letter from the B.C. Ministry of Health identifying Jarad as a blood (or blood product) recipient between January 1985 and June 1990. The letter stated "the provincial government has set up a toll free hepatitis C information line." The letter went on to encourage us to get our son tested for hepatitis C as soon as possible. The B.C. government announced on Tuesday, April 15, 1997 that it would finally conduct a look-back study of the letters they sent out to over 52,000 blood transfusion recipients who resided in B.C. At least the Red Cross had begun to follow through on a look-back/trace back study.

Over the summer the hepatitis C news front was pretty quiet, as victims in every province conducted meetings to test the waters for their own class action lawsuits. By summer's end, two more provinces, Quebec and Ontario, had filed class action lawsuits seeking compensation on behalf of their province's victims as they followed the B.C. lead.

And we all eagerly awaited the final report from the Krever Inquiry.

After fifty-eight years in the blood business, the beleaguered Canadian Red Cross received their pink slip by the health ministers, firing them as the country's blood managers. The Red Cross continued to blame everybody else [in this case the provinces] for their mistakes. ". . . because they hold political responsibility for the blood system," the Red Cross spokesperson explained.

The provinces paid the Red Cross more than $300 million each year to collect and redistribute blood and blood products. The real truth was that the federal government, provincial governments, the Canadian Red Cross, pharmaceutical companies, and a handful of doctors all had approved the procedures that lead to the hepatitis C disaster.

On Justice Krever's recommendation the independent Canadian Blood Services was formed as the successor to the Canadian Red Cross. It was agreed by federal and provincial health ministers that the day-to-day operations of the new blood agency should be kept at arm's length from its funding sources. It was clear the Red Cross had a flawed chain of accountability that emphasized financial concerns over medical ones. But the Prairie Provinces (Alberta, Saskatchewan and Manitoba) were reluctant to give up their control over potentially expensive spending decisions that involved new testing procedures.

Jarad and I were invited to join a handful of representatives of the Hepatitis C Society of Canada on Parliament Hill, in Ottawa when the Krever report was unveiled and distributed to each delegate. First we stopped in Toronto to attend our third Hepatitis C Society of Canada Annual General Meeting and the board meeting that immediately followed it. The winter had definitely set in, and it was so much colder in Ontario than in B.C. that, no matter how many layers of clothing, Jarad complained nonstop about the frosty weather. There was a feeling of excitement about the AGM this year, and the board members were eager to conduct business. There were so many rumors circulating through the membership, with everyone guessing just how far Justice Krever would go with his final report findings and recommendations. We could not wait for the meetings to end and to board our flights for Ottawa, and were accompanied by a large delegation of victims. I was reelected to the board and this year as Vice President. Because of the litigation I agreed to take on this more responsible role.

Jarad and I flew into Ottawa the day before the report's release, and checked into our room at the Chateau Laurier, the charming old CN hotel. After all of the lengthy delays and appeals, we were all eager consumer groups ready to hear the findings. There had been so much speculation over the past months that no one knew what to expect. I was so nervous—all of my anxiety surfacing at one time—that I could not sleep, and so upon our arrival, I focused on settling a vomiting Jarad down for the night.

The focus groups met in the early morning for breakfast with the lawyers to plan our strategy. We had spent many hours together over the years leading up to this moment, and had all gotten to know each other quite well. We were told that we would have three hours to familiarize ourselves with the report and formulate our opinions before we would face the media to answer their questions. We planned to work as teams, each of us studying a section of the report. We agreed to break after two hours to discuss our content and collectively prepare for the press conference.

So it was with great trepidation when I entered the room, holding tightly to Jarad's hand, as I stoically realized the fate of every transfusion recipient would soon be revealed. As we were called into the two separate ballrooms by name, we were handed our own copy of the report—I stared in disbelief at the three volumes, and its 1,138 pages!

While I struggled with this task at hand, I opened the report to the foreword and read: **"In the pages that follow, an account is given of a public health disaster that was unprecedented in Canada and, if we have learned from it, one that will never occur again."**

Tears flowed freely down my cheeks. From beside me, I heard Jarad's soft small voice ask, "Why are you crying Suki?"

"Justice Krever called this a public health disaster, Jarad. Do you understand how serious that statement is?" I felt myself crumble inside as I gazed into my precious boy's big brown eyes. "What would come of all of our suffering?" I wondered. "I have to do this for Jarad," I told myself as I sucked it up and pushed on through my reading. I frantically scribbled notes. A voice broke the silence every thirty minutes as it announced the time remaining. I was rushed by the end, and could not believe the two hours had flown by so quickly. Thank goodness we had tackled this task as a team!

The press conference was brutal as, one by one, we were asked for our opinion and what was coming next. I felt some relief given the long-awaited report was in front of me—even if the report was overwhelming in its scope. After all of the hype, we were all physically, mentally and emotionally drained and ready to head home to curl up and spend time digesting the entire report.

The Commission of Inquiry on the Blood System in Canada was estimated to have cost to Canadian taxpayers more than $40 million and now I could see why.

Justice Krever had begun to collect documents in 1993 (two years before we were aware of Jarad's infection) and continued throughout the course of the Inquiry. "Approximately 175,000 documents, totaling between 800,000 and 1,000,000 pages were collected. Approximately 19,750 documents were filed as exhibits. Most of the documents were bound into 436 exhibit briefs that were distributed to all persons and organizations that were granted standing. Justice Krever heard the testimonies of 474 persons during the 247 days of hearings. He received written submissions from 89 persons and organizations that had an interest in the blood system. More than 300 persons called a toll free hotline, and their messages were relayed to Justice Krever. These testimonies and submissions produced a total of 50,011 pages of transcripts and 1,303 exhibits consisting of nearly 100,000 pages."

In the final report Krever's number one recommendation: ***"It is recommended that, without delay, the provinces and territories devise statutory no-fault schemes for compensating persons who suffer serious, adverse consequences as a result of the administration of blood components or blood products."***

In all Judge Krever provided fifty recommendations. He was tough but brutally fair in his assessment of what had caused this disaster.

The following day's newspapers announced, "Justice Krever displayed true heroism in standing his ground throughout the blood inquiry. Sixty-seven-year-old Krever, dressed in his business suit, is an unlikely national **hero**. This country reserves that word for hockey stars, Olympic athletes and helicopter pilots on wilderness rescue missions."

Finally, Health Minister Allan Rock officially apologized on behalf of the Government of Canada for their role in the tainted blood affair. "We are sorry for all that has happened. We want to reassure the victims of this tragedy and Mr. Justice Krever that his work and their suffering will be remembered, will be respected and will be acted upon." It was too little and far too late but at least it was an apology!

No other governments, hospitals, doctors, or individuals had so far offered any form of apology except the Canadian Red Cross' Douglas Lindores—just before he was fired.

By the end of the year the RCMP announced that, based on Krever's findings, they were conducting an investigation to determine if criminal charges were warranted in the tainted blood affair. I was called and asked if I would give a sworn statement on Jarad's behalf to Inspector Rod Knecht.

It appeared that the government of Canada was finally acting on Krever's findings.

As another year rolled to a close, I reflected back over all that had happened. I was Vice President of the Hepatitis C Society of Canada and spent a lot of time on the Internet, the telephone and in meetings. Jarad and I made numerous flights across the country. No sooner was Jarad named as representative plaintiff, than he was removed when we were forced to choose between taking care of Jarad medically and seeking justice on his behalf. Jarad was able to see medical doctors again, although my trust in them was severely shaken. The long-awaited Krever report was released with his fifty key recommendations that suggested compensation for **all** who received contaminated blood. The Canadian Blood Agency was formed to collect and distribute blood in Canada removing the 58-year responsibility from the Canadian Red Cross. I was being called to swear an official complaint in the RCMP's criminal investigation into the tainted blood disaster. And we had finally received a long awaited apology! A breakthrough year in all but Jarad's condition, as my little boy's health continued to deteriorate.

CHAPTER TEN

Escape and Corruption

Jarad's compromised health resulted in him missing more school days than he was able to attend during the year. We were forced to accept his pediatrician's recommendation that he be enrolled in a hospital homebound program, where a teacher would come to our home and provide Jarad with one-on-one tutoring. It would be advantageous, we were told, so that Jarad would not fall further behind in his studies. I questioned their suggestion. I was only in half-hearted agreement because there were times when I honestly felt Jarad didn't have many more days on Earth. I cannot say why, but I really bought into the notion that school was not important because he was going to die anyway. Besides, school in general was a huge cause of the stress for him and me. Between Tyler and Ashley bringing home germs that regularly landed Jarad in the hospital and the reality that Jarad was already so far behind, it just did not make sense most days to force our sickly boy to study subjects he would quite likely never use—especially in light of the prognosis I knew other people with the disease were receiving.

Sadly, as Jarad was so sick and he could no longer attend classes at the school, I saw this somewhat like the beginning of the end and felt little hope that Jarad would likely ever attend school again. He was experiencing so many more sick days and was vomiting daily, and my fear of him infecting someone if he did go back to school was growing larger from all that I learned about hepatitis C and its routes of transmission. I felt more in control of his exposure if he stayed at home, where I could keep watch over my special boy. Besides, having a teacher at home tutoring Jarad would free me up to work on my hepatitis C projects.

When the Penticton School Board sent Michael Kimmis to our house to meet with us, Jarad was immediately drawn to him; Mike was a great teacher and, for Jarad, a welcome relief from his sickness and he was lot of fun to be around. As we would soon learn, Mike was always running late and Jarad loved this about him, while I grumbled because his tardiness often interfered with my plans. And as they got to know each other better, Jarad had begun hatching a scheme of punishment worthy of Mike's crime.

Jarad loved sour candy of all kinds—the sourer they were the better he liked them. Mike, however, did not share Jarad's taste in candy! The first time Mike accepted one of Jarad's goodies, his face immediately contorted with shock of the sour flavor! Jarad was so taken with his reaction that he prepared a stash of the sourest candies he could find to enact his punishment each time Mike was late.

Jarad worked hard to dutifully complete each task Michael assigned him, and thoroughly enjoyed the kudos he received from Mike as well as the enjoyment of sharing his time with him. Although Jarad rarely talked about his feelings, it was clearly evident that he liked to make Mike laugh. The two of them became "playmates" for a few minutes before and after each session, as they kibitzed back and forth. Mike gave Jarad homework when we headed to conferences or meetings. When we returned, he engaged Jarad inquiring how the trip went, what he had seen and what he had learned. Mike listened intently as Jarad shared stories of our travel adventures. The fact that they loved each other was understood and felt by all who ventured into our home during their class time—they shared a very special bond.

I really believed it was during this time with Michael that Jarad began to develop his keen sense of humor. On the good days, when Jarad was not throwing up, he would clown around engaging everyone within earshot with his antics and subsequent belly laughter. For however long, these breaks were a welcome relief for all of us.

At the time I was particularly serious—worried, sad, hurt, and often confused. Life was difficult and watching my son suffer added a burden that tugged on my heart. It was just not easy for me, and I worried my failing marriage was affecting the children and adding a further negative impact on Jarad's fragile life. As the good days became few and far between, his antics and laughter would go a long way to brighten my day—if only temporarily. It made my heart sing to see him happy and smiling, and I attributed these interludes to Michael's presence.

It was heartwarming to take Jarad to the store where he would carefully hunt for and eventually purchase "sour candies" as his supply was depleted. He got such a kick out of searching for the sourest candy he could find. To be sure, Mike's reaction would cause Jarad to crack up, as his teacher wince in pain!

While Jarad was still classified as a "failure to thrive," he was gaining a bit of weight, albeit very slowly. At ten years of age, he remained below the 10th percentile for weight on the boy's growth charts. This became a cause of concern for not only the doctors but more so for me. I blamed myself for being somehow negligent despite all of my efforts to fatten him up.

Despite the doctors pointing out the "failure to thrive" status of my son, I tried not to just focus on his weight. As his wise cardiologist encouraged me, "Look at the whole boy. Do not just focus on what is wrong." After the cardiologist's thorough testing, he reassured me that Jarad was growing and, from a cardiac standpoint at least, he was healthy. At nine years of age, his heart had finally healed and was the same size as other boys his age. His lungs also finally appeared totally normal on x-rays. He did add that Jarad had developed tachycardia, and he explained this condition was responsible for his fast metabolism. "I doubt Jarad will ever be overweight," he told me.

Jarad had also passed a full psychiatric assessment and appeared to be a "normal boy" in this regard. The testing showed Jarad was, in fact, dealing with nausea and that he was not "faking" his illness. There never was a doubt in my mind, but there were a few people who thought otherwise, and I continued to watch him closely for signs of contradiction. While Jarad really loved travelling on airplanes and being the center of attention at hepatitis C events, I was worried that he may be over doing it. He did engage with a lot of new people, and I became concerned about "over exposure" from what I was reading and learning about hepatitis C on the Internet. I did not want to see his whole life wrapped up in hepatitis C.

We were beginning to see some favorable news on the hepatitis C front when on February 4, 1998 the federal government finally announced they were willing to contribute $300 million to the 1986 - 1990 Compensation Fund.

Later that same month the Royal Canadian Mounted Police announced a full-scale criminal investigation to decide whether individuals involved in the tainted blood fiasco could be charged criminally: " . . . based on evidence of misdeeds that had been accumulating over the past eight to ten years," announced Jeremy Beaty, President of the Hepatitis C Society of Canada.

The R.C.M.P. appointed a twenty-member taskforce. In the subsequent media blitz, they encouraged every victim of the HIV or hepatitis C "crimes" to call their toll-free hotline. This was a key development considering senior government and blood-system officials had already been convicted of similar crimes in France, Germany, Switzerland and Japan. Dr. Michelle Brill-Edwards was quoted as saying, "The RCMP investigation will be hampered by the destruction of crucial evidence from the Canadian Blood Committee." [It was learned during the Krever Inquiry that important documents had previously been destroyed.]

Still later that month the provincial health ministers and federal health minister, Allan Rock, met for two days to debate compensating **all people** infected with hepatitis C through the tainted blood (not just those infected between the 1986 and 1990 time period). Most agreed it would be better to offer compensation now than face an endless series of lawsuits. But the regional governments were worried about the cost, which could easily run into the billions of dollars given the estimated large number of victims. At this point the grossly exaggerated media estimates ranged from 60,000 to 90,000 people infected with hepatitis C through tainted blood. However, the victims from the 1986 - 1990 timeframe believed those numbers were grossly exaggerated to frighten the taxpaying public.

By the end of the two-day meeting, there was no signed agreement on compensation, but it was believed some of the victims would eventually share in $1.118 billion award. However, they did agree the offer of compensation would only be extended to those transfused between 1986 and 1990 when [they wanted us to believe] screening tests were available but not used. While the meeting ended with no signed deal, Allan Rock suggested the federal government (Ottawa), "Might go it alone on compensation," leaving the provinces and the Canadian Red Cross to battle it out in court against the victims.

In March 1998 I made another emotional trip to Toronto; this time it was for a press conference to hear the federal and provincial health ministers had agreed and would "officially" announce the offer of $1.118 billion in compensation to those victims infected only between January 1, 1986 and July 1, 1990. "Shame, shame," we shouted, as many angry demonstrators crashed the announcement site. One Toronto attorney, David Harvey, vowed following the announcement, "I will proceed with a national class action suit on behalf of people infected pre-1986 and post-1990," arguing the proposed compensation deal violated the Canadian Charter of Rights. It was leaked to the media that of the 1.118 billion in compensation, a good chunk would be taken off the top to compensate those victims secondarily infected with HIV, and it would also have to cover all legal and administrative fees for that group.

Hepatitis C became a hot topic in the media as headlines in all of the national and provincial newspapers screamed: "No to blood money!" and daily stories from all of the enraged victims filled the front pages for the next seven weeks.

Soon I was on a plane headed to Ottawa for another protest on Parliament Hill. This time we placed white crosses over the entire Parliament lawns to symbolize the hepatitis C victims who had already lost their fight for life. The hepatitis C issue dominated the House of Commons question period. Federal Health Minister Allan Rock suggested the health care system would go bankrupt if he were to back down on his stand and compensate all victims. Many scare tactics were employed in an attempt to lose public support for compensating all of those transfused with hepatitis C. Pressure continued to mount on the federal government to honor Justice Krever's recommendations and fairly compensate all those infected and their families. Victims and family members began a mass campaign to contact members of parliament (MP) and senators by letters, emails and telephone calls. The pressure became palatable across the country.

In the *Globe and Mail* an article claimed: "Victims turn [a] non-issue into the hot topic." They quoted doctors, lawyers, company vice presidents, nurses, bus drivers, and TV personalities regarding an upcoming vote in the House of Commons. In the article, they referred to me as "another high-profile person in the battle for compensation, whose 13-year-old son Jarad was infected by tainted blood shortly after he was born." The boy's appearance at the Krever inquiry helped put a face on the disease that few were taking seriously prior to young Jarad becoming their poster boy.

From studies beginning in 1958, there was significant evidence that had the blood been tested for enzyme activity, it would have indicated the presence of hepatitis in the blood. A major US study from the early 1970s, with preliminary results in 1975, confirmed ALT screening was effective.

The final study results were published in 1981 and caused private blood banks all over the world to implement the surrogate ALT testing. All blood banks in the U.S. had initiated the testing by 1986. *It was unfathomable to me that tests were available seven years before Jarad was even born and that, if implemented, he would never have been infected!*

The compensation debate became heated as Federal Health Minister Allan Rock maintained there was only a proven test available after 1986. To his comment Dr. Brill Edwards countered, "Rock is misleading the public at best, and flat out lying at worst."

Medical documentation confirmed the surrogate test was, "An old, old test that has been used in hospitals throughout the world since 1958 and it is still used today to test for liver infection." It was also reported that, "In Japan and France the relative ministers of health were prosecuted and in some cases jailed" for not initiating the testing in a timely manner. Yet Canada chose to "study" the matter.

The prelude to these events had actually occurred in the summer of 1984. John Turner was the prime minister and was engaged with fighting a doomed election campaign against the progressive conservative leader Brian Mulroney. Monique Begin was the Minister of Health, and at that time she reported directly to deputy Prime Minister Jean Chretien. On August 27, 1984—as disclosed at the Krever Inquiry—Dr. A. J. Clayton, the director general of the Laboratory Center for Disease Control, wrote to then Deputy Health Minister A. J. Liston [who was also the director of the Health Protection Branch]. Clayton warned the minister the AIDS virus was in the blood supply and it threatened to become an epidemic. "There is . . . mounting evidence that this virus has already spread to the general population and that there is potential for an explosive outbreak in the next few years . . ." Clayton said.

At the same time the health protection branch was recommending new regulations that would have given them direct regulatory control over blood product manufacturing and distribution.

The regulations, completed during the liberal term in 1984, were **never** implemented and the Alliance for Public Accountability (APA) wanted to know why. "There is a really important memo demonstrating the government's full knowledge of the contamination of the blood supply," said Gabe Kampf from the APA. "Had the regulations being passed into the Food and Drug Act at that point, it would have made it clear to the Red

Cross that it had a duty to act [upon the warning]. The people infected with HIV and hepatitis C after 1984 would all have been protected."

"You have to ask yourself who stopped the process. It wasn't the senior bureaucrats because they'd done their work," said Kampf. "That puts it up to the politicians and the cabinet ministers."

Dr. Michele Brill Edwards had discovered the draft regulations in 1996, while doing research for submissions at the Krever Inquiry. When the regulations became known, it touched off a storm of debate. "Monique Begin was the liberal health minister in the 1970s to 1984. Prime Minister Chretien was not involved in health, but at the end of 1984 he was the deputy prime minister. That connection potentially brings him [Chretien] into the criminal culpability issue," Dr. Michelle Brill-Edwards explained. The government refused to turn over thirteen documents, and opposition politicians wanted to know why those draft regulations were never given to the Krever Commission in the first place. When Justice Horace Krever subsequently asked federal lawyers to produce the documents, as well as all documents pertaining to the decision not to implement the new regulations, the government refused. "Further documents pertaining to this issue exist but will not be probed as they are protected by the Canada Evidence Act," said their attorney Donald Rennie, who was defending the government. From the National Democratic Party (NDP) and a Member of Parliament, Svend Robinson subsequently wrote to Chretien urging him to allow the Krever Commission access to all of the documents. In response to Robinson, Chretien claimed "cabinet privilege" and refused to produce the documents.

The RCMP had begun their criminal investigation of the tainted blood scandal, and had promised the Canadian public that their probe would not stop at the doors of the government.

There was to be a vote in the House of Commons intended to determine the time frame for compensation. The motion read: "This House urges the government to act on a recommendation of Justice Horace Krever to compensate **all victims** who contracted hepatitis C through tainted blood."

In advance of the vote, Prime Minister Jean Chretien ordered all Members of Parliament to cancel any previous plans and to be present in the House for the vote. The prime minister's office told reporters that no liberal MP would be allowed to "free vote" on this issue, and that all MPs were told to support the government's 1986 to 1990 timeframe. The liberals could not vote their conscience nor vote against the government.

The press leaked, "In the past, Prime Minister Chretien has not hesitated to discipline MPs who go against the party line." The liberals only held an eleven-seat majority over the combined opposition parties, so if only a few liberals were absent or broke ranks and voted in favor of compensating all victims, it would topple the current liberal government. The fate of the current liberal government and that of Prime Minister Jean Chretien was dependent on the vote.

Dr. Michelle Brill Edwards, co-director of the Alliance for Public Accountability, said, "Even Prime Minister Jean Chretien could come under criminal investigation if the government was found culpable for hepatitis C infections prior to 1986." Dr. Brill Edwards went on to say, "What we're providing is the motive for why they're lying to the Canadian public. The false 1986 timeline is a political device to limit criminal culpability to the conservative era, therefore protecting liberal ministers in power up to September of 1984."

When the vote took place, Jarad and I had joined a small band of hepatitis C demonstrators on Parliament Hill, in Ottawa. Most of the protesters were, "Very sick individuals who reluctantly had been cast into the role of activists," said colleague and friend Joanne Manser.

As I sat in the gallery, among colleagues and friends, we held our collective breath as the vote was taken. The Reform Party motion was defeated by a vote of 155 to 140. It was one of the most emotionally charged days ever in Canada's House of Commons. Jarad and I, as well as other colleagues, were escorted out of the gallery for booing and clapping. The opposition members shouted our battle cry from across the floor of the House, "Shame. Shame!" or they taunted the Liberals with sheep sounds (bah, bah). One of the politicians, who supported the bill, said of Prime Minister Jean Chretien, "He's a bully and a tyrant and he's a dictator and I despise that."

Previously proud liberal Members of Parliament [and many who when speaking with their constituents claimed to support compensating all victims] hung their heads in shame and just stared at the floor. The vote was quickly referred to by the prime minister as a vote *of confidence* in the leadership of the liberal government. Had the Liberals been allowed to vote their conscience and the bill passed—the vote would have clearly been one of non-confidence in the current Canadian government leadership. But no liberals broke ranks with their party that day, especially the former

Hepatitis C Society of Canada board member, Carolyn Bennett, whom we were all counting on to support the bill.

In an interview immediately after being removed from the House of Commons, I told reporters, "This battle may be lost but the war is far from over."

Following the vote Federal Health Minister Allan Rock said, "The file is now closed in terms of compensation." But by this he meant only those who contracted the disease between 1986 and 1990 would be entitled to receive compensation.

But Rock was the only person in Canada who truly believed that statement. We were not about to give up and proceeded with the Pre-1986 Post-90 lawsuit. David Roberts of the *Globe and Mail* was quoted in the *Times Colonist* newspaper in Victoria BC, "The Liberal government can't hide its nervousness by refusing to help many of those who need it most. Compensation will not be based on those who need it most, but on an arbitrary timeframe that ignores the fact that the government knew as far back as 1978 that there was a mysterious form of hepatitis that was carried in the blood."

As it stood this newspaper argued the policy was "untenable" and then "an unforgiveable betrayal . . . Health Minister Allan Rock cannot hide behind the defense that there is an inherent risk in all medical procedures; the only risk hepatitis C victims took was . . . [believing] that Canada's blood supply was safe. Canadians are dying because of the situation our government helped to create," he reported.

A few days later our national newspaper headlines screamed, "Blood deal may be reopened!" We had successfully kept the pressure on the government and held the attention and support of the Canadian public. But the provinces began to split on the concept of compensation. B.C., Ontario, and Québec urged the federal government to extend the package to cover everyone, while the federal government was once again discussing the possibility of going it alone.

The prime minister and federal health minister accused the provinces of cynicism and hypocrisy for attacking the deal just five weeks after agreeing to it. The provinces were in agreement that, while offering compensation to everyone who was transfused, the federal government should pick up the bill and not expect the responsibility to fall on the provinces. "The federal Liberal government must bow to public pressure," the Québec Premier Lucien Bouchard announced.

At this point all of the hepatitis C support agencies, including the Hepatitis C Society of Canada, the Canadian Hemophilia Society, the Alliance for Public Accountability and others, continued to lobby for equal compensation for everyone with no limit on the date of infection. It appeared that would translate to as many as 22,000 infected individuals that may additionally receive this compensation, but that number too could have been grossly exaggerated.

The legal case for victims seeking to prove negligence may have been strongest for infections received between 1986 and 1990, because in 1986 the Canadian Red Cross and the Canadian Blood Committee decided not to implement the so-called surrogate test being used successfully in other countries to detect blood tainted with hepatitis C during that period of time. But there existed volumes of documentation that confirmed the surrogate tests had been used as far back as 1958, which called into question the 1986 cut-off date, and made a strong case for all transfused victims. Besides, compensating all was one of Justice Krever's recommendations.

Between 1986 and 1990, the managers of the blood system had launched an elaborate study to determine the effectiveness of this test. This test involved giving high-enzyme blood to thousands of Canadians who came through some of Canada's largest hospitals. As a result thousands of innocent people were infected with the virus. The results of this study proved what the rest of the world already knew—the surrogate test substantially reduced the rate of infection in countries where it was used. In 1990, another test that could directly detect the hepatitis C virus was developed and introduced in Canada.

In early 1998, although Jarad was doing very well from a cardiac perspective, his health was deteriorating in many other ways. I was becoming increasingly frustrated by the lack of acknowledgement by medical professionals about hepatitis C, many of whom did not consider it the cause of his deteriorating health. As my colleagues openly talked about how hepatitis C affected them, I wondered how much of what Jarad was experiencing—headaches, nausea, and vomiting—were simply a result of the disease. After being told on three separate occasions that Jarad had irritable bowel syndrome and it was the cause of his problems, I continued to reject this diagnosis and questioned why the medication prescribed for that condition did nothing to change his symptoms. I believed the doctors were simply wrong about his IBS diagnosis. But then who was I to question them? The doctors still maintained hepatitis C did not manifest itself in children the way it did in adults. With Jarad's overall health on the decline and no pediatric gastroenterologist convincing me of the cause, I sought out a new doctor in nearby Summerland to keep an eye on Jarad and treat his overt symptoms—nausea, vomiting, and headaches.

Intuitively I knew Jarad was getting sicker. I could see that his weight was dropping, the color drained from his face, his skin dry and sallow, and his eyes sunken in his cheeks. What was worse his smile had gone, and a serious, pained expression had replaced the light in his eyes. He was increasingly having more bad days and less good days. The way he felt was shaping what our family would be able to do on a given day, and I saw the negative impact of his ill health on his siblings. Although they were concerned about their little brother, their resentment was obvious as our daily plans changed or were cancelled all together. More often than not, we travelled in the car with a bucket, as the small trash bags could no longer contain the contents of his upset stomach.

My travelling increased as I became recognized as a knowledgeable speaker, and my presence was requested at more hepatitis C events. Conference calls were an option at times and were certainly welcomed for being less disruptive for the family. They afforded me the luxury to remain at home and allowed Jarad to rest in more comfortable surroundings. However, my physical presence was requested most of the time, and I felt torn knowing how my absence affected all three of my children. What kept me going were my sick colleagues and my good health; someone needed to represent all those too sick or poor to travel. With us living on the West Coast, and all of the activist activity centered on the federal government in Ottawa, the head office for HeCSC in Toronto, or the Courts in Toronto or Hamilton, I was often required to make long cross-country flights.

During many of my presentations, I was asked for my opinion on the proposed compensation settlement and what I was going to do on Jarad's behalf. Since stepping away from the class action lawsuit to return Jarad to the care of his doctors, I had followed but not signed Jarad up for the pending lawsuit. I told my audiences I had no intention of signing on to the compensation deal. I was not particularly happy with it because it only addressed the needs of the adults infected through blood transfusions. I had read the actuarial reports cover to cover, and I believed children's needs, as well as family expenses and services, were not adequately covered. There was no compensation to support families with infected children, who could not access their money until they turned nineteen. For families with a sick eight year old, it appeared there was no money to hire a caregiver; yet for adults, wage-loss compensation and money to pay a caregivers were provided. I saw that as very unfair and publicly said so. I felt that Camp, Church and the other lawyers involved agreed to the swiftest settlement possible so that they could be reimbursed for all their hours and expenses over the past two and a half years. The lawyers were paid millions for their time—the victims would receive no more than $250,000, if they qualified to receive anywhere near that figure!

Peter and I were in agreement that the mounting evidence indicated serious wrongdoing on the part of those responsible for our sons' infection. We contacted the new Royal Canadian Mounted Police taskforce to lay out our complaint.

When we were interviewed and subsequently gave sworn statements to Inspector Rod Knecht of the RCMP, I was instantly relieved. Our hopes were high, as we trusted our complaints would result in a *full scale criminal investigation* into the blood system in Canada. We were hopeful criminal charges would be drawn against government officials to bring to justice those responsible for the infection of so many people. However, we knew their punishment would not heal our son, bring health to the other innocent victims, or restore life to the thousands who had already succumbed to the hepatitis C virus. Within days of giving my statement, I received multiple requests for media interviews. Given that the RCMP had previously investigated the destruction of Canadian Blood Committee documents without leveling charges, they wanted to know why we believed they would find someone criminally responsible this time. The RCMP had been privy to all of the shocking evidence presented at the Krever inquiry, and for two years remained silent on the subject. Despite Health Minister Alan Rock's apology, why would we now make a formal complaint and expect a different result?

The media also asked us to justify the amount of money this had already cost and how much more should be borne by the Canadian taxpayers. "That is easy," I said. "The Canadian public will now be able to put a real face on this disaster by seeing our little boy's 90-pound body, the horrific journey our family has been forced to take, as well as the cost we have personally incurred through no fault of our own [we were taxpayers too]. And besides, it is the right thing to do!" Secretly I hoped and naively believed that since so much focus had been put on Jarad and our family, and because Peter was a longstanding member of the RCMP, the investigators would take a closer look at the evidence and seek justice for the son, of one of their own.

In a mounting effort to take the negative attention away from the nonprofit Canadian Red Cross and to reinstate confidence in it, the media focused on the new Canadian Blood Services. It was officially beginning operations as the transfusion arm of the old blood matriarchs—Red Cross Blood Transfusion Service and the Canadian Blood Agency—which began their final shut down. It was hoped this move would improve dwindling donations for the Canadian Red Cross as well as increase the depleting donor blood supply.

Towards the end of 1998, Camp, Church and Associates send me a letter threatening a defamation lawsuit. They demanded I retract some of the derogatory statements that I made regarding the proposed compensation settlement, and warned me to refrain from repeating them. In talks I was giving, and in emails I had disseminated, Camp, Church claimed that I was damaging their reputation. In particular they took exception to my statement: "Camp Church is not going to court and is not interested in the largest settlement, but the speediest one," which they claimed was both untrue and defamatory. The registered letter I received said, "We require you to retract these statements and cease and desist from republishing them. Failure to do so will result in prompt action by Camp, Church and Associates." In response, I told the media that my comments accurately represented "my understanding of the situation," and I had no intention of retracting them.

Dr. David Mazoff, the chairman of the Victoria Hepatitis C Society of Canada support group, told me he had received a call from J.J. Camp. Camp had attempted to dissuade his group from having me come to Victoria to speak with the hepatitis C support group. Mazoff said that Camp told him "my statements could leave his chapter open to legal action," and that J. J. Camp had tried to intimidate him. To an investigating reporter, the lawyer denied that he was trying to silence me or even to discourage the Victoria group from having me speak to them. I failed to see how my opinion would dissuade the infected from accepting the compensation package. So many were struggling now with mounting medical/travel bills, and the relief the compensation would bring was within sight.

On December 18, 1998, the remaining details of the proposed hepatitis C compensation plan were revealed after much negotiating. It became obvious to me that the collection process would not be made easy for the claimants. To begin with, there was so much proof required before anyone would qualify. I had begun encouraging transfusion recipients to contact the Red Cross to confirm their transfusion results years earlier. "Make sure that you get all of your paperwork in order," I urged them through the media "including all of your receipts for all out-of-pocket expenses." For many of the transfused, expense receipts were long gone and could never be retrieved.

Although Peter and I were united on the hepatitis C legal and criminal issues and showed the face of a cohesive family involved in a struggle, our home life and marriage was in ruins. My role as an activist and hepatitis C advocate contributed to our compounding issues. Although I saw my roles and involvement as positive, both Peter and the children began to resent the outside demands on my time. I felt like I was being pulled in many different directions as I shared my limited time and energy with my family and the hepatitis C community. I saw this critical time as a tiny window of opportunity that truly afforded me no alternate choices. Without my involvement and voice, so many of the transfused I was assisting would fall through the cracks. I knew deep down I was severely hurting myself as food became my best friend when I travelled, was frustrated, or I found myself alone. I was constantly purchasing clothes to cover my growing body, and I knew from his comments that Peter began to detest my overweight presence.

At home I excused my increasing weight gain by saying walking was not an option since Jarad was sick and could not walk very far. Peter suggested I join a gym, but after only one visit, I knew that was not for me. We had purchased a special-needs stroller; however, this did not prove practical in the dead of winter when roads were slippery, nor in summer when temperatures soared into the 100s. A treadmill purchase sat in the basement holding clothes destined for the ironing board.

Facing years of mounting out-of-pocket medical expenses, we were forced to declare personal bankruptcy early in 1999. The bank took possession of our home and limited the amount of assets we could retain. Peter and I had to attend debt counseling classes and prove we understood what had caused this to happen. For us, it was little more than another wedge in our relationship as we blamed each other for careless spending. Although the debt counselors were sympathetic to our situation, they did not in any way excuse our reckless spending habits. However, they did show compassion for the extra stress our bankruptcy added to our already shipwrecked marriage.

At the same time I watched in horror as yet another blood story was emerging in the media. This time the story crossed our borders reaching Arkansas and Louisiana and brought to light how the blood supply had clearly become a "profit-motivated business." It was reported that these states bled prisoners weekly, which provided $7.00 per unit to the inmates and "rehabilitate[d] them" by teaching them to give back. The blood processing plant—Pine Bluff Biological Products—grossed 2.5 million in 1986; $350,000 of which went to pay inmates and $249,600 was paid to the State of Arkansas. A money maker indeed!

Michael McCarthy became the lead plaintiff in a $660,000,000 lawsuit filed against the Canadian Government and several private companies, who imported the blood in boxes simply marked "DOC" (Department of Corrections) and used the blood products to make Factor 8 to treat the Canadian hemophiliac population.

The Arkansas Prison Blood story was documented by Michael Galster, using the pen name Michael Sullivan, in his novel *Blood Trail*. It was covered by many media sources and brought to light that Canada foolishly purchased this Arkansas prisoners blood in the 1980s. From 1980 to 1985 over one thousand Canadian hemophiliacs were exposed to U.S. prison plasma, which had been collected from convicts who were known to be at high risk for hepatitis C and HIV. "They knew that just one infected prison donation would contaminate huge lots of plasma that would be made into hemophilia product," McCarthy was quoted as saying. The FDA cited the following problems when the prisons were finally stopped from bleeding the prisoners: 1) disqualified donors were allowed to continue to donate, 2) plasma was inadequately stored, 3) records were altered, 4) there were instances of willful disregard for standards, 5) plasma center staff were inadequately supervised, 6) people in management at the center tried to hide that they were either initiating or condoning the destruction or alteration of records concerning these activities—despite these facts, **the plasma was allowed to be sold and exported to Canadian pharmaceutical companies**.

Sadly the lawsuit was not allowed to cross the border nor could it implicate any of the politicians who were involved. There were many lessons to be learned from those responsible for the decision-making process where blood was concerned. When health care and excessive profits are involved, the cost in human lives—not the profits—was on the losing side.

In May 1999, a settlement valued at 1.118 billion plus interest was reached among all the parties for the 1986 to 1990 transfusion recipients. Much to the disappointment of the recipients, they were told this amount included compensation for those individuals secondarily (from the primarily infected partners or parents) with HIV. [In the 1989 federal government settlement, 1068 HIV-primarily-infected-transfused individuals each received $120,000 over four years. In addition in 1993, the provinces agreed to pay each primarily infected person an additional $30,000.00 per year for life.]

To most it appeared the hepatitis C fund might one day run out. Because many HIV claimants, who were secondarily infected, received a far superior compensation package, it seemed unfair to take more money from the poor cousin hepatitis C victims.

In the settlement, hepatitis C-infected individuals would be eligible for compensation based on the severity of their disease. They would also be able to receive compensation for loss of services in the home, costs of care, costs of hepatitis C drug therapy, costs of uninsured treatment, medication and out-of-pocket expenses. Sadly, since many had long ago tapped out their savings and were living on small disability pensions, they did not have the money to pay for such outlays and had few receipts to be reimbursed for past expenses. Many would continue to do without. The infected would be able to come back to the fund to apply for more compensation as their disease progressed, up to a maximum $240,000.

In addition, a death benefit category would compensate the patient's estate should their death be directly attributable to hepatitis C, through the blood supply between the dates January 1, 1986 and July 1, 1990. It was announced the compensation would be tax free and would not affect social assistance benefits. Individuals wanting to accept the compensation package would be required to sign a waiver giving up their right to sue the Red Cross and the federal, provincial or territorial governments.

On November 24, 1999 the courts approved the 1986-to-1990 Class Action lawsuit for hepatitis C compensation. Finally it was agreed upon by all parties.

CHAPTER ELEVEN

Our Peruvian Lifesaver

By March of 2000, Jarad was just eleven years old and had been sick for most of his short life. The Internet was relatively new, and I spent much of my spare time searching it for anything that might restore my young son's health. After being told repeatedly that there was no prescription medication to treat hepatitis C, in anyone under the age of nineteen (at least in Canada), I decided to follow up on every alternative treatment I could find. I realized that most of these were not sanctioned by the medical establishment. But by that point, given that nothing the medical doctors had offered him had worked, I was getting desperate.

Jarad had chosen to opt in to the Hepatitis C Compensation Settlement Plan, telling me, "I do not want you to fight anymore." He wanted me to stop traveling and stay home, and would accept any amount they offered. I submitted the claim on his behalf, but couldn't help but wonder if he was going to be around when he turned nineteen, the age when he'd be eligible to collect his compensation.

While Tyler and Ashley were excited about the school year winding down, Jarad had become increasingly lethargic. We found ourselves postponing and cancelling summer plans because Jarad was too sick to do most activities. It impacted all of us, but nobody complained. We just wouldn't go ahead without him.

We all had our own way of handling the sickness and sadness. I was desperately angry at the medical industry and those responsible for the blood contamination. There was no amount of money that could take away our pain. I felt fearful all of the time, and I ate constantly. Perhaps this was a way to compensate for Jarad's lack of appetite and subsequent physical deterioration. I worried and found it hard to concentrate. Would he die suddenly the moment he was out of my sight? I could not leave his side. Ashley—our little nurturer—waited on him hand and foot. She read him stories; played his favorite games, got him any toy he asked for, fluffed his pillow, offered him treats she hoped he would eat and pulled the blanket over his tiny body when he had fallen asleep. Tyler went about his business. He was an A student and never had to study. He loved to draw, kept busy with his paper route, and he used the money he earned to buy his first BMX bike. He loved to ride and competed at the local track and in neighboring cities. This was his way of escaping the pain of watching his sick brother fade away. Although they didn't say it, I knew both Tyler and Ashley held some resentment toward their younger brother. In the past we had cancelled family outings because Jarad had gotten sick. Now that he was sick all the time, there were just no plans being made. No talk about the future. Every day was spent at home. I know this wasn't easy on my growing teenagers.

By now Peter and I had exhausted our counseling services and were tired of trying to change each other's minds. My husband continued to be in denial that anything was seriously wrong with our youngest child and continued to ignore my concerns.

One day when Ashley and Jarad were watching TV, I went downstairs to Peter's workshop where he spent much of his time. I was sick of watching him retreat from our problems.

"You should be upstairs with the children," I snapped.

"Why? They don't need me. In fact none of you need me," he said. I was too exhausted to waste my time arguing with him. By that point I felt incredibly alone in our relationship. Peter had moved out of our bedroom long ago. With Jarad so sick, I let him sleep in our queen-sized bed most nights. Just like when he was a tiny baby, I could not bear to let him out of my sight. I was so worried he would die alone in the middle of the night. Jarad suffered horribly from violent vomiting and bouts of diarrhea and unexplained rashes. His appetite had all but disappeared. He understood the relationship between eating and throwing up and as a result was hesitant to put anything in his mouth. He spent a good deal of his day curled up in the fetal position on the couch, sleeping or softly moaning. His weight had dropped to sixty-six pounds. A visit to our doctor revealed that, in addition to everything else, Jarad had also contracted an upper respiratory infection complete with a bad cough. In his weakened condition he could not shake it. His lymph glands were swollen. Vomiting increased to three times or more per day. Any nibble of food I could get him to eat did not stay down for long. He mainly existed on sips of ginger ale. The anti-nausea drugs from the doctor gave him no relief. So in June, one month shy of his twelfth birthday, I took him back to the doctor.

By that point his weight had fallen to forty-six pounds. He was so weak I had to carry him from the car into the doctor's office. Our family doctor, checked him out thoroughly and glanced over at me. We exchanged worried looks, and I told her that the irritable-bowel and anti-nausea drugs had not helped. It was a miracle he was not dehydrated and in need of IV fluids. I knew without actually hearing the prognosis that Jarad was quite possibly only weeks away from dying. His will to live was sinking fast. Nothing could make him smile. He spent more and more time sleeping. I did not know whether Jarad sensed his end was near, or if he was just fed up with being sick. Back at home, I cuddled my sick son in my arms. I physically hurt everywhere, as if I was absorbing some of his pain—and I would have gladly done so, if only it would have made Jarad better.

Jarad was usually exhausted when his hospital homebound teacher, Vanda Wilson visited. Some days they spent an hour or so together reading, writing and doing arithmetic. But Jarad was losing his enthusiasm for life and his attention often wavered. Sometimes he just slept through Mrs. Wilson's entire visit. Watching this little boy suffer and miss out on so much of his childhood was torture. I wasn't sure how long we'd be able to bear it.

One day, Jarad weakly asked, "Will I throw up when I get to Heaven? Will I still have headaches, and be so itchy?" But it was his next question that caused my heart to break. Years before, Jarad and Ashley had nicknamed me "Suki" after the sophisticated Siamese cat in their favorite book, *The Cat's Wedding*. One day he asked me, "Suki, will you put red roses on my grave?" I couldn't respond, but secretly wondered where these questions were coming from. For days after that, he continued to ask me difficult questions about dying. I was stumped. How could I possibly provide him with the answers he was seeking when I did not know the answers myself?

Jarad's line of questioning prompted me to examine my own relationship with God. I searched the bible for answers.

"I'm scared Suki," he said one day. "Will you be there?"

Although it nearly killed me inside, I shakily answered as best I could. "I will likely be here on earth, Darling, but one day we'll see each other again."

He thought about my response and asked, "Who will take care of me? Will I ever see Rolly (his nickname for his sister, Ashley) again?"

The last thing I needed was this conversation. I wanted to cover my ears, and say "La la la" and forget he had ever opened this conversation. How could I live without him? I had given so much of my heart and soul to his health and the cause of hepatitis C. I decided my life would simply not be worth living without him. I prayed all day, in one breath asking God to take both of us, and in the next, asking for a miraculous cure to fix all of our broken lives.

Everything I did during the course of my day reminded me of Jarad. When I walked past the boys' room and spied Tyler playing on the floor, all I could think about was how Jarad would not get to do this. When I did laundry and folded his tiny clothes or when I stopped to pick up toys laying on the floor, it reminded me just how sick Jarad had become. He was at the center of my universe.

I became quite militant about protecting Jarad. His immune system was broken and we didn't want any other germs invading his body. If I was not by his side, I was within earshot. I kept him isolated from sick people when we were out and about. But the safest place for both of us was usually at home. That way I was spared explaining why he was not at school or giving updates to friends we bumped into. I limited the friends Tyler and Ashley could have over for play dates. I told family and friends that if they were feeling sick they should stay away. This left me alone with Jarad day after day. I became hyper-focused on his failing health and quickly spiraled into a depression. My whole family felt the pain of Jarad's long-term illness; it was the black cloud that followed us everywhere. Most nights I cried myself to sleep as he slept fitfully beside me.

This whole ordeal made me edgy. I snapped at those I loved the most. I was angry all the time. My health suffered. I had begun eating for two, as if I were pregnant, subconsciously attempting to make up for Jarad's lack of appetite. My body swelled, and my blood pressure, cholesterol and blood sugar levels all reflected my troubled life.

Some doctors continued to downplay the seriousness of Jarad's condition. My intuition was screaming, "You are wrong, you don't know him, he is going to die!" More than once I heard them suggest that I was the problem. Doctors often told me to see a psychologist. But I didn't feel strong enough to tear myself away from Jarad to go see one. Even my husband, Peter, seemed to doubt that things were as bad as I made them sound. I saw the way he looked at me. He no longer went with us to Jarad's doctor appointments. Maybe, I thought, he simply couldn't deal with being torn between what the doctors were saying, and my interpretation of the situation.

At least our general practitioner was on my side. She knew our situation better than anyone else and had witnessed Jarad's deterioration firsthand. She had been our family doctor for years and she saw the dramatic decline in his health and mine. After all we had been through I wondered what else the other doctors could be covering up but still at times I doubted myself. Could I possibly be wrong? I spent almost all of my time with my sick son. If he were well, wouldn't he be doing more? His sad face told the truth and his vomiting and weight loss were certainly more than symptoms of being a "failure to thrive." As the days passed, I was plagued with headaches and extreme anxiety. I continued to pack on the weight. I punished myself by caring less about everything around me. If Jarad was going to die, he was going to take me with him.

My friend Robin grew concerned watching what hepatitis C was doing to Jarad and me. Robin was a good friend I had met through a hepatitis C forum I had hosted. She was also infected through a blood transfusion. I called her following Jarad's last appointment with Dr. Severide.

"Remember I told you about Michael?" she asked her voice brimming with excitement.

"No," I told her impatiently. I guess I had promptly forgotten our conversation as soon as I hung up the phone a few weeks ago. Apparently an acquaintance of Robin's, Michael, had hepatitis C, too. He recently tried a tonic and tea from Peru and had experienced a complete transformation.

"Remember I told you that he had taken Interferon and felt horrible?" Robin reminded me. "Well, today I got the doctor from Peru's phone number. I bet he can help Jarad, too. It can't hurt. It's an herbal tonic and Mike said he hasn't experienced any side effects."

"Does the doctor in Peru claim this is a cure?" I asked. "How much does he charge?" Robin said she wasn't sure. Money was tight given all of our medical expenses. I owed it to my family to proceed cautiously. I knew I couldn't deal with any more dead-end searches for help. I followed up on every lead, but sadly I had heard too many promises, and paid out too much money, for zero results. I was simply not ready to have my hopes dashed again. But then again, we had nothing to lose. I told myself I just wouldn't hold expectations this time.

"Okay Robin, give me his number. I'll talk to our general practitioner and see what she says about this."

Of course, I wanted my son to be healthy, but I could not handle another setback. I was drained from watching him spend his days curled up on the couch and moaning gently with a bucket beside him. It was a struggle for me to just be in his presence these days, but I also could not bear to be too far from his side. Ashley especially drew closer to Jarad and became blatantly aware of his decline in health. It had been obvious since Jarad's birth that they shared a very special bond. She had always helped me: getting diapers, bringing clean clothes, watching over as I bathed our new bundle in the sink, and now caring for him as he suffered. She was his little mother.

After a particularly upsetting check-up with our general practitioner, who could give me no hope or solace, I finally picked up the phone and made a desperate call to Dr. Jose Cabanillas. He did not answer my call. After weighing my options once more in my head, I left him a message.

A few days later, our house phone rang. My heart skipped a beat or two as I heard Dr. Jose Cabanillas say, "Hello is this Leslie Sharp?" Although I struggled to understand his broken English, Dr. Cabanillas introduced himself and carefully explained how the tonic detoxified the liver and allowed it to rest, so that the liver could heal itself and fight off infection. That was the case, "As long as Jarad followed the strict diet and got plenty of rest."

"No worries there," I told the doctor, and explained that all Jarad *could* do was lie on the couch and doze on and off all day. The doctor told me that his other patients who had taken the tonic—all with different types of liver disease, including hepatitis C—had experienced miraculous recoveries and had seen their health restored. His encouraging words gave me a glimmer of hope, but I was still skeptical. I had heard "miraculous" bandied about too many times.

However, the good doctor had gotten my attention. His sincerity shone though during our conversation, especially since he didn't ask for any money. In the past every time someone told us about a potential treatment for hepatitis C, it always came with a price tag. I had dragged Jarad to a Native American medicine man ($325.00 plus a tobacco offering), a pranic healer ($500.00), and a naturopath (thousands). We had received many invitations from naturopaths, MLM companies (selling Tahitian Noni Juice and a variety of supplements), chiropractors, faith healers, and snake oil salespeople offering us the "only" cure available. While legally they couldn't state that their product cured certain diseases, they always implied that "theirs actually did." I got sucked in by many of these "cures" for the first few years and over time, shelled out more than $15,000.00 on alternative treatments that did not work.

I expressed my doubts to Dr. Jose that a tea made of twigs and roots would in any way appeal to my sick son, given that he vomits up everything he eats. Dr. Jose consoled me by saying, "If Jarad feels better when he takes it, he will ask for more." He urged me to let Jarad's body decide.

"Please Leslie, I make no promises and offer no guarantees. But I have seen this tonic work some miracles, and I have no reason to doubt that Jarad's liver will experience a similar healing." The doctor assured me that either way it would cause my son no harm. He explained how he had admitted himself to a hospital in Peru to test his tonic on himself. He had it infused directly into his veins while doctors monitored his vitals for harmful side effects. He reported that he had suffered no harm by taking massive doses.

Although I desperately wanted to accept his offer immediately, I told him that I would have to discuss it with our family doctor. He went on to assure me that the tonic "contains all natural ingredients made from plants, flowers, vegetables and herbs—no chemicals." He explained that I just needed to boil up the contents of the paper bag to make a "tea," and add a filled dropper of the elixir. Based on his size, Jarad would need to drink two cups of tea each day with a teaspoon of the tincture added to each. Doubts were spinning in my head.

I thought to myself, "Maybe this is a desperate, stupid gamble, but if Jarad feels better, nothing else matters." To his credit Dr. Cabanillas did not use the word "cure" when describing the effects of his herbal treatment. He never asked us for money, and just requested that I keep in touch and let him know how Jarad was doing. "Please, just let me know how your son feels over the next couple of weeks," he pleaded.

My mind was made up when I called our general practitioner to ask her opinion. She offered the encouragement I needed to hear by saying: "You have nothing to lose." My gut feeling was that at the rate Jarad was vomiting and losing weight, he would be lucky to live another couple of weeks. I wanted this to work so badly for Jarad. I started to daydream about the possibility that he might actually enjoy a quality of life that had eluded him for the past five years. I thought about how all of our lives would change. The remote possibility of Jarad feeling better was more important to me than anything else.

But, I couldn't help but think about how this might appear to medical professionals and the legal system. In Canada there was danger in administering untested treatments, especially from third world countries. If Jarad's health deteriorated further after taking the tonic, I could be charged with criminal negligence and be sent to jail. However, that didn't matter to me now. Just as our doctor said, we had nothing to lose.

At this point, it took very little to make Jarad gag and vomit. I was buying all different kinds of food hoping to find something he would keep down. He turned his nose up to most food with an emphatic, tight-lipped, shake of his head—and then I ended up devouring it myself, out of frustration. I knew that if he didn't like the smell of the tonic, it was highly unlikely that he would even taste it.

The gentle Peruvian doctor reassured me that if Jarad noticed a relationship between taking the tonic and feeling better, he would naturally ask for more. Dr. Cabanillas felt confident that Jarad would feel a little better with every liter he drank. He would give us enough to make a liter each day for about a month. Dr. Cabanillas had left some with his brother-in-law and arranged for us to meet the brother-in-law and pick it up in Keremeos, a town forty-five minutes away from our home. Now I just had to tell Jarad about the plan.

"Jarad, I spoke with a doctor who has a liver tonic that might make you feel better. I spoke with our general practitioner and she agreed it would be worth a try." He looked up at me, his eyes sunken in his thin face. His first question was, understandably, "What does it taste like?"

"I don't know, Sunshine," I said, thinking on my feet, "but I do know someone who has taken it and now he feels better. What if we go and talk to him?" Jarad gave me a weak nod. I quickly called Robin and asked if she thought Michael might talk to Jarad and share his experience. She called me right back and said, "Can you go right now?"

"Yes," I told her.

"Okay, I will be by to pick you up in ten minutes." Robin lived just around the corner. I carried Jarad out to her car and we headed out to Michael and Musha's home in Kaleden, about 20 minutes away. I sat in the back seat holding Jarad close.

We drove up to their basement door as a beaming Michael came out to greet us. I was immediately struck by how healthy he looked.

"This must be the little Jarad I have read and heard so much about", he said. "Welcome and come on in." Michael sat Jarad down and described his experience with the tonic. His wife, Musha, relayed her perspective of the experience as well. She said Michael had gone from sleeping most of the day to being able to work.

"Mike is a new man! His energy has returned, his appetite is great and he is finally gaining weight." Her words were music to my ears. Her enthusiasm was contagious. Jarad listened and then asked Michael, "What does it taste like?"

"Honestly", Mike said "a little like dirt." Jarad managed a weak smile. "But it was not as bad as some of the other medicines I have taken, and those never made me feel this good." Jarad seemed a little brighter at the hope of the nausea and headaches going away. But I could tell the trip had been long enough for Jarad, and he asked if we could go home.

"What do you think?" I asked on the drive home.

"I guess so," he answered feebly. As I looked out the window my heart was heavy and tears streamed down my cheeks. It was as if we both understood this was our last hope for him.

I did not tell Peter of our plan to drive to Keremeos. Since he was a member of the Royal Canadian Mounted Police, I was afraid that he might try to stop me, or that he might get in trouble for my actions. I felt a little foolhardy going to a tiny village in the middle of nowhere to pick up a mysterious package. But it was a risk I was willing to take for my son. Although our marriage was on the rocks and we rarely communicated, I still didn't want to jeopardize Peter's RCMP career by involving him.

The day we were scheduled to run this errand was hot. As soon as my husband headed out the door to work after lunch, I scooted all three children into the car and we headed off to Keremeos. I was both nervous and excited to meet up with the doctors' brother-in-law, Penn Dragon. Something told me I was making the right choice, and I couldn't wait to get there. I quickly told the kids that Mommy had something special to pick up that might make Jarad feel better. Tyler asked what it was.

"It's an herbal liver tonic Robin told me about," I said. "A doctor from Peru gave it to a friend of Robin's," I explained, "and he feels so good now. He had no side effects." Jarad was very quiet but a renewed sense of hope filled the car as we headed down the highway.

Soon I rounded the corner onto the rocky driveway. It was early afternoon, and tall trees shaded the drive. Ashley pointed out a man standing in the driveway just in front of the big, old rustic house. I noticed the wood siding was rough and worn, and it had three stories. It blended right into the country setting. I quickly turned my attention to the man. He had a very handsome face. He was tall and slender, with long dark hair tied back in a ponytail. His skin was light brown as if kissed by the sun. "Could that be him?" I thought. My eyes went immediately to two medium-sized paper bags in his hands. I told the kids to wait in the car. I slowly opened my door and walked towards him, shyly asking "Penn Dragon?"

He smiled reassuringly "It is I," he said as he handed me the two bags. His face shone brilliantly in the afternoon sun. I brought him over to the car and introduced him to the kids. They, too, were fascinated by this man with the medieval name and the long ponytail!

He explained that the instructions were in the bags and said his goodbyes as he turned back towards the house. I was almost giddy with anticipation. I felt a twinge of guilt for not telling my husband, but most of all I felt that a spark of hope had returned to our darkened lives.

Relieved that we had gotten our "goods," I was momentarily distracted by our possibilities. One of two things would happen: Jarad would get better, or he would get worse. I chose not to focus on the latter. I sat for a minute unable to start the car. I gave my head a shake as Ashley asked if she could hold onto the two bags. I told her to hold on tight; concerned she might drop the precious contents, as I turned the car around and made the slow drive up the bumpy driveway.

Ashley was very curious about the contents, and she was also very protective of her sick little brother. She checked inside the bag. "Be careful," I warned, as I watched from the rearview mirror. Ashley described the contents. "It's just a bunch of sticks!" she said disappointedly, but there were also "two small glass bottles" of the elixir that the doctor had described in the bags.

As I entered the divided highway, I could feel the atmosphere in the car change from one of trepidation to lightness. Tyler slid their favorite cassette tape into the car stereo, and we all sang along to Akuna Matata (from the Lion King) as we headed for home.

As soon as I walked into the house, I excitedly took the bags of herbs to the kitchen. I cautiously opened them and peeked inside to see twigs and roots as Ashley had described. There were also some dried flowers and chunks of sticks and strips of bark in the bags. I carefully read the instructions, refreshing my mind on what Dr. Cabanillas had said. I poured a gallon of distilled water into a soup pot and emptied the contents of one bag as instructed. I boiled it on medium-high for twenty minutes and watched the mixture become a very dark red color. I used a strainer and poured the boiled tea into four quart glass jars that would store Jarad's concoction, and silently said a prayer that he would not only drink it but would keep it down. The tea smelled somewhat like dirt, just as Michael had warned, while the tincture smelled like a combination of soya sauce and scotch whiskey. It was not an appealing smell for anyone—let alone a sick boy with a very sensitive nose!

I did not share these thoughts with Jarad. I went to the living room to check on him and saw that he was curled up on the couch fast asleep. "That's good," I told myself, as I went back to the kitchen and placed the jars in the fridge. "His nap will give the tea time to cool."

Jarad slept for just over two hours, and when he woke up he asked if his new tea was ready. "It sure is," I told him, as he rubbed his sleepy eyes. I carried him to the kitchen, not taking the chance that he might vomit on the living room carpet. I sat him on the kitchen counter as I poured him a cup of tea and added the tincture. Ashley and Tyler came in to witness the first sip.

Jarad said, "Humm, smells good . . .!" And then he plugged his nose and drank it down. We all laughed as he reluctantly added, "Not bad!" But his contorted facial expressions indicated the very opposite of what he had just said.

We watched for signs of the liquid coming back up but that didn't happen. In fact, a few minutes later he asked, "When can I have some more?"

Not only did the tea stay down, but he asked several times that afternoon, "Is it time for my tea?" The next day, he went to the fridge and poured a glass for himself, pinched his nose and downed it. Unlike pretty much anything else he ate, I never had to coerce him to take his "liver tonic."

It was soon obvious that Jarad was feeling better. Within two days he reached a level of energy and activity that we had not seen from him in over a year. He left the couch to tramp up and down the stairs to his second-floor bedroom. The twinkle returned to his previously dark sunken eyes. His cheeks were flushed, and his legs and arms found strength. He even went out to ride his bicycle and take off on his rollerblades or skateboard. Soon enough, he was meeting up with the neighborhood kids to play.

Three days after beginning the tonic, I was panic-stricken when I realized that Jarad was missing. The last time I had seen him, he was playing in the driveway. I later learned that Jarad was out on our quiet cul-de-sac when some boys his age were walking home from school, and they invited him to join them at one of the boy's homes.

Because Jarad had been so ill for the past few years, he had never gone off to play with anyone. He spent his days indoors or maybe, on a good day, in our yard. So, I had never had to teach him to tell me where he was going and when he would return. That day he had innocently accepted the boys' invitation. Tyler, Ashley and I walked the neighborhood, calling his name and knocking on doors, looking for any signs of him. Hours later, when I was ready to give up and call the police (or at least his Dad), Jarad came sauntering down the street. He was grinning from ear to ear, happier than we had seen him in years. I simultaneously wanted to hug and smack him. But, before I could give him a stern lecture on telling me where he was going, Jarad asked if it was time for his "medicine." Hand in hand, we walked back to the house, and I watched in awe as he gulped down his tea.

It was crystal clear to me that if Dr. José Cabanillas had not entered our lives when he did, Jarad would not have lasted another two weeks. I called him in Peru and gave him an update. He was thrilled by Jarad's recovery, and to hear that by following the doctor's strict diet, Jarad had put on twenty pounds in less than two months.

Peter was as amazed and overjoyed as the rest of us, and the family had a wonderful summer together. We went to the beach, waterslides and parks. We visited with my sister and her family often, now that Jarad could make the drive to Kelowna without vomiting. We even travelled to Vancouver and Gibson's to drop Tyler off at Camp Elphinstone. For the first time in years, we all relaxed and Jarad started living like a normal boy. He wanted to compete in BMX racing and did it. Our reporter friend, Gary Symons, wrote a feature story about Jarad's recovery that swept through provincial and national newspapers, creating a sensation. He interviewed our general practitioner who confirmed Jarad's miraculous recovery but could not explain it. But I knew the answer.

Jarad took his medicine every day—he never missed a dose! However, we soon realized that our supply was going down fast and we needed more. I called the doctor and he arranged for us to pick up another batch from his brother-in-law. He cautioned that after this delivery we would have to wait until the next time he came from Peru. He assured us that he would be back before Jarad ran out again, but months later his return had been delayed. I decided to cut Jarad's daily dosage in half in an effort to stretch out what we had left.

I had been invited to speak at a Hepatitis C Summit near Seattle, Washington about hepatitis C in children. So early Friday afternoon I packed up my children and we headed for the border. We were just twenty minutes from crossing to the United States at Sumas, Washington when panic seized Jarad. We all held our collective breath as Jarad started to whimper and asked for a "barf bag". The half-dose of medicine was obviously not enough. The vomiting had suddenly returned with a vengeance. The fear in his eyes was horrifying. We had gotten so comfortable with him being well that we were totally unprepared for this devastating moment. He spent the entire weekend vomiting. He did not leave our hotel room, except to get in the car when we drove back to Canada.

For the next month, we watched in anguish as Jarad got progressively sicker. This was so difficult for us as a family, as Jarad's brief stint of wellness brought a new tragic depth to the returning sickness. The panic on his face was gut-wrenching as each wave of nausea returned in full force. There was nothing any of us could do but wait until the doctor returned from Peru. On his return, the doctor was detained at customs. The precious fluid was taken from him and dumped by immigration officials.

But, as a precaution, the doctor had managed to send us a parcel that arrived on the Greyhound bus. Excitedly, I rushed down to the bus station to pick it up. As soon as I returned home, I proceeded to boil the first full batch of medicine that Jarad would have in a month. He drank every drop of that first cup. I believed that he immediately felt the effects. Within two days, his energy was up and he was back at school. He resumed playing outside with his new friends and thoroughly enjoying his new passion—BMX biking. Seeing him on the BMX track, you would never know what this child had gone through over the years. He gave the racing his all, a testament to him feeling good again and living life to the fullest.

Over the next year, the medicine would become scarce and unavailable a few more times. Each time, Jarad would sink into a depression. Soon the vomiting and diarrhea would return and take control of his life again. There was no mercy from the effects of his hepatitis C for this sweet child whenever the medicine ran out.

I applied to Health Canada under the Special Access Program to import the life-saving tonic from Peru. I secured letters from our general practitioner, as well as Jarad's pediatric gastroenterologist. Both gave high marks to the tonic and praised Jarad's miraculous recovery. They urged Health Canada to grant us permission to import a six-month supply of the medicine. After waiting many weeks, we finally received their reply: the access was denied unless we were willing to hand over the list of ingredients, the quantities of each ingredient, and the method used to create the liquid. I was shocked. These bureaucrats did not care whether my son suffered or died, but only wanted to maintain their petty control over this medical treatment.

I was glad I didn't know any of the required information, because for Jarad's sake I likely would have given it up. The doctor's patents were not yet in place, and so it became imperative that the liver tonic's ingredients be kept under wraps. I knew it was important to proceed cautiously and protect the doctor, the medicine and his manufacturing rights.

Jarad's life once again hung in the balance. I was furious and called our reporter friend Gary Symons to notify him of their response to our appeal. He chose to write another story for the local newspaper, which was picked up both provincially and nationally, and we were interviewed on national radio. Within days I received a call from the talk show host Vicki Gabereau. She asked if Jarad and I would come to Vancouver and appear on her show. She wanted to bring national attention to the treatment we were receiving by the very government responsible for poisoning Jarad in the first place.

On October 1, 2001 Jarad and I appeared on national TV to tell our story about Health Canada's refusal to let us import Jarad's life-saving tonic. This ruffled some feathers in government. More importantly, many people came forward—businessmen, pilots and flight attendants—who travelled to Peru on a regular basis. They offered to bring the life-saving medicine back for Jarad. The public response to our situation was incredibly moving. There was no way we would ever run out of this life-saving tonic again.

But sadly, there was another side to this public disclosure. The CTV station received over eight hundred phone calls from families who had someone infected with hepatitis C; they all wanted to know how to get this tonic for their loved ones. The TV station told me they had never had such a response to a program. Some viewers even found us and begged me to share our medicine with them. They called on behalf of their moms, dads, children, parents, and other family members and friends. To say their pleas were overwhelming and heartbreaking is an understatement. But there was nothing that Dr. Cabanillas or I could do to supply the tonic to anyone else. Until the Canadian government approved it, only a limited amount of the tonic could be processed and imported at a time.

In the first year of the treatment, Jarad grew in height and gained more than sixty pounds. He was happy, healthy and active. He loved going to school and hanging out with his new friends. He tried all kinds of new activities and truly showed no fear. His passion for BMX biking soared, and he steadily improved his skill at it. At the awards banquet at the end of that BMX season, Jarad was presented with the "Rookie of the Year" trophy for the most improved new biker, a testament to his newfound health.

Jarad took the mystery fluid for the next four years. When the decision was made by Dr. Jose to take him off of the tonic, believing his liver had fully recovered, none of us feared his symptoms would return. When the last drop of our supply was gone, we celebrated Jarad's health and his new disease-free life. But mostly we celebrated the modest doctor who had generously provided us with the tonic and his business partner, Brad Clarke, who continued to keep Jarad supplied after that first stressful year when we ran out periodically. My deepest thanks go to both of them for believing in the miracles of the rainforest and for sharing them with a young boy and a very broken family.

It was Ashley who summed up the benefits of the liver tonic best when she said, "Jarad may have taken the medicine, but our whole family got better."

CHAPTER TWELVE

A New Beginning

Although it was only June, I had already begun my homework and signed Jarad up on the hospital homebound program for the 2000-2001 school year, commencing in September. His teacher, Mrs. Wilson, planned to stop by later that afternoon to wish Jarad a good summer vacation and to give him his report card. She was unaware he had been taking the Peruvian liver tonic. I could tell she was nervous walking up to the house, since the last time she had seen him ten days ago Jarad was very sick. When I called to tell him Mrs. Wilson had arrived and he walked into the room, shock registered on her face. She could not believe her eyes! He was alert, awake, and active. Mrs. Wilson had **never** seen a "healthy" Jarad! She smiled as I said, "It is truly a sight to behold, isn't it!" Happy tears welled up in both our eyes. As a mother she could relate to the miracle that stood proudly before her.

After years of counseling and fighting, Peter and I separated in September of 2000. With Jarad feeling so much better and back in full time attendance at school for the first time in years, the time had come for me to return to the workforce and earn a living. My parents had gifted me the down payment on a townhouse, which was not far from where they lived and just a couple of blocks from Ashley and Jarad's schools. We were all eager for the fresh start.

I felt lighter than I had in years, but when I looked into the mirror, I was horrified to see what the years of sickness and stress had done to my body. Somehow my weight had ballooned to over two hundred and fifty pounds. My health was also suffering as a result: I had an underactive thyroid, high blood pressure, high cholesterol, and pre-diabetes. I was taking a plethora of medications, as Jarad had wound down to just one: his jungle cure. I had been running on adrenaline for years looking after everyone except myself.

The decision to end my marriage, although difficult for me and the children, had actually brought me some peace of mind. Peter and I had been at odds about everything in our lives, from Jarad's illness and beginnings, to me championing the hepatitis C cause, for way too long. Jarad's miracle recovery only proved my point. He was a sick little boy and his liver was the cause. It was not car sickness, and he was not faking it. While Peter was as happy as we were about Jarad's recovery, the years of Jarad seriously illness had only created a greater divide between us.

From kindergarten through the fifth grade, Jarad had been too ill to attend school for more than a few hours each day, if at all. So it was a big shock when we drove Tyler and Ashley to their respective schools on September 5, 2000, and Jarad asked, "Suki, can I go to school, too?" I almost drove off the road! My initial reaction was to blurt out "NO," but since Jarad was on the road to recovery, why not? As much as I wanted to keep him home with me and protect him, I was actually relieved that he was finally healthy enough to attend school full-time and I supported this whole heartedly! Later that day we registered him for the sixth grade and Jarad became a regular attendee in middle school.

I then decided that, if Jarad was going to be in school, it was time to do something about my health. As I dropped all three children off at school the following morning, I drove to the new ladies-only gym, Curves for Women that had recently opened in Penticton. As I walked in on the vigorous aerobics circuit, I felt confident this would be a life-changing first step towards my own recovery!

My Dad came over that afternoon to help me with the hepatitis C support packets. It had become our routine to get together for a few hours every afternoon. He helped me answer mail, compile information packages, and was the first to critique my speeches, but most of all he had always supported my activist role. I knew how proud he was of the work that I did and the woman I was becoming. In his retirement, he loved to spent time with his grandchildren, and living so close he would often pick them up from school and get them started on their homework. Mom's primary ambition in retirement was to travel and see the world, and her constant complaint was, "Getting your father to go anywhere is like pulling teeth!"

I had requested intervention from the Public Trustee for British Columbia regarding Jarad's compensation package. The 1986 to 1990 hepatitis C compensation program did not take into account the long-term effects of the disease on the children and their young bodies. It certainly offered very little support for the families that had infected children. Besides, it appeared to me that the only ones to truly benefit from this settlement were the lawyers.

Four days later the Public Trustee told me that I should consult legal counsel regarding legal alternatives. As usual, at least where government representatives were concerned, we were assumed to have unlimited funds to pay for attorneys. Despite the paperwork we were required to submit, they appeared to be unaware that Jarad's needless hepatitis C infection had already cost our family hundreds of thousands of dollars in lost wages and expenses.

In early 2001 the province of Manitoba announced the first pre-1986 post-1990 compensation of $10,000 per infected person. Although this was a pittance, it was at least an acknowledgement of wrongdoing by the Manitoba government. I wondered if perhaps all of the provinces and territories would follow suit. And then four additional provinces added to the pot: Ontario paid $25,000 to primarily infected individuals and Quebec $24,500. British Columbia created a fund of 6.5 million to be split among qualified claimants, and Alberta offered their HCV transfused residents an additional 22.5% of the compensation provided by the federal settlement.

After months of planning and travel between Penticton, B.C. and Montréal, Québec, On May 1, 2001 I attended the first Canadian Conference on Hepatitis C. The conference offered four days of speakers and breakout sessions, and brought together the very best hepatitis C researchers from all over the North America. For me this was a great opportunity to connect face to face with many people that I had communicated with over the past four years.

Sadly, now that the hepatitis C compensation package had been awarded, the Canadian government felt little pressure to continue the educational process that had begun when the disease was a hot topic and in the daily news. Unfortunately, little did we realize that it would also be the last conference of its kind paid for by the federal government.

In late June of 2001, I was approached by both Brad Clarke and Dr. Jose to gather together a group of hepatitis C-infected friends for an all-expense paid trip to Peru to experience the same tonic that had so radically changed Jarad's life. Many people I knew had begged for the opportunity to take the life-saving tonic, and making the selections was no easy task. For weeks I interviewed people and decided the best way to approach this trip was to make a list of the sickest people who had dependent family members. I was told to select them from both western and eastern Canada. The first person that came to mind was Brian Baskin (Ottawa, Ontario). He was so sick his doctors even advised him against taking the trip to Peru and had literally given him only weeks to live. His wife had passed away two years earlier from cancer, and he had two teenage daughters dependent on him. If ever there was a challenge, Brian presented a monumental one to this trial.

The others that immediately came to mind were Joanne Manser (Ottawa, Ontario), Rita Wegsheidler (Penticton, B.C.), Ross Short (Kelowna, B.C.), Robin Dolynuk (Penticton, B.C.) and Patrick Peterson (Ottawa, Ontario). I was told that all six of the patients had genotype 1—the most difficult to treat.

With the final candidates selected, we began to fill out the mountain of forms necessary to make such a trip possible. We had just over three months to prepare for and finally make the journey to Lima, Peru. Unfortunately, on September 11, 2001, air travel came to a standstill when hijacked planes crashed into the twin towers of the World Trade Center. It was uncertain if anyone would be making the trip to Peru. The plan was for me to leave three days later, September 14, and I would arrive a week before the Canadian patients. My job was to pave the way for them by stocking the clinic rooms with all the comforts of home for our patients. I had plenty of things that I needed to do and only a week, if my flight went as scheduled, to accomplish them. "Oh please, open up the skies to air travel again and let me get safely to Peru," I prayed.

As planned on September 14, I boarded a plane bound for Lima, Peru, with a connection in Los Angeles. Security was so tight I had no fear whatsoever of flying. I quickly realized that LAX was quite likely the safest of airports and the skies were better policed as they had ever been. It was a very long flight, and I had never been this far away from my children or my home.

The airport security was frightening in Lima. There were men armed with machine guns everywhere. As we approached security gate, everyone in the line-up held their breath because at the whim of a stoplight, it was determined whether you were getting searched (red), or if (green), you collected your luggage and could leave the airport. Thank goodness I got the green light. The experience was extremely nerve-wracking, and there was no doubt I was no longer in Canada or the United States.

As I entered the main part of the terminal, I was met by the Dr. Jose Cabanillas and his entourage. I was so grateful to see his familiar face—all of this travel and the soldiers with machine guns had me exhausted and nervous. I also wished that I understood the language everyone was speaking, since only Dr. Jose spoke English. We headed outside to his car; I was, at first, shocked by the chill in the air, even at 5,000 feet above sea level. We drove to the hotel near Dr. Jose's apartment. The doctor came in and spoke with the registration clerk. Dr. Jose said he would send the car around to pick me up at noon - allowing me to do as I pleased on my first morning in Lima. I had not slept well on the flight and decided to catch up on my sleep. I tossed and turned for an hour, too exhausted to sleep and a little nervous about being here and on my own.

In the morning I decided to take a walk. It was a little unnerving with the uniformed soldiers armed with machine guns patrolling in front of my hotel and along its waterfront street. However, the waterfront cliffs were spectacular, and I did enjoy the chill of my first morning in Peru. But the fog socked in the entire waterfront, and where I walked you could not see the clouded ocean below. As I walked along I gradually relaxed at the sight of children playing. They were biking and skateboarding at the large BMX Park along the boardwalk. I took pictures to take home for my boys, both of whom were avid BMXers. There were so many people out walking and riding bicycles, despite the steep streets of the city.

Each morning for the next three days, I was taken to a different shopping mall in Lima. My job was to shop for all of the amenities one would find in Canadian homes—sheets, comforters, pillows, bedside tables, lamps, and towels. I also assisted with the grocery shopping by purchasing familiar foods and beverages. Dr. Jose took me to the outdoor market stalls where local crafts were bright and plentiful. He also drove me around to show me the sights of the picturesque city of Lima and took me to restaurants and introduced me to local foods. Everything was colorful and so fresh.

On my fourth day in Peru we drove to Chaclacaya. We arrived at the clinic compound and waited at the guardhouse for the gates to open. I was surprised by the metal security gates and the high walls surrounding the entire facility. I learned these were fairly common even for family compounds in South America because poverty was so prevalent. My first night there I was invited to accompany Doctor Jose to an evening of cock fighting that was taking place on the property.

On the far side of the compound, there was a large ring with "COLISEO CHACLA'S CAMP" written in big red letters on the white cement inner wall. It was obvious this was a very popular sporting event as the men placed their bets and talked loudly about the night's competition as they drank their beer. There were mesh cages that housed the "armed" roosters. We sat on bleachers built on the side of the high rock wall. The competition was fierce and the bystanders boisterous. I spent most of my time there sitting with my hands covering my eyes. When cheers or booing would occur, I would peek out through my fingers to see what was happening. I had never witnessed such violence in my life as the roosters with sharp razors attached to their legs battled to the death. I was horrified by the blood splattered everywhere in the ring.

The next morning the housekeepers had prepared a fabulous fresh breakfast for me to start my day. Afterward they silently collected my dishes and disappeared. The huge house attached to the clinic was empty, as the doctors and staff met elsewhere to prepare for the incoming patients. I was all alone. The girls had washed all of the new linens, so I went to work making the beds, putting out the towels, and deciding the sleeping arrangements based on the level of mobility for each patient. I used the pictures, clocks and throw pillows we had purchased on our shopping trips to decorate the rooms. Later that afternoon, I was invited to sit in on the medical team meeting. I was able to update the doctors on all of the patients' histories, personalities and their family backgrounds with the help of an interpreter. There were, however, many questions asked that I could not answer. Although I had collected the patients' medical information packages before leaving Canada, the envelopes were sealed only to be opened by the doctors when I got to Peru. I shared information gathered from the original interviews and conversations, and obviously my knowledge was based on how well I knew each one of them.

Brian and Joanne were the sickest. They suffered with nausea, vomiting, weight loss, jaundice, and brain fog. Both had arrived in Lima with pneumonia. Rita had surgery and was transfused when she was much younger, and she was selected because of her advanced age and length of time of her infection. Patrick was unsure how he was infected, had a handful of symptoms, and like Ross had very young children. Ross suffered with minor symptoms and was infected in the line of duty, doing police work. An incident where a needle pierced his skin while searching for evidence in a dumpster was the starting point of symptoms. Robin, the healthiest of the bunch, was transfused with half a unit of blood following a C-section.

On September 19, I was incredibly excited as we climbed the car to make the trip back to Lima. The six patients were arriving—three on one flight and three on the other, and we had only one stop to make before the airport.

We pulled into the doctors Jose's apartment building and parked his car. A twelve-passenger van was waiting there. We had the van and the chauffer for the next five weeks.

We were at the arrivals gate as Brian, Joanne and Patrick, the three from Ontario, made their way out of the customs and immigration area. Brian and Joanne were brought out in wheelchairs. They looked exhausted but happy to see us. We went to a coffee shop to await the arrival of Robin, Rita and Ross from British Columbia, who were due to land about an hour later.

Once the luggage was loaded in the van, we were taken from the airport to the compound in Chaclacaya. Everyone was exhausted from the long trip from Canada to Peru. On route we stopped briefly at a roadside fruit stand to purchase fresh produce. The local fruits were cool and sweet and so refreshing.

The doctor explained that the young girls holding babies and begging on the street corners had borrowed or rented the babies for the day to arouse the tourists' sympathy and make more money. He also pointed out shrines and some local points of interest as we drove our tired guests back to the compound.

The patients were eager to get settled in their clinic home. This was where they would call home for the next five weeks. The compound was beautiful, despite being surrounded by high walls and security gates. Armed guards allowed only authorized people to enter.

However, behind the gates there were gorgeous grounds with a huge swimming pool, a fabulous clinic/home, and even a small a petting zoo containing exotic parrots, an ocelot, alpacas, large box turtles, monkeys, peacocks and guinea pigs. The property had rows of kennels that contained

Peruvian hairless dogs for breeding. During our first week there, a litter of puppies were born.

I was so happy to be able to spend time with my friends and to help them get settled. We talked, walked around the compound, swam in the pool, or watched the petting zoo animals. The next day the patients daily physical and medical testing began; urine was analyzed and blood drawn every day. They had their teeth checked by the dentist who had flown in from Florida. They were subjected to procedures including ultrasound imaging of soft tissue organs and x-rays. After all of the patients were initially tested, the doctors called me in for a private consultation.

"Brian," they told me, "may not live to see the end of this week. He is gravely ill, in liver failure and his lungs are full of fluid as a result of his pneumonia." They asked me if I would accompany him back to his home in Ottawa right away. Although I did not want to leave Peru early, I understood that one of the patients dying here during treatment would certainly be detrimental to the results of this study. Dr. Jose said they would give him two more days here, and if he did not show any sign of improvement, they would have to send him home. He asked me not to say anything to the other patients, although it seemed everyone was aware of Brian's deteriorating condition. Both Brian and Joanne had been unable to make it to the dining room for meals since they arrived, spending all their time in bed. The doctor made sure they were receiving treatment for their pneumonia as well as their liver tonic. I was hopeful, after seeing the miracle that transformed Jarad's health in three days, that all of the patients would respond just as quickly.

We all ate like kings and queens during our stay. The cooks prepared the most amazing, healthy and fresh meals that any of us had ever tasted. We were all introduced to foods we had never eaten. My favorite had become the Andes fruit called the cherimoya, which Mark Twain called "the most delicious fruit known to men." Every other day we were treated to short sightseeing trips. We travelled to the Inca ruins, went to view the area's diverse ecosystems from cactus gardens, to the jungle along the Amazon River with all the incredible beauty and mystery that was Peru. The only real complaint from the patients was the sketchy Internet service at the clinic compound, as it was their only way to stay in touch with their loved ones back home.

What an incredible experience it was to witness, in person, the gradual but steady improvements in the patients' strength, appetite and vitality.

Each day new blood tests and ultrasounds confirmed positive changes in their liver enzymes and their disease-battered livers. Like Jarad, their bodies responded very quickly to the healing effects of the A4+. Within the first ten days, Brian and Joanne were both wheelchair-free and were able join the other patients in the dining room for meals. They were mobile and could get there on their own steam! Brian's crisis was averted, and my work was now completed here.

After three full weeks in Peru, it was time for me to leave. After I wished all of the patient's good luck and gave my tearful goodbyes, Dr. Jose drove me to Lima. On the way there we dined on ceviche at a wonderful restaurant and stopped at the outdoor market for me to pick up gifts for my children and a few friends at home. While I was shopping, he asked me to pick out either an alpaca jacket or one of the many beautiful alpaca blankets in the market booths as his gift to me. Although I saw this gift as an extravagance, I realized tourists were expected to leave Peru with something made of alpaca. I chose an incredibly soft, white, thigh length jacket.

At the airport, Jose walked with me to the departure desk. He waited until I was out of sight and safe under the tight airport security before he headed back to Chaclacaya and his patients. I boarded the plane with the incredible memories of all I had just experienced fresh in my mind. I returned to my home and family, confident that I had left the patients and my friends in the competent hands of the medical team.

CHAPTER THIRTEEN

The Silver Lining

At Brad Clark's request I arranged a dinner in Kelowna for all of the patients after their return from Peru in October 2001. Joanne and Patrick attended, but Brian chose to stay home with his two teenage daughters and ease back into his most important role as Dad. He sent his best to all of us and said that he had not had so much energy in years. Joanne was feeling so good that she had left Ontario and moved to B.C. At the dinner Patrick announced that in three months he too would be moving west. I cannot describe the joy I felt as I looked upon the smiling, healthy faces at the table. This eclectic group of friends had bonded and become family during their time in Peru. I recognized that like a mother hen I had missed all of my chicks. It was wonderful to see everyone together one more time, all dressed up and radiating health and wellness.

They had all seen their doctors and received excellent reports from their physicians who were so impressed with their transformations! They all shared great stories about their days at the clinic compound in Chaclacaya. Over the five weeks there, they had become intimately familiar with each other's cases, and their group support had helped each one in their recovery. They also shared how the doctors broke the monotony of their confinement by bringing in musicians to entertain them and children who they entertained. We all left dinner that night promising to keep in touch and share progress reports as our lives moved on.

By the end of March, 2002 I suddenly realized that Dad had been sick for a few weeks. This upset me because my Dad was rarely ill. At first he had been to see his general practitioner, who treated him for a sinus infection and gave him a prescription for antibiotics and sent him home. When that seven day prescription ran out, he went to the walk-in clinic where the doctor wrote him a prescription for stronger antibiotics, agreeing with the previous diagnosis. When the next ten day protocol of drugs was gone, and his condition had not improved, he went to the emergency department of our local hospital. He was examined and once again sent home with a ten day prescription for even stronger antibiotics. Given Jarad's medical history, neither of us held much faith in doctors and their ability to accurately diagnose health problems, and this time his symptoms sounded a little more serious to me than a sinus infection. Dad's case was sadly no exception.

On April 2, 2002 I called my parents, and Mom answered the telephone. This was very unusual, as Dad always jumped up to silence their ringing phone. I asked where Dad was, and Mom said "He is trying to get up the stairs but isn't moving very fast." She explained that Dad was short of breath. This was not a symptom that I associated with a sinus infection.

I left the children doing homework, and I quickly jumped in my van and drove over to their house. When I arrived, Dad and Mom were sitting at the kitchen island playing a game of Ginny-O. Dad, who was never one to complain about his health, quickly dismissed all of my questions concerning his slow climb up the stairs. We talked for about an hour then I said I had to go home to put the kids to bed.

Dad stood up to walk me out but in the dining room, he suddenly turned grey and quietly whispered for me to take him to the hospital. I immediately ran out the front door, up the hill to my van, and drove it down to their front door. I helped Dad get into the front seat, while Mom insisted that he was fine. She yelled that if I took him to the hospital, they would likely kill him. His color and lethargy told me if he stayed home he would not survive.

In the Emergency Room the nurse correctly identified the grey pallor of dad's skin, and admitted him to the cardiology section. He was being helped onto the stretcher as I arrived from parking my van. The nurse had already alerted the doctor on call and hooked Dad up to the heart monitors. Blood work was ordered and labeled 'STAT." The blood test results arrived within thirty minutes, and the Emergency room physician decided Dad needed to be admitted to the hospital based on some suspicious markers. He went on to explain they would do further testing early the next morning and would call in the cardiologist to examine him. I was impressed with the speed with which this had taken place, given the usual long waits we had experienced over the years in the Emergency department. The doctor asked me to go to the admitting counter and fill out the necessary paperwork. I took Dad's wallet with me, gave the clerk his personal information, and signed the required release forms on his behalf.

When I returned to Dad's bedside, he was again experiencing difficulty breathing. He seemed frightened because he was not exerting any energy. He pointed to the nursing station and asked me to get the doctor. Both of us were confused by this episode, since he was flat on his back in bed. When I returned, dad was gasping for air, with a look of confusion masked on his pale face. As the doctor reached him, the monitoring machines began to blare in alarm. I heard the doctor call a "Code Blue." I knew within seconds, standing against the wall and watching in shock, horror and disbelief, that my Dad's spirit had passed silently from this world despite all of their efforts to revive him. His death was officially called just a few minutes after midnight. The doctor expressed his condolences to me and asked if they could perform an autopsy to determine the cause of death. I told him I would ask my Mom. I went to the pay phone in the lobby and solemnly placed two phone calls—one to my sister and one to my ex-husband, Peter. My sister said they would come to Penticton sometime the next day. Peter came immediately to the hospital, desperate to make sense of our loss. I drove to my parent's home to tell Mom that Dad was gone. Initially she laughed and thought I was joking, but when she saw Peter was with me, she knew it was true. I fully expected she would want to go to the hospital to say her goodbyes right away. Instead Mom said that she was tired and that she just wanted to go to bed.

Peter and I drove back to the hospital. I picked up Dad's clothing, jewelry, and wallet and then he dropped me off at my townhouse. Although I knew I was in shock, I had never experienced pain that was this crippling. I was crushed and tried to wrap my head around all that had happened. I recalled the night long ago when Jarad was left in ICU, and Dad had poured me a Grand Marnier.

I stood up and stumbled to the liquor cabinet. I found a bottle of Grand Marnier and poured myself a glass. I spent the rest of the night sitting in my living room reflecting on dad's life and questioning how I was going to live without him. He had always been the one steadfast, constant in my life, and now without him it was just me and my children to look out for ourselves. Dad was my rock.

We were shocked a week later when the autopsy results revealed Dad had a nine centimeter blood clot that had lodged in the branch between his lungs. His death happened in an instant, and there was nothing the doctor or anyone else could have done to prevent it. But I wanted to scream at someone; people don't die from sinus infections how was this missed?

The morning after his death I found a letter in my parents' safe outlining his post-death wishes, which we followed. His body was cremated and the ashes sprinkled under the willow tree along my parent's favorite walking path at Skaha Lake. As his wishes stated, and on a sunny day the following August, family and friends joined us from across Canada and the United States to celebrate the very special life and legacy of a wonderful husband, father, grandfather, uncle and friend. At the time I had no idea that his death would change the course of my life forever.

A little over a month later Peter and I received our divorce decree. It was bittersweet as years of my anger and resentment finally began to melt away. I had been on my own with the children for over a year now, and we were all thriving in our new home. I gained my confidence as regular exercise reduced my stress, and mindful healthy eating helped me to drop pounds and reclaim my health. I had lost almost sixty pounds, and the dosage of my medications had all been reduced. I thoroughly enjoyed the ladies I worked out with at Curves and exercised at the gym five days a week. I met so many inspirational ladies there who were gaining control of their health.

> I was hired by Amma Corporation (Brad Clark and Dr Jose Cabanillas) to be a liaison between people with hepatitis C and the company. There were talks of doing another trip to Peru and this time taking American and Canadian patients.
>
> Jarad continued to take the "miracle tonic," and he was reaping the increasing benefits of energy, stamina, and steady weight gain. He was working hard in school and really enjoying every day as a "regular" student. He was

motivated to attend school dances for the first time in his life and became a friend to most of his sixth grade classmates. He brought to school his minor "celebrity" status and an attitude towards life that worked like a magnet. He loudly proclaimed that "I love school," and it showed! He was positive and joyful all of the time. If he wasn't cracking up, he was telling jokes and everyone around him was laughing.

The doctors who had been treating him were shocked by his rapid recovery and at the new life he had claimed for himself. However, after they had written their letters in support of the tonic, there was nothing more the doctors, or the medical establishment itself, could do to make the tonic available to the suffering people who needed it. I desperately wanted to see this alternative treatment approved for the tens of thousands of people who were dying from hepatitis C in Canada and around the world. But that drug approval process, I learned, would require millions of dollars just to get off the ground.

All three children loved our new home and its close proximity to their school, their friends, and the beach. At the age of eighteen Tyler got his drivers' license and had already saved enough for a used car by working at the bike shop and *Starbucks*. It was great to have a second driver in the house now I had accepted a full time job at *Curves* and was working the afternoon shift. Since I now closed every evening, I wasn't available to take the children to their activities. Tyler, pitching in, offered to get his sister or brother where ever they needed to be was such a big help to me.

After a five-year criminal investigation in to the blood distribution scandal in Canada, on Wednesday, November 20, 2002, Royal Canadian Mounted Police Blood Inquiry Taskforce finally entered charges of "criminal negligence causing bodily harm" and "criminal negligence causing death," and added charges of "common nuisance by endangering the public," as well as a charge of "failure to notify under the Food and Drug Act regulations." These charges named Dr. Roger Perrault, Dr. John Perez, Dr. Wark Boucher, the Canadian Red Cross, Armour Pharmaceutical Co., and Michael Rodell, who were all part of Canada's top medical decision-makers along with their agencies. In their positions they certainly knew what was happening with the blood supply, the potential consequences of their decisions, and at the very least they should have known better!

Part of the hepatitis C settlement allowed for families of the victims to make financial claims for reimbursement of out of pocket expenses. After submitting a box full of spreadsheets and receipts, we finally received a check from the compensation Plan administrator via the Public Guardian and Trustee for British Columbia. The check was for just over $10,000.00, a fraction of the $486,000.00 that I had submitted in receipts and lost earning statements. A mere pittance after being forced to declare bankruptcy in our attempts to save our son's life.

I had lost 120 pounds by now and had finally reached my goal weight. Ashley and I had trained for the Vancouver Sun Run and decided we would do it together with some of my *Curves* colleagues. We had a blast in Vancouver all weekend and after the run, the kids drove back to Penticton while I headed south down the Pacific Coast highway. I was mentally and physically exhausted and needed some time to reassess my life. With two children grown and Ashley soon to be out of high school, I had to start nurturing myself. Jarad was so healthy and I knew my nest would be empty soon. I drove for two weeks, stopped when I wanted, slept when I wanted, and listened to what I wanted to hear on the car stereo. While on my adventure, I worked out at a *Curves* franchise on my route Monday through Friday, as if it were my job. I planned driving distances and destinations so I would not miss my exercise. I believed I was in search of a *Curves* franchise I could purchase. When the two weeks were over, I returned home with a clear head and a plan.

Upon my return I talked to the children and explained that I needed to get away from hepatitis C and the support environment I had created in Canada. I told them I wanted to buy a *Curves* franchise because I was living proof of the positive impact the workout could make on my life.

I had started taking online university courses in nutrition, exercise physiology, women's health, and kinesiology in hopes of earning a degree. I needed a new direction and saw that it was not in Penticton, but of course my children did not want to leave.

Dad's death made me realize the truth in the saying "life is short and uncertain." I had done my best to look after Mom since Dad had passed away, but our relationship was strained. I felt she was still angry at me for taking Dad to the hospital, after she had warned me they would kill him there. I understood without Dad, our family dynamic would never be the same and, if I had to, I was ready to let Peter take on the responsibility as caretaker of Jarad and Ashley now that they were older. Tyler was living on his own and he had expressed the same sentiment as Ashley and Jarad: they did not want to accompany me to the U.S. while I searched for a new home and business opportunities. Instead they asked their dad if they could live with him. He readily agreed. I made it very clear they could join me at any time!

Over the next few months I sold my townhouse and gave away most of my furniture and possessions to the children, Peter or my sister. Peter had rented and furnished a new home and was looking forward to forging a closer relationship with his children. The pressure and stress of dealing with governments, lawyers, hospitals and sick people all these years had taken its toll on me. While I may have been a hero in the hepatitis C community, I had been maligned by the medical establishment and even some taxpayers who resented the billion-dollar government settlement accomplished in part by my activist role. While the hostility was never overt, it was there and I believed that I would eventually crack if I continued to live in Canada under this dark cloud. For me, losing Brian and so many other colleagues and friends to their hepatitis C infections was a daily reminder of how close I had gotten to losing my precious son. Mostly I just felt that this chapter of my life was over, and I had served a purpose. Now that Jarad was doing so well, I needed to leave Canada and get a fresh start somewhere else.

My online courses could be taken anywhere, and I knew they would provide me better opportunities as a business owner and personal trainer. I packed up the few important personal belongings I decided to keep. On the night of Ashley's prom and a week after her official graduation, I jumped into my Acura, opened the sun roof, and headed toward California to reclaim my life. Although I knew I would be lonely without the children, the exhilaration I felt at that moment made me feel more alive than I had in a long, long time. I knew I was doing the right thing, and in my heart I knew that eventually my grown children would all end up under my roof again. I recalled telling them, on one of our many four-hour drives to see doctors in Vancouver, "One day I am going to get in my car, drive south and never come back!" The only difference was, at that time, they all thought it was a great idea and were ready to join me!

On August 16, 2004, just a month and a half after I had left B.C., I received an email from Dr. Jose. The time had come for the next phase of the Peruvian tonic study. All of the other patients had been taken off the medicine at varying times over the past two years, and all but Brian, who had died in 2003, continued to do well. Jarad was the only one remaining on the tonic, and there were no assurances that he would not get sick again if he quit taking it. Dr. Jose wanted to determine the effects and establish a timeline for beginning and terminating the tonic, to see when it would be safe to stop the treatment and if a patient would need to restart it. So, as soon as another round of ultrasounds and blood work were completed, he asked Jarad to stop taking it. We had all of Jarad's final reports sent to Dr. Jose in Peru and to Brad Clark in Calgary.

Jarad had suffered no side effects while on it, or after he had been off it for a few days. The doctor conveyed his fear that, "Jarad could develop a tolerance to the tonic and I am concerned that eventually it may quit working for him." Instead Jarad continued to thrive. His health remained stable—no nausea, vomiting, headaches, rashes or heartburn. His liver enzymes remained at a healthy level and his viral load was negligible. It appeared his liver was now healthy.

After BMX biking and skateboarding, Jarad's passion soon turned to snowboarding. At school he participated in all school activities. He continued to enjoy a healthy appetite and regained all of the weight he had lost plus some. After four years on the liver tonic, his weight was up to 120 pounds, still skinny but at least he was gaining steadily. Jarad had not looked back and neither had I!

In 2005, a year later, the Canadian Red Cross pled guilty to distributing contaminated drugs (blood) and was fined $5000.00 under the Food and Drug Regulation act. Jarad and I were in the Hamilton, Ontario Superior Court courtroom when their plea was announced. Jarad and I were given this opportunity to present our Victim Impact statements shortly after hearing the plea, in the case of "Her Majesty the Queen VS the Canadian Red Cross" to the Canadian Red Cross executives, the judge, and the defense attorneys. In fact the court room was packed with other victims, the support agencies of various affected groups and to be sure, full of reporters. It was our one and only opportunity to tell the courts how the hepatitis C tainted-blood transfusion Jarad received had affected his life and the lives of all of his family members. For the first time we were given an opportunity to express publicly our horror at their admission of guilt.

In exchange for the guilty plea and paying the paltry fine, all Criminal charges against the Canadian Red Cross Society were dropped. The Canadian Red Cross also agreed to donate 1.5 million dollars to the University of Ottawa for a research and a scholarship fund available to the children of adults infected with hepatitis C. It was obvious immediately this plea bargain was once again favoring the infected adults, as neither Jarad nor his siblings qualified to apply for this scholarship fund. Again, the Canadian Red Cross made available no further compensation for the infected children or their siblings.

On January 1, 2006 Ashley and I moved to Honolulu, Hawaii where I would finally fulfill my dream of owning and operating a *Curves* franchise. We left California, where both Jarad and Ashley had joined me months earlier, to set up our home and prepare the club for its February 1st opening day. Jarad joined us in Honolulu in mid-January and resumed his final semester of high school. He was looking forward to graduation, but as it approached he told me he wanted to return to B.C. and his friends as soon as school was finished. I agreed that if he actually graduated he could go back. So the day after he received his final report card from Henry J. Kaiser High School in Honolulu, he boarded a plane to return to Penticton. Although he had enjoyed skateboarding, surfing and the laid back lifestyle of Hawaii, Jarad preferred the cold climate in B.C. and of course snowboarding had become his passion.

In the fall of 2006 the *Friends of Jarad* trustees voted to donate the balance of the fund, established to help Jarad and our family with medical related expenses, to Okanagan Similkame'en Neurological Society in hopes that it could help other families in the city of Penticton. We had a healthy young man now and heartily agreed the funds should help other families.

HeCSC, the Hepatitis C Society of Canada officially closed its doors on March 30, 2007 ". . . due to a lack of committed funding for the next fiscal year 2007-08." The organization, founded by Dr. Alan Powell in 1994, was the first of its kind to deal primarily with the outbreak of hepatitis C in Canada. "Now that the compensation issue is finally drawing closer to resolution, I think our mandate in practical terms is over," said Tim McClemont, the executive director. The Society's achievements included press conferences, brochures and information packages, advocacy for victims, setting up a national 1-800 support hotline, and creating more than forty-five chapters and telephone networks. It also was instrumental in keeping media pressure on the federal, provincial, and territorial governments that eventually lead to the out-of-court settlements for those infected through the tainted-blood crisis.

Like many other people, I got my first information about hepatitis C from Dr. Powell's "big yellow book" in 1995, just weeks after Jarad was diagnosed. I think I sat and read it in one sitting. It satisfied my ravenous need to understand the disease that had crippled my son's life, and for this I was very thankful, as I'm sure were many other newly diagnosed and their family members throughout Canada. "I am hopeful that someday soon people in government will truly get it, see the need and fund hepatitis C appropriately . . . until then, take care and be well," said Tim McClemont as he locked the office doors for the last time.

Just before his nineteenth birthday, Jarad returned to Honolulu. He was excited to be back in the Islands and asked for his first stop to be Zippy's restaurant, where he would indulge in his favorite 'chicken katsu' meal. The next morning he asked if I would file the required paperwork for him to apply for the release of his compensation. Finally, he could collect the financial restitution for the first twelve years of his life when he had been so sick and even near-death.

The check arrived a week following his nineteenth birthday and he was overjoyed. He carefully planned a family celebration dinner and treated all of us to a delicious meal. We could always count on Jarad's generosity when he had money, and this would be no exception. He went out shopping and purchased special gifts for Tyler and Ashley as soon as he received his check for $69,062.69. I had attempted to talk to him about taking responsibility for this windfall and offered suggestions for investing it for long-term benefit. I was upset when the Public Trustee for British Columbia did not offer him any financial counseling. Who in their right mind would hand a large check to an immature nineteen year old? What were they thinking? Within a few months the entire proceeds were gone, and sadly Jarad had little to show for it! But I knew Jarad had a great time being "rich" while it lasted. Many of his friends also reaped benefits from his temporary wealth!

After years of waiting, a hushed silence fell over the Ontario Superior courtroom in Toronto, on October 1, 2007, as the remaining group of four doctors: Dr. Roger Perrault, Dr. John Perez, Dr. Wark Boucher, Michael Rodell, and Armour Pharmaceutical Company were acquitted of all criminal charges. Activists and lawyers for the victims lashed out in anger. "There was no conduct that showed wanton and reckless disregard," said Superior Court Justice Mary Lou Benotto in her judgment. "The events were tragic; however to assign blame where none exists is to compound the tragedy," we were told.

James Kreppner, a colleague, a lawyer and friend who had contracted both HIV and hepatitis C, could not believe what he heard in court. "I find it distressing to call that professional conduct; you just can't justify that."

John Plater of the Canadian Hemophilia Society could barely contain his bewilderment at the announcement. He explained, "If you, on the one hand, have a study that says there's a problem, and on the other hand have a study that says maybe there isn't a problem, any reasonable person takes the product off the market. They didn't. People were infected, and people died. How that could be considered reasonable behavior is beyond us . . . A lot of money and time was spent and it all just ended today with a 10-minute speech from the Crown."

He continued, "There are a lot of people out there that are hurting as a result of what happened and they are going to walk away from this very confused, very upset, with a lot of questions. People can say that the system has failed them once again."

A national newspaper summed up our feelings:

"It was not the outcome those who received tainted blood in the worst medical scandal in Canadian history were expecting. An Ontario judge has acquitted the former director of the Canadian Red Cross and three doctors accused in the incident, which saw blood products contaminated with HIV given to hemophiliacs and those in need of transfusions back in the 80s and 90s . . .

"Thousands of patients were left suffering from HIV and hepatitis C as a result of the foul-up, which sparked a lengthy inquiry headed by Justice Horace Krever. The incident drastically changed the way blood is collected and distributed in Canada. In 1998, the Canadian Blood Services took over from the Red Cross.

"Those who were affected by the mistake – and are still alive – were hoping someone would be held responsible for their plight, but instead the four individuals at the centre of the case aren't seen as accountable."

An article from the *St. Catherine's Standard* stated, "Victims of what's been called one of this country's worst public-health disasters were left bewildered and frustrated.

"The 10-year criminal probe came on the heels of the Krever inquiry, which didn't lay direct blame for the scandal in which more than 1,000 people were infected with HIV after receiving tainted blood products in the 1980's. Another 20,000 people contracted hepatitis C. It's not clear how many people have died as a result, but the death toll was 3,000 as of 1997."

This was to be the official end to the tainted-blood matter. As I watched the press conference on the Internet, tears rolled down my cheeks. I was sickened to see all parties except the Canadian Red Cross got away with murder. I couldn't help but wonder if the lawyers for the Canadian Red Cross were now kicking themselves for entering a guilty plea, since all who chose to fight the charges were acquitted.

Postscript:
To add insult to injury, nuisance charges against Dr. Roger Perrault, the former Canadian Red Cross director, were dropped the following year. To quote a news article: "These charges stemmed from an allegation he endangered the public by failing to properly screen donors, implement testing for blood-borne viruses and warn the public of the danger regarding hepatitis C and HIV."

Mom had been enjoying life at Sun Pointe Retirement Community since shortly after I had left B.C. Her health was declining as well as her cognitive skills, and she required some assisted care that my sister could no longer provide. Sun Pointe brought in entertainment, activities and provided many services on site for their residents. Despite my weekly phone calls, Mom sounded down and quite often expressed confusion of everyday situations. She continued to articulate her anger with Dad passing away before her. She reminded me they had a pact; they agreed that he would stick around until after she had passed away. Instead the exact opposite happened and Mom resented being left behind. She was quite despondent. In May of 2009, Mom fell and fractured her hip. She had hip replacement surgery days later and spent a few weeks in the hospital before being transferred to rehab.

In late June I returned to Penticton to visit my family. During my trip, Jarad and I went to see Mom and my sister Sue, and her son Rob before we left the Okanagan Valley. It was a difficult visit because Mom had deteriorated so much. She was not the same lively and often argumentative mother of years past. She simply sat quietly in her wheelchair and looking down at her lap. Her few recent attempts to walk on her weakened legs had resulted in falls, and so she had resigned herself to just sit and allow people to push her in the wheelchair. Jarad and I did all of the talking, telling her about Hawaii, snowboarding, work and the latest news on Tyler and Ashley. This shell of a woman was the only parent and grandparent we had now. Mom had difficulty now recognizing her grandchildren, all of whom had also moved away and now rarely got to Kelowna to see her. My heart broke at the distant look in her eyes, so unlike the last picture we had taken together. This visit was not how I would have chosen to remember her.

Little did I know that visit would be the last time I would see her. It was a warm December evening when my phone rang just as I was heading off to bed. My nephew Daniel called to say that Mom had just passed away. I sat out on my lanai and watched a spectacular lightning show that began just as I hung up the phone. I could only imagine Mom stepping up to the pearly gates to the clash of thunder as she was greeted by Dad after being apart for seven years. She said her piece as the thunder clapped again. Then just as quickly I could see her and Dad—both restored and together, walking hand in hand, again like they did on their daily walks in Penticton. I am doing well on my own but there are so many times I reach for the phone to ask them a question or just to say hello.

Epilogue

It had been almost nine years since I last experienced a Christmas in British Columbia. On December 20, 2013 I was at the Honolulu International airport waiting, at the gate, for my Air Canada flight.

I was hoping to spend Christmas day with all three of my adult children. But, with them living so far apart, their busy work schedules and holiday travel plans, I was content that I would be able to see all three of them on my trip, but at different times and in different places.

My Air Canada flight from Honolulu to Vancouver was uneventful, but as I arrived at the gate to board my plane for Castlegar the departure sign began to flash "annul/cancelled." I placed a quick call to Ashley and asked her to go online and search for other forms of transportation right away.

The representative at the Air Canada counter explained there were no flights available until December 24, but then there was no guarantee my plane would be able to land when it arrived in Castlegar. She did not offer the stranded passengers any other alternatives. There had been a huge snow storm, unusual for Vancouver, the day before and all flights within B.C. had been cancelled for the past twenty-four hours. Everyone was scrambling to find alternative transportation to get home for the holidays.

As the stranded passengers began to talk to each other, we quickly learned there were no empty seats on the Greyhound bus to Castlegar, no rental cars available, and we were told that all flights to the regional Kootenay airports were already oversold. After all, it was just four days before Christmas.

Ashley sent me a text message saying that WestJet airlines showed two seats available for their flight to Kelowna leaving within the hour. Since

Castlegar was a 10 ½ hour drive from Vancouver, the 4 ½ hour drive from Kelowna seemed much more manageable, that is, if the roads were passable.

I was so fortunate to snag one of those empty seats, and while standing in the lineup to enter the boarding gate, I overheard one of my fellow travelers mention "Castlegar." My ears perked up and I asked her if she was on the Kelowna flight and going to Castlegar. She said, "Yes. You want a ride?" My heart sang as I realized my problem was just solved, and I would actually arrive in Castlegar just a few hours behind schedule!

I was so grateful to Stephanie Smith and a wonderful husband Shawn, who had driven all the way from Castlegar to Kelowna just to pick us up. It was my first Christmas miracle!

They dropped me off in my daughter's driveway—I could not believe this door-to-door delivery service, as they literally lived just down the street. Ashley and her husband Jamie, my grandson Riley, and their little Min Pin dog, Alize, were watching out the window for me to arrive. As soon as we pulled into the driveway, they all came outside in the bitter cold to thank my rescuers for their generosity. We wished Stephanie and Shawn a Merry Christmas as we quickly went inside with Jamie schlepping my two large bags for me.

The house was beautifully decorated for Christmas. The first thing I noticed was the smell of the fresh evergreen tree that sat proudly in the middle of the living room. We never get to smell such fresh-cut Christmas trees in Hawaii.

We sat down and caught up on all that had happened since my chaotic adventure had begun. I sat mesmerized as I watched and listened to my 2 ½-year-old grandson, Riley. His eyes were wide as he pointed out all of the special Christmas decorations. However, fatigue soon overtook me from my twenty-four hour trip. I was exhausted and I announced I needed to go to bed before I fell over.

The next morning Ashley and I headed out to the gym. Overnight a snowstorm had blown in to town, and we couldn't even see the road in the blinding snow. Ashley simply kept the car between the telephone poles on either side of the buried pavement. It was freezing cold out—colder than I ever remembered a Canadian winter. I quickly made a mental note that they needed to come visit me in Hawaii next Christmas.

Our plan was to pick up her older brother, Tyler, who would arrive at the Greyhound station, across the street from the recreation center where we would be exercising. Tyler's bus was scheduled to arrive at 10:30 A.M.

This gave us just under an hour to work out and head across the street to pick him up. While we were in the gym, Ashley received a text message from Tyler saying the bus was running at least an hour late due to the treacherous roads. Ashley and I discussed going home or staying for a longer workout; we decided, because the roads were really bad and the snow was still falling, to just stay put until he arrived.

When Tyler texted that the bus was about five minutes away, we walked out of the rec center and got into Ashley's car, but it would not start. There was a gentleman parked in a truck beside us, and so I went over and asked him if he could give us a hand. He readily agreed to boost the battery, got out of his truck and attached the jumper cables and started Ashley's car for us. We thanked him and sat in the car with the engine running to recharge the battery. Just as we were leaving the parking lot, we saw Tyler walking towards the center dragging his large suitcase behind him through the deep snow.

We got out and exchanged big hugs, and quickly climbed back inside the warm car. On the drive home Tyler shared the harrowing experience of his eighteen-hour bus ride from Edmonton, Alberta through the blizzard. We were both thankful he had made here safely.

On Christmas morning we went upstairs to see Riley staring wide-eyed at all the gifts under the tree. He was a little overwhelmed but excitedly cautious as he patiently waited for an okay from his parents to open his gifts. Once given the go-ahead, he ripped the wrapped presents open, and their little dog, Alize, helped him by tearing at the paper. It was a joyful sight for me watching my only grandson on Christmas morning and brought back so many fond memories of my own children at that age. They had experienced some very stressful Christmases after Jarad was born, but Peter and I always put a lot of effort into making Christmas as joyous as possible. At least now everybody was healthy and getting on with their lives, and their health and happiness was by far the best present of all for me.

I cooked our family's traditional breakfast—garlic pork on toast with sliced oranges—and both Tyler and Ashley exclaimed how the smell brought back so many wonderful memories from their childhood in their grandparents' kitchen. My parents had always been the mainstay of stability in our family circle when the children were younger, and we all missed them, especially at this time of year.

After all of the gifts were opened, I received a text message from Jarad asking if I would like my gift now. "A gift from Jarad," I wondered. I had never received one from him. I thought this was kind of a strange request now, as he knew I would be seeing him in Whistler in just a few days. My initial reaction was, "No, I can wait," but after urgings from Tyler and Ashley, I realized this gift must be very special and one that they too wanted me to see. Ashley explained she would videotape my reaction to the gift, so that Jarad could see it firsthand.

I have to give the reader a little history here. Jarad had never called me "mom" his entire life. It was always "Suki." This stemmed from when Tyler and Ashley were very young, and we read a book called *The Cats' Wedding*, and later added its sequel *Three Little Kittens*. These books, written by Linda Jane Smith, told a story of Suki, a sophisticated female Siamese cat, and a black-and-white tomcat named Barney. After proper courting and permission to marry by Suki's father, they were married, and had three kittens Barney Jr., Rolly and Yaki. These books were the favorites of all three children and were read so often that we all knew every word in them by heart.

Somehow to Jarad my name was Suki and that is all he has ever called me. Peter was nicknamed Barney; Tyler – Barney Jr.; Ashley – Rolly, and Jarad – Yaki, to match the fictional family in the story. But those nicknames have come and gone over the years. Suki, however, remains my name to this day.

In addition, Jarad has taken a liking to tattoos. He has so many that I have lost count. But when I see him, after time's passage, I always asked if he has a tattoo with my name on yet. He always smiles as he tells me, "Not now, but one day!"

So with cameras rolling, tears filled my eyes as Jarad shared a picture of his right hand and I studied it carefully on my cell phone. He had tattooed on the back of his hand, a heart and a rose around the name "Suki." I was speechless. It was very tastefully done, and I saw it as an honor bestowed upon me by my youngest child.

Jarad's explanation for getting the tattoo was as follows: "Number one, because of how much you mean to me, and because you and I have been through a lot of hell together. If it weren't for you, I wouldn't be alive today so I wanted to honor you and permanently show you what you've meant to me. I didn't want it to be one of those 'in memory of' tattoos after you died. I wanted you to be able to enjoy it." After a few sobs from me, Jarad continued, "As I get older, I am more able to appreciate what you really did for me, and I see that you were pretty much on your own through it all. So, I admire your strength and determination." Although I have made a point of letting my children know I am not a fan of tattoos, this tribute from Jarad touched my heart deeply. For me, this was Christmas miracle number two!

After Riley's nap on Christmas Day, we headed out to Jamie's childhood home in Thrums. Jamie's dad, Al and his girlfriend Sandy greeted us and ushered us in to their toasty warm home. The wood stove was blazing in the corner of the living room. I watched as Ashley took off Riley's jacket and then proceeded to strip him down to his onesie shirt; I thought, "This is odd for her to be undressing him. We are supposed to go sledding."

The answer was quickly revealed as I read Riley's T-shirt. Across his chest the words "only child" were scratched out and below it read "big brother." I quickly looked at Ashley and asked if she was trying to tell us something. She gathered everyone around her and announced their Christmas surprise: They were expecting another baby—my second grandchild—in August. Again, for the second time that day, I was overcome with emotion as we hugged each other and offered the parents-to-be congratulations. Christmas miracle number three! Their announcement was followed by the anticipated sledding party, and then congratulatory toasts around the fire pit at the bottom of the hill. I had forgotten how frigid a Canadian winter could be—my blood had thinned out living in Hawaii. Between the fire and the Christmas cheer, we were all enjoying the warm glow of Christmas day both inside and out!

Sledding was followed by a delicious home-cooked turkey dinner with all the trimmings—a Canadian Christmas tradition that I had missed since moving to the United States. In Hawaii, with its large Japanese population, families often opt to serve fish for Christmas dinner.

On the morning of the 27th, as I was packing up to head to the airport for my flight to Vancouver, I received a call from Air Canada to tell me that, once again, my flight had been canceled. I quickly called Pacific Coastal Airlines to see if they had any seats available. I was informed their flight from Trail would be departing an hour after my scheduled Air Canada flight. I would arrive an hour later than I had expected, but I was relieved that I could find a flight to Vancouver at all. I called Jarad, and he confirmed that he would be there to pick me up when the plane landed at the new arrival time.

Although it was hard to say goodbye to Tyler, Ashley, Jamie and Riley, the second leg of my vacation was about to begin. I was flying to Vancouver and driving with Jarad from there to Whistler. Since I had not seen Jarad snowboard in eleven years, I had agreed to watch him compete at the King of the Rail snowboard competition at Whistler on the 28th.

In Vancouver Jarad kept me waiting at the airport for more than an hour. I kept going outside to check for him, but would quickly retreat back inside; it was so cold! I wasn't angry, just anxious to throw my arms around him and give him a huge hug. I was so touched by his tattoo tribute that I wanted him to know how much the sentiment had meant to me. It had been almost two years since I had last seen him. I had already learned so many lessons from this young man, and this occasion was certainly going to be another educational opportunity. I had never watched Jarad "do rails"—snowboarding on elevated stunt rails—before and I was worried he might get injured like some did in the snowboard competitions he insisted I watch on TV.

Jarad and I had a history forged together, as they say, with blood, sweat, and tears. How I missed spending time with my son! On the drive to his home in Whistler, Jarad asked me about my life in Hawaii. I could tell something had changed . . . my son was truly growing up. I asked him about his new positive attitude towards life. His happiness was contagious. My tall, thin, long-haired son explained, "Suki, I have no reason to be angry or bitter towards anyone, even the doctors who played havoc with my life." Jarad was a loving, gentle giant with the most caring heart, always cracking jokes and lightening even the most stressful situation. He believed that he was living his dream simply by being able to live in Whistler Village, working as a boot fitter for Showcase (a clothing and snowboard company), and by being sponsored in competitions by five companies, besides being able to snowboard in his spare time. Ultimately, his happiness was all I could hope for after all he had been through.

On the drive to the tiny house he shared with his roommate, Turbo, my son explained that, "No one in Whistler uses their given names." When we arrived, I was shocked by how small and crowded the main floor was. There was barely space to walk through it, but Jarad said, "This is normal for rental accommodations in Whistler, since everybody spends their days at work or outside."

We talked about the upcoming King of the Rail competition. It was the first competition of the season in Whistler. I could feel his excitement!

He described some of his earlier crashes and subsequent injuries, and I wondered if I would even be able to watch him compete in this event, or if I would be hiding my eyes like at the cock fights in Peru. I could tell by the sheer joy on his face that he was eager to be sharing his passion with me. I loved that he was exactly where he needed to be and doing exactly what he made him happy, even if I was concerned about him getting hurt in the process.

We talked about his introduction to the sport, about the day he received his first snowboard, boots and bindings from Brad and Dr. Jose. For him this was the best gift he had ever received, second only to having his health restored by the doctor. I kidded him about how he took the board to bed with him that first night. We reminisced about him learning to snowboard at Apex Alpine in Penticton, and how many boards he had broken since then!

As much as I dreaded it, I would have to endure watching him snowboard "the rails"—for this was the purpose of my trip here—I had come to Whistler to finally see firsthand Jarad's grownup life and to support him in it. I had been there in the early days of his blossoming, but after living outside of Canada and its' winters for nine years, I needed to see Jarad in action—whether I was ready for it or not!

The upcoming competition was the talk of the village and you could feel the energy in the air. Everyone we met walking around town asked Jarad if he was competing, and they all wished him good luck. Many said they would be there to watch. Jarad happily introduced me to all of his friends—it seemed like he knew everyone in the village!

On competition day we ate a late lunch and just hung out at his home watching sports on television, as he psyched himself up for the competition. He was quiet and focused. He prepared his snowboard by applying more stickers from his five sponsors: Endeavor Snowboards, Skull Candy, Vans Canada, Airhole Facemasks and Smith Optics.

He had an Internet connection and so I busied myself checking e-mails and updating friends and reading the news. I proudly watched his preparations out of the corner of my eye. He dressed slowly—carefully picking out his competition garb which consisted of a bright orange hoodie. "All the better for you to see me," he announced.

My mind reverted back to Penticton just before his twelfth birthday when my dreams for any type of a future for my youngest son were shattered by his sudden decline in health. With him unable to even walk and his days spent sleeping, I was unable to foresee Jarad doing any type of physical activity in his future, if he had one—and certainly not one like this that required so much skill and energy. Jarad drew me out of my reverie. The competition was to start at seven P.M. He wanted to be in the village by 6:15 to register, retrieve his snowboard and boots from Showcase, and then be on the hill ready for warm ups when they called for the riders to join the judges on the slopes. So we headed out to the center of the village.

Rumor had it that more than seventy riders had signed up for the competition. I found my viewing spot on the side of the slope and watched some of the early competitors. A few of them crashed, slamming their chests and lower abdomens into the rails so hard that it caused a collective groan to rise among the crowd of spectators. I eagerly searched for Jarad's bright orange sweater to make sure he was still upright on his board. I watched as Jarad attacked the rails, peeking from behind my gloved hands just in case he crashed.

Both Jorja, Jarad's girlfriend, and Turbo explained the difference between the three competitive rails—downtube, down flat down-rails, and down flat down-box—and explained in detail the judges' criteria. As the evening progressed, Jarad showed unbelievable endurance as he ran past all of the competitors and made his way back up to the top of the hill for their next ride down. There were no chairlifts on this lower part of the hill, and after several runs I could see some of the participants beginning to tire, but not my Jarad! I got tired just watching him!

The further the competition moved along, it appeared that 'sticking the rail' was becoming more of a challenge for Jarad. The mayhem became more evident as the dwindling number of participants tried to impress the judges in the final minutes, which was a cause for concern as I scanned the crowd searching frantically for my son.

While Jarad was definitely not giving up, all the physical exertion of running back up the hill and the competition runs themselves was taking a toll on him. Again I was reminded of my sickly little boy, now a man, but not as robust as some.

Jarad did not win the competition that night, but there was no doubt in my mind that he had the drive and determination, along with the heart, spirit, and attitude of a winner. In the meantime, I prayed he would stay safe and healthy in his crazy quest for King of the Rail.

As we were leaving the venue, I was bursting with pride at all that Jarad had accomplished by himself. Although Jarad was quiet and reflective, it was heartwarming to see how well liked and respected he was among his peers in this bustling ski resort full of the "rich and famous." I could see his passion through the struggles to simply make his way.

Later that evening Jarad, Jorge, Turbo and I went out for a light dinner. We talked about the competition, which his buddy Teol Harle had won. Jorja and Turbo critiqued his performance and made suggestions that would help him improve his technique for the next competition. Jarad listened with interest, and it was evident that he was open to their suggestions.

Before we went home, Jarad shared his plans for the following day: He wanted to take me on a personally guided tour of Whistler and Blackcomb mountains. He was bursting with pride as he told me all about the famous resort. Jarad explained that the interconnected Whistler/Blackcomb Mountains made up the largest ski resort (8,171 acres) in North America, and the area was second only in size to those in Europe. He went on to say that Whistler boasts having an "atlas" to display their over two hundred marked runs! He warned me to expect "crowds," as he heard the resort was anticipating 20,000-plus visitors to ride the chairs and gondolas to the top the next day. Many of those would ski or snowboard but quite a few, like us, would be there only to sightsee. Then he asked if I would be ready to leave the house by ten in the morning. I laughed and said, "If you get me home soon, and I can get a decent night's sleep!"

The next morning Jarad reminded me to a bundle up warmly as we were leaving his house. We drove to Whistler Village and rode the gondola to the top of Whistler Mountain. There we walked over to the Peak 2 Peak gondola, the world's largest, and most breathtaking, unsupported cable span; it ran 1.87 miles between the tops of Whistler and Blackcomb Mountain.

As we stepped aboard, I was shocked that the gondola we were riding in would dip so low into the valley. With no towers to guide and support the gondola, it was a gentle downhill ride and a steep climb up to the Blackcomb peak. It was like being on top of the world, except the gathering fog and clouds made visibility rather poor. I could only see straight down but not the distance across the valley.

As we walked around the top of Blackcomb Mountain amid the thousands of skiers and snowboarders, Jarad asked if I would like lunch. We went into the chalet and enjoyed a hot bowl of vegetarian chili. To my surprise lunch was Jarad's treat because part of his mountain privileges included a 50% discount at the mountaintop restaurant.

As we ate our delicious lunch we watched as some young snowboarders repeatedly slid and fell. Jarad offered insight on how they could better get down the mountain. He explained how their weight was not being transferred to their heels as their toes came up in order to control the board—"much like releasing the gas pedal in a car to slow the engine," he explained. This was called side-flipping. He really knew his stuff and possessed a unique ability for helping friends who had repeatedly tried to master snowboarding finally become successful.

He had wanted to show me his house from the glass-bottom gondola cabin, but we did not want to wait in the long lineup. Jarad had wanted to take the glass-bottom gondola down the hill, but sadly the weather did not cooperate as clouds socked in all around us.

Considering the unseasonably nasty weather that had set in and the fact that seeing anything on the way down through the clouds and fog was questionable, I agreed with him. We chuckled as he pointed out the sign at the top of Whistler's Peak that read: "Today's weather: <u>COLD</u> Forecast: HIGH -1°." Despite all of my layers of clothing, I was chilled to the bone!

The tour and the scenery was secondary to simply enjoying being in Jarad's company. His chipper mood, the broad smile plastered on his gorgeous face, and the friendly way he greeted everyone he knew, was a balm to my spirit. Nothing made me happier than to watch him being so joyful. He was truly in his element! When we returned to the village, he informed me that our day was not over yet. "Tonight Whistler hosts the weekly Sunday night show called 'Fire and Ice.'" He explained that it involved skiers and some of his snowboarding buddies performing jumps and flips through a huge lit hoop of fire—hence the name fire and ice. As we approached the venue, I could not believe how many people were standing outside in the cold as snow lightly fell from the sky. And there was still an hour before the show was to begin!

Neither of us wanted to just stand there waiting in the cold, so we walked around and found a vantage point on the second floor of a restaurant just above the ring-of-fire landing platform. The show started with what appeared to be Hawaiian fire dancers. The family that was standing next to us, we learned, were there on vacation from Kauai.

We watched as the boarders and skiers were towed up the hill behind skidoos. I smiled and asked, "Why do they get rides and you he had to run up the steep slope the night before?" He grinned back at me as if he could read my mind . . . at least now he had the energy to expend on getting up and down on his own!

As the participants warmed up, we watched in horror as one of the jumpers crashed hard and lay unmoving in the snow. The crowds' collective groan drowned out the MC's "welcome announcement." But the skier quickly stood up, and it was just in time, as the participants headed towards the first jump and the huge, burning ring. They did front flips, backflips, and side flips. These young daredevils mesmerized the crowd. When they flew through the ring of fire, and some of them appeared to touch the ring, the crowd cheered loudly. The announcer had a way of revving up the crowd, and everyone was cheering and clapping for the boarders and skiers and their magnificent display of dexterity. The show was a definite highlight of my trip. After the show, Jarad and I headed to the KEG Steakhouse for a late dinner.

I could not remember the last time I had been to a KEG restaurant. Jarad and I talked about when they used to have a salad bar, and we reminisced about how much I ate on my last visit. I laughed as I took off my jacket and we ordered our drinks and food. "Remember?" he said, "we would load up our plates from the salad bar and then eat appetizers as well as the main course and dessert. Suki, you look so good now. How much did you used to weigh?"

I told him, "Over 270 pounds! We were both sick in those days." The Keg food was delicious and better than I recalled, and we both left there feeling comfortable, but not over stuffed! It was no wonder with the stress of Jarad's illness, my lack of exercise and sleep, and me overstuffing myself that my weight had ballooned so much. At 150 pounds I was now enjoying the best health that I had experienced in years; no diabetes and normalized blood pressure and cholesterol without medication. And it was obvious that Jarad was too. We had both come a long way since those stress-filled days in Penticton.

When it was time for me to return home to Honolulu, I sadly made my way to the international departures terminal at Vancouver International Airport. I completed the appropriate paperwork and handed it to the immigration officer after answering a few questions at the counter. I was welcomed "home" by U.S. Homeland security screeners as I headed toward the Air Canada gate to board a 767 to Honolulu. Traveling across the vast ocean that separates the mainland from Hawaii, tears flowed freely down my cheeks as I recalled in vivid detail the adventures on my first Canadian

Christmas in years. I loved spending time with my family, but I was really happy to be heading home.

Suddenly I realized I was on a plane full of Canadians who were going to Hawaii on vacation to escape their frigid winter temperatures. At once I said a prayer of thanksgiving that Honolulu was now home for me, and I no longer had to endure the bitter cold winters, unless I chose to go there. I knew once my feet hit the ground and my nose smelled the exotic scents of the island flowers that my head and my heart would once again remind me that this was now my home.

This time, however, I returned with my story completely down on paper, a project that has spanned the past thirty years of my life and that of my family. With it finally told, it is time for me to switch gears and think about my future. I believe my future would culminate in a published book. And I am ready to embark on a career in health coaching seniors. For now I have perpetual sunshine, warm breezes, and a circle of friends who never knew me as an obese, angry activist but had come to know the organized, thoughtful health coach and trainer I had become.

But now with this life project behind me, I am ready to put all of my life experiences into practice and make another shift, to take on something new, demonstrating to my three adult children you are never too old to change your path and begin again.

As I slid the key into the door of my cottage, I knew this is where I belonged. As much as I miss my family, I also realize that my children are grown and have little need of a mother in their busy lives. We do maintain regular contact through text messaging, phone calls and Skype, and there are always family vacations where we choose a destination and get together to laugh and reminisce about the days gone by—be it Mexico, a Hawaiian Island cruise, Las Vegas or Texas—and when we all get together, the time that we had spent apart is forgotten. We share a closeness few families can claim. But after what all of us had been through when the children were growing, our bond was strengthened forever.

My oldest son, Tyler is now happily married and lives very close to the Dallas/Fort Worth area of Texas. After many years he has become a legal permanent resident of the United States. He and his wife Katherine share two beautiful kittens.

My daughter, Ashley is also happily married to Jamie and lives in Castlegar, British Columbia. They have two beautiful boys, Riley is 7 and Spencer is 4. They have two dogs – Alize and Thor.

In the winters, Jarad could be found fitting snowboard boots at the board shop or on one of his snowboards among the Whistler/Blackcomb Mountains. He was pursuing his passion and had attained three levels of snowboard instructor certification. He is currently single and getting ready to make a big move to Victoria, B.C. He also thoroughly enjoys skateboarding and surfing. He continues to take A4+ for a two week period every six months. His heart and liver have never been healthier. He is grateful for the amazing restored wellness that he continues to enjoy every day!

I have learned so many lessons from my children and all of the experiences life has thrown my way. I live daily with deep gratitude, and in hindsight I can see all of the good that has actually come from the trying years of Jarad's illness and near-death experience, along with my advocacy for the victims of the Canadian tainted-blood crisis. My life resembles nothing that I could ever have imagined, but in so many ways it has been much, much better! Had anyone told me twenty years ago when I was struggling, that I would one day be living on a beach in Honolulu, Hawaii, I would have thought them crazy! But here I am, and all is finally right in my world: my children are independent, healthy and happy. I am fulfilling my dreams, enjoying my early-morning workdays at the Y.M.C.A., managing fabulous properties in Diamond Head, recently graduated from the Institute of Integrative Nutrition, healthy, and living a life of gratitude in Honolulu. To top it off, on October 18, 2011, I became an American citizen.

I would, however, be remiss if I didn't acknowledge in this closing that there has never been a doubt in my mind that Jarad would have died when he was 12, if not for the miraculous liver tonic he started taking, in what looked to be his final days on this earth. I will be forever grateful that both Dr. Jose Cabanillas and Brad Clark came in to our lives when they did—an answer to my prayers that, as I said earlier, Ashley summed up so well, "Jarad may have taken the medicine, but our whole family got better!"

The company that is manufacturing the liver tonic, A4+, for use in Canada is Sabell Corporation, in Calgary, Alberta. For the past eighteen years, they have been proving that this product is safe and effective for human consumption and a treatment for those with hepatitis C and other liver disorders. Research on the A4+ was conducted at McMaster University in Hamilton, Ontario, University of Alberta, in Edmonton, Alberta and University of Calgary, in Calgary, Alberta.

The liquid version was given "an exemption number" by Health Canada's Natural Health Products Directorate (NHPD). The capsule version was approved by Health Canada and received license July 29, 2012.

Dr. Jose Cabanillas lives in Iquitos, Peru and is continuing his work as a doctor and shaman.

About the Author

Leslie Sharp graduated from the British Columbia Institute of Technology in 1979 after studying Accounting and Business Management. After the strain of her son's long-term illness, she found herself overweight by 120 pounds. At that point she shifted her focus to fitness training, taking courses in Health and Wellness Services from Thomas Edison State. On January 1st, 2006 she moved to Honolulu, Hawaii and achieved her dream of purchasing and operating a Curves franchise. In 2015 she obtained a National Health Coach certification from the Institute of Integrative Nutrition. Today, she successfully runs Health Compass International and uses her accumulated skills to support her clients through their health challenges.

During the tainted blood crisis, Leslie was a board member of the Hepatitis C Society of Canada and gave numerous newspaper, television and radio interviews about the crisis and its' fallout. She was a vocal advocate for the billion-dollar compensation package for its victims. She also wrote articles that appeared in the Penticton Herald, the Pony Express Magazine, and the Canadian Journal of Public Health. It was her unrelenting search for a cure that brought to light the Peruvian liver tonic, A4+, which ultimately saved her son's life.

Made in the USA
Middletown, DE
03 February 2019